Strategic Marketing Management

Planning and Control

2003–2004

Helen Meek
Richard Meek

BUTTERWORTH
HEINEMANN

AMSTERDAM BOSTON HEIDELBERG LONDON NEW YORK OXFORD PARIS
SAN DIEGO SAN FRANCISCO SINGAPORE SYDNEY TOKYO

Butterworth-Heinemann
An imprint of Elsevier
Linacre House, Jordan Hill, Oxford OX2 8DP
200 Wheeler Road, Burlington MA 01803

First published 2003

British Library Cataloguing in Publication Data
A catalogue record for this book is available from the British Library

ISBN 0 7506 5965 3

For information on all Butterworth-Heinemann publications
visit our website at www.bh.com

Typeset by Integra Software Services Pvt. Ltd, Pondicherry, India
www.integra-india.com
Printed and bound in Italy

Contents

preface
welcome to the CIM coursebooks

A message from the author

This coursebook is designed specifically to meet the needs of students studying for the Chartered Institute of Marketing's Strategic Marketing Management: Planning and Control exam. The structure of the coursebook mirrors the Planning and Control syllabus and reflects the relative weighting given to each aspect of the syllabus. The Planning and Control module acts as a foundation on which the other Diploma subjects are based. This module builds on the operational aspects of marketing that have already been covered at Certificate and Advanced Certificate level. However, this module is firmly focused on the strategic rather than the operational aspects of marketing. It is expected that students will already be competent in all areas covered in the Certificate and Advanced Certificate modules.

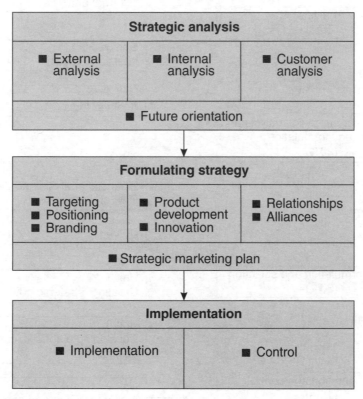

Figure 1 Process of strategic marketing
Drummond and Ensor, 2001

The syllabus reflects the importance of strategy development, and in particular the critical areas of implementation and control of plans. There is now slightly less emphasis placed on planning and the planning process. The following are key themes of the syllabus:

o   Developing a view of the future through various forecasting techniques
o   Innovation and creativity
o   Branding
o   Implementation and control of plans which now equates to 15% of the syllabus
o   The use and evaluation of marketing tools and techniques.

The process of strategic marketing is shown in the figure above. The coursebook is structured around this framework. The syllabus is broken down into five distinct areas:

o   Market-led approach to planning (10%).
o   Analysis (25%).
o   Techniques for analysis and strategy development (20%).
o   Strategy formulation and selection (30%).
o   Implementation and control (15%).

The following figure provides a diagrammatical overview of the book and how it relates to the various components of the syllabus.

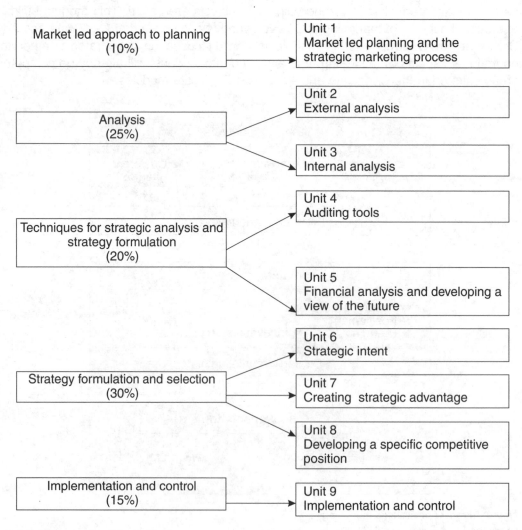

Figure 2 Overview of the book

This coursebook is designed to bridge the gap between the theory of strategic marketing and its practical application; this is achieved by providing students with practical examples and encouraging them to reflect on their own knowledge and understanding by the inclusion of relevant exam questions and mini-cases. Many of the case examples have been sourced using www.Lexis-Nexis.com.

Strategic marketing is a vast subject and there is a wealth of books, articles and on-line materials available for students studying the Planning and Control module. The recommended reading for the Planning and Control module is extensive and many students feel overwhelmed by the number of recommended and additional texts on the reading list. This coursebook is designed to act as a 'map' for students to lead them through the syllabus and to refer them to relevant further reading where necessary. The text is designed to complement the texts on the reading list, not to replace them. It is essential that students demonstrate both 'depth' and 'breadth' of knowledge of strategic marketing, and this can only be achieved by reference to other core and supporting texts. A key role of this book is to provide students with signposts to further reading.

The examiners are looking for evidence that you have the ability to apply the theoretical concepts of strategic marketing to practical situations. Therefore it is suggested that you develop a portfolio of examples that will demonstrate key aspects of the syllabus. There are numerous sources of materials – such as *The Financial Times* and other quality newspapers, websites and other on-line resources and marketing journals such as *Marketing, Marketing Week* and *Campaign*. By building a portfolio of articles you will arm yourself with relevant examples that you will be able to use in the Planning and Control exam.

An introduction from the academic development advisor

In the last two years we have seen some significant changes to the CIM Professional Series initiated by the Chartered Institute of Marketing. The changes have been introduced on a year-on-year basis, with Stage 1 (Certificate) changes implemented last year in 2002, and the Stage 2 (Advanced Certificate in Marketing) changes being implemented this year. It is anticipated that next year in 2004 the Stage 3 (Postgraduate Diploma) changes will be implemented.

As a result the authoring team, Butterworth-Heinemann and I have aimed to rigorously revise and update the coursebook series to make sure that every title is the best possible study aid and accurately reflects the latest CIM syllabus.

The revisions to the series this year included continued development in the Stage 1 and Postgraduate Diploma Series, and complete re-writes at Stage 2 to align with the radical overhaul of the CIM syllabus. There are a number of new authors and indeed Senior Examiners, in the series who have been commissioned for their CIM course teaching and examining experience, as well as their research into specific curriculum-related areas and their wide general knowledge of the latest thinking in marketing.

We are certain that you will find these coursebooks highly beneficial in terms of the content and assessment opportunities and a study tool that will prepare you for both CIM examinations and continuous/integrative assessment opportunities. They will guide you in a logical and structured way through the detail of the syllabus, providing you with the required underpinning knowledge, understanding and application of theory.

The editorial team and authors wish you every success as you embark upon your studies.

Karen Beamish
Academic Development Advisor

How to use these coursebooks

Everyone who has contributed to this series has been careful to structure the books with the exams in mind. Each unit, therefore, covers an essential part of the syllabus. You need to work through the complete coursebook systematically to ensure that you have covered everything you need to know.

This coursebook is divided into units each containing a selection of the following standard elements:

- o **Learning Objectives** Tell you what you will be expected to know, having read the unit
- o **Syllabus references** Outline what part of the syllabus is covered in the module
- o **Study guides** Tell you how long the unit is and how long its activities take to do
- o **Questions** Are designed to give you practice – they will be similar to those you get in the exam
- o **Answers** (at the end of the book) suggest a format for answering exam questions. *Remember* there is no such thing as a model answer – you should use these examples only as guidelines
- o **Activities** Give you a chance to put what you have learned into practice
- o **Debriefings** (at the end of the book) shed light on the methodologies involved in the activities
- o **Hints and tips** Are tips from the senior examiner or examiner which are designed to help you avoid common mistakes made by previous candidates and give you guidance on improving your knowledge base
- o **Insights** Encourage you to contextualize your academic knowledge by reference to real-life experience
- o **Key definitions** Highlight and explain the key points relevant to that module
- o **Definitions** May be used for words you must know to pass the exam
- o **Summaries** Cover what you should have picked up from reading the unit.
- o **Further study** Provides details of recommended reading in addition to the coursebook.

While you will find that each section of the syllabus has been covered within this text, you might find that the order of some of the topics has been changed. This is because it sometimes makes more sense to put certain topics together when you are studying, even though they might appear in different sections of the syllabus itself. If you are following the reading and other activities, your coverage of the syllabus will be just fine, but don't forget to follow up with trade press reading!

About MarketingOnline

With this year's coursebooks Butterworth-Heinemann is offering readers free access to MarketingOnline (www.marketingonline.com), our premier online support engine for the CIM marketing courses. On this site you can benefit from:

- o Tutorials on key topics every two weeks during the term, comprehensive revision support material and access to revision days from Tactics – the highly acclaimed independent trainer for CIM courses.
- o Fully customizable electronic versions of the coursebooks – annotate, cut and paste sections of text to create your own tailored learning notes.

o   Instant access to weblinks related to the coursebooks.

o   Capacity to search the coursebook online for instant access to definitions and key concepts.

Logging on

Before you can access MarketingOnline you will first need to get a password. Please go to www.marketingonline.com where you will find registration instructions for coursebook purchasers. Once you have got your password, you will need to log on using the onscreen instructions. This will give you access to the various functions outlined below.

Using MarketingOnline

MarketingOnline is broadly divided into four sections which can each be accessed from the front page after you have logged on to the system:

1. **The coursebooks** Buttons corresponding to the three levels of CIM marketing qualification are situated on the home page. Select your level and you will be presented with the four coursebook titles for each module of that level. Click on the desired coursebook to access the full online text (divided up by chapter). On each page of text you have the option to add an electronic bookmark or annotation by following the onscreen instructions. You can also freely cut and paste text into a blank word document to create your own learning notes.

2. **Revision material** Click on the 'Revision material' link and select the appropriate CIM level and coursebook to access revision material.

3. **Useful links** Click on 'Useful links' to access a list of links to other sites of interest for further reading and research.

4. **Glossary** Click on the 'Glossary' button to access our online dictionary of marketing terms.

If you have specific queries about using MarketingOnline then you should consult our fully searchable FAQ section – again, this is accessible through the appropriate link on the front page of the site. Please also note that a **full user guide** can be downloaded by clicking on the link on the opening page of the website.

unit 1
market-led planning and the strategic marketing process

Key definitions

Societal marketing – Holds that the organization's task is to determine the needs, wants and interests of target markets and to deliver the desired satisfactions more effectively and efficiently than competitors in a way that preserves or enhances the consumer's and the society's well-being (Kotler, 2000).

Market orientation – Entails: one or more departments engaging in activities geared towards developing an understanding of customers' current and future needs and the factors affecting them, sharing of this understanding across departments and the various departments engaging in activities designed to meet select customer needs (Kohli and Jaworski, 1990).

Corporate strategy – Is concerned with what types of business the company as a whole should be in and is therefore concerned with decisions of scope (Johnson and Scholes, 1999).

Marketing strategy – Can be characterized by: analysing the business environment and defining customer needs, matching activities to customer needs and implementing programmes to achieve a competitive position relative to competitors (Drummond and Ensor, 2001).

Objective – Statement of what an organization is trying to achieve. Ideally objectives should be SMART (Specific, Measurable, Actionable, Realistic and Time bound).

Strategy – Broad statement of the way in which objectives are to be met.

Tactics – Represents the details of the plan – who, what, when and how.

Contingency planning – Planning for uncontrollable events.

Culture – Aaker (1998) suggested that organizational culture involves three elements: (1) a set of shared values or dominant beliefs that define an organization's priorities; (2) a set of norms of behaviour; (3) symbols and symbolic activities used to develop and nurture those shared values and norms.

Study Guide

- ○ This unit will take you about 3 hours to work through
- ○ We suggest that you take a further 3 hours to do the various activities and questions in this unit.

Introduction

The marketing concept is inherently simple – satisfying customers whilst at the same time achieving organizational goals. Few people would disagree with this principle, however many organizations find it very difficult to put the concept into practice. Marketing planning is highly challenging because it takes place against a backdrop of continuous environmental change, increasing competition, changing customer needs and limited resources. Marketing strategy has therefore become a vital component of organizational success. This unit will provide an overview of strategic marketing planning, discuss marketing's relationship with corporate strategy and in particular introduce the concept of market-led strategic change. The components of a strategic marketing plan will also be outlined.

Marketing revisited

There are numerous definitions of marketing and it is not the purpose of this study text to provide a definitive list. Instead, it will highlight the key issues in relation to the many and varied definitions of marketing that exist. Crosier (1975) reviewed more than 50 definitions of marketing and concluded that definitions of marketing could be classified into three distinct groups:

1. The *marketing process*, which is concerned with connecting the supplier and the customer
2. The *marketing concept* (philosophy), which suggests that marketing is concerned with exchange between willing parties
3. The *marketing orientation*, which is the phenomenon that makes the marketing process and the marketing concept achievable.

Activity 1.1

Defining marketing

1. Write down your own definition of marketing
2. Using a range of texts and/or articles, identify six different definitions of marketing
3. Compare and contrast these definitions, identifying any differences or similarities, and categorize them according to Crosier's classification
4. What conclusions can you draw?

Despite the numerous definitions of marketing, it is clear that marketing can be discussed from two different perspectives. Firstly, it can be seen as a functional activity concerned with operational aspects such as promotion, pricing, product development, distribution or market research. It can also be seen in the wider context as a business philosophy that seeks to put the customer at the centre of an organization's activities. This philosophy is often referred to as the *marketing concept*.

There is now, generally, a universal agreement that marketing is a way of doing business, i.e. a philosophy that is driven by the customer rather than a purely functional activity. Most definitions of marketing include two dimensions: the need to identify and satisfy customer needs (more effectively than competitors) and to achieve organizational goals. These goals do not necessarily have to be related to profitability. For many organizations, in particular not-for-profit organizations, there will be other types of goals that are just as important such as environmental or employee goals. It has been argued that an organization's primary (and only) responsibility is to its stakeholders in terms of maximizing their return. However, others argue that organizations have a responsibility not only to their customers and stakeholders, but also to society in general. Kotler (2000, p. 25) states that:

> *Some people have questioned whether the marketing concept is an appropriate organizational philosophy in an age of environmental deterioration, resource shortages, explosive population growth, world hunger and poverty, and neglected social services.*

Are companies that do an excellent job of satisfying consumer wants necessarily acting in the best long-run interest of consumers and society? The marketing concept sidesteps the potential conflicts between consumer wants, consumer interest and long-run societal welfare.

He goes on to suggest that, due to these potential conflicts, companies should adopt the societal marketing concept.

Definition

Societal marketing – Holds that the organization's task is to determine the needs, wants and interests of target markets and to deliver the desired satisfactions more effectively and efficiently than competitors in a way that preserves or enhances the consumer's and the society's well-being (Kotler, 2000).

There are many examples of organizations, such as the Body Shop, Iceland, Cafedirect (a fairtrade product) and the Co-operative Bank (see below), that are seemingly keen to adopt this societal marketing concept. However, many other organizations have failed to acknowledge their responsibilities to wider society, and indeed still struggle to satisfy their customers. The extent to which organizations are internally or externally focused can be illustrated in Figure 1.1. This matrix highlights the importance of being not only customer-focused but also competitor focused.

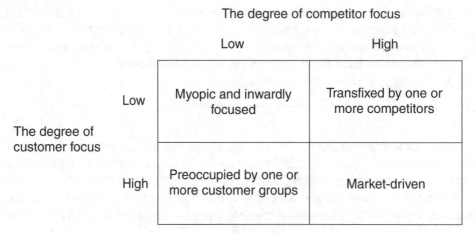

The degree of competitor focus

	Low	High
Low	Myopic and inwardly focused	Transfixed by one or more competitors
High	Preoccupied by one or more customer groups	Market-driven

The degree of customer focus

Figure 1.1 The management team's customer and competitor orientation

It is clear that those companies who adopt an 'outside in' approach to business (as opposed to an 'inside out' approach) are more likely to be aware, not only of changing customer needs, but also of activities of established and potential competitors, and will therefore be more able to anticipate and adapt to environmental change. The characteristics of these 'market-oriented' organizations will be explored in the next section.

Case history

The Co-operative Bank – the importance of being ethical

The Co-operative Bank uses its ethical banking policy as a major means of differentiation. It has recognized the increasing interest of customers in ethical issues. MORI was commissioned by the Bank in 2000 to undertake a survey of customer attitudes to ethical products. The results suggest that across all consumer markets, as many as 30% of consumers will demand ethical products and services. The Bank has recognized the increasing importance of the societal marketing concept and has therefore adopted an ethical investment policy, based on extensive consultation with its customers. Through its Web site, the Bank actively encourages customer participation and feedback. The Bank demonstrates its commitment to the societal marketing concept in its ecological mission statement:

We, The Co-operative Bank, will continue to develop our business, taking into account the impact our activities have on the environment and society at large. The nature of our activities are such that our indirect impact by being selective in terms of the provision of finance and banking arrangements is more ecologically significant than the direct impact of our trading operations. However, we undertake to continually assess all our activities and implement a programme of ecological improvement based on the pursuit of the following four scientific principles:

o Nature cannot withstand a progressive build-up of waste derived from the Earth's crust
o Nature cannot withstand a progressive build-up of society's waste, particularly artificial persistent substances which it cannot degrade into harmless materials
o The productive area of nature must not be diminished in quality (diversity) or quantity (volume) and must be enabled to grow
o Society must utilize energy and resources in a sustainable, equitable and efficient manner.

We consider that the pursuit of these principles constitutes a path of ecological excellence and will secure future prosperity for society by sustainable economic activity. The Co-operative Bank will not only pursue the above path itself, but also endeavour to help and encourage all its stakeholders to do likewise. We will aim to achieve this by:

Financial services

Encouraging business customers to take a pro-active stance on the environmental impact of their own activities, and investing in companies and organizations that avoid repeated damage of the environment.

Management systems

Assessing our ecological impact, setting ourselves clear targets, formulating an action plan and monitoring how we meet them, and publishing the results.

Purchasing and outsourcing

Welcoming suppliers whose activities are compatible with both our Ethical Policy and Ecological Mission Statement, and working in partnership with them to improve our collective performance.

Support

Supporting ecological projects and developing partnerships with businesses and organizations whose direct and indirect outputs contribute to a sustainable society.

Legislation

Adhering to environmental laws, directives and guidelines while continually improving upon our own contribution to a sustainable society.

The Co-operative Bank has developed a detailed ethical policy that outlines how customers' money should or should not be invested. It is based on extensive consultation with their customers. Their position includes a stance on investments in relation to human rights, the arms trade, corporate responsibility, genetic modification, ecological impact, social enterprise, customer consultation and animal welfare. For example, their stance in relation to human rights and the arms trade is as follows:

Human rights

Through our investments, we seek to support the principles of the Universal Declaration of Human Rights. In line with this, we will not invest in:

o   Any government or business which fails to uphold basic human rights within its sphere of influence
o   Any business whose links to an oppressive regime are a continuing cause for concern.

The Arms Trade

We will not invest in any business involved in:

o   The manufacture or transfer of armaments to oppressive regimes
o   The manufacture of torture equipment or other equipment that is used in the violation of human rights.

The Co-operative bank has recently extended its concern for the environment into their mortgages. When customers take out their 'green mortgage' the Bank will make an annual donation, for the duration of the mortgage, to Climate Care, a scheme developed to tackle global warming. They also make donations to the Customers Who Care campaign. For every £100 their customers spend on their Co-operative Bank Visa credit and debit cards, they will donate 1.25p to the latest Customers Who Care campaign.

Source: www.co-operativebank.co.uk and Mason 2000, www.Lexis-Nexis.com

Market orientation

In a company that is market-oriented, all departments (not just the marketing department) would be customer-focused, and the aim of providing superior customer value would be seen as everybody's responsibility (i.e. that everybody is seen as a part-time marketer). Some authors refer to this as market orientation, while others as marketing orientation. Often the two terms are used interchangeably. However, Piercy (2001) argues that *markets* are what are important, not *marketing* and therefore more emphasis should be placed on 'market orientation'. Many studies have attempted to identify the key characteristics of market-oriented companies. Kohli and Jaworski (1990) identified that:

A market orientation entails:

1. One or more departments engaging in activities geared towards developing an understanding of customers' current and future needs and the factors affecting them
2. Sharing of this understanding across departments and
3. The various departments engaging in activities designed to meet select customer needs.

In other words, a market orientation refers to the organization-wide generation, dissemination and responsiveness to market intelligence.

Narver and Slater (1990) developed the following model that highlights the key components of a market orientation (Figure 1.2).

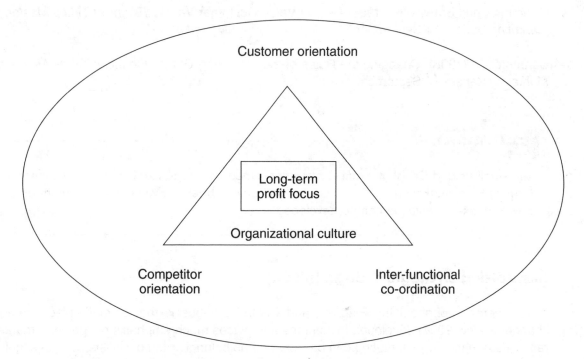

Figure 1.2 A model of market orientation
Adapted from Narver and Slater (1990)

  o Customer orientation – concerned with understanding customers so that you can better meet their needs
  o Competitor orientation – having an awareness of competitors' capabilities
  o Interfunctional co-ordination – all aspects of the business striving to create value
  o Organizational culture – a culture that facilitates organizational learning
  o Long-term profit focus – as opposed to a short-term perspective.

Activity 1.2

How market-oriented is your organization?

Hooley et al. (1998) in their Marketing Strategy and Competitive Positioning have developed a framework for evaluating market orientation. Complete the assessment presented in pp. 11–13 of their book, by applying it to your own organization. To what extent do you think your organization is market-oriented, and how helpful is this framework in understanding the key components of market orientation?

When considering an organization's market orientation, it is also essential that the external environment be taken into consideration because this is continually changing and will impact on the development and implementation of market orientation. The external environment is discussed further in Unit 2.

Extended knowledge

The Financial Times ran an excellent Marketing series, entitled 'Mastering Marketing' in 1998. Find and read the following articles that provide a useful discussion of market orientation.

Meehan S. and Barwise P. (1998) Do you Value Customer Value? *Financial Times Mastering Marketing* Series, 14 September.

Carpenter G. (1998). Changing the Rules of the Marketing Game. *Financial Times Mastering Marketing* Series, 14 September.

Exam hint

The Analysis and Decision exam is often concerned with organizations that are suffering from a lack of market orientation. It is often part of your brief to give recommendations as to how a market orientation can be developed.

Market-led strategic change (MLSC)

A key theme throughout the Planning and Control syllabus is that of market-led strategic change. Piercy (2001) developed this phrase and places much emphasis on 'going to market' rather than marketing. Marketing can be regarded as belonging to specialists, whereas 'going to market' is what companies do and should be the responsibility of all employees. It may be argued that marketing departments could disappear in a truly market-oriented organization but going to market will always endure. Piercy (2001) identifies a number of important differences between 'going to market' and marketing:

- o Strategies are based on customers and markets
- o Internal processes of change and external actions are driven by those strategies
- o Focus is on delivering a customer-focused strategy
- o Relationships are fundamental (customers, competitors, intermediaries)
- o Information technology underpins new ways of doing business.

Many successful companies have succeeded, not because of their structured marketing programmes but because of their understanding of the *customer* and their ability to sense the market. Marketing functions such as promotion, marketing research and NPD are all important aspects of the process of marketing.

Piercy (2001) suggests that managers need to concentrate on three key issues:

- o Customers – understanding customers
- o Market strategy – segmenting the market, selecting target markets and developing a strong competitive position
- o Implementation – getting the strategy to the marketplace.

Too often these important issues are not given priority because immediate problems get in the way. Managers should be concentrating on these strategic issues rather than getting involved in the tactics. Many strategies fail, not because they are poor strategies but because they have been poorly implemented. Managers need to focus as much on the implementation as they do on the contents of the strategy. This issue will be discussed further in Unit 9 – Implementation and Control.

Piercy (2001) acknowledges that the process of going to market is not easy, may require substantial change in the way organizations are run and that a key role of marketing is to encourage and facilitate change so that employees are more likely to accept and embrace it willingly. Piercy acknowledges that the market is dynamic and that for companies to maintain their competitive advantage they will have to respond to the following new challenges:

- o New customer demands and expectations – customer expectations are increasing and they are less willing to accept second-class service.
- o New competitors – competition is coming not just from established competitors but also from new entrants, such as the entrance of Virgin into financial services and easyJet into car rental.
- o New types of organizations being established – many organizations are downsizing and becoming more narrowly focused. Others (such as Time Warner and AOL) are entering strategic alliances and collaborative partnerships.
- o Whole new ways of doing business are being developed, e.g. electronic marketing.

It is imperative that marketers continually adapt and respond to these new challenges in order to gain/maintain competitive advantage.

Extended knowledge

Market-led Strategic Change by Nigel Piercy (2001) is essential and entertaining reading for this topic. Read at least Chapter 1 – Whatever happened to marketing?

Chapter 1 of Hooley et al. (1998) also provides a comprehensive discussion of this topic.

Question 1.1

Market-led strategic change

Answer Question 5 from the June 1999 Planning and Control paper on market-led strategic change. Go to www.cimeduhub.com to access specimen answers for this question.

Drivers of change

Change is inevitable and companies that wish to maintain a market-led approach must take into consideration both cyclical and evolutionary change when developing their marketing strategies. The rate at which the external environment changes varies according to the nature of the business, but increasingly all organizations are facing escalating levels of change. Therefore, according to Drummond and Ensor (2001, p. 5),

> *'it is important to see the concept of change as an integral part of strategy'.*

Drummond and Ensor (2001) suggest that the concept of change can be evaluated in terms of the following questions:

1. What drives change? The continually evolving environment in terms of political, economic, social and technological developments (PEST) is driving change
2. How does change impact on our markets/business environment?
3. What is the result of change on the organization's strategy? The change may result in either opportunities in terms of changing customer needs, or conversely, organizations may become complacent and drift away from the needs of the marketplace.

The change drivers (PEST factors) are discussed in detail in Unit 2.

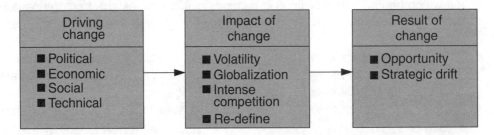

Figure 1.3 The three questions posed by Drummond and Ensor (2001)

Activity 1.3

Drivers of change

In the context of a particular industry sector, select a significant change driver from the marketing environment (PEST) and:

    a.   Consider how the selected driver impacts on markets/business environment?
    b.   What opportunities or potential strategic drift may result?

Change is inevitable. To survive companies need to adapt and to convert the threats created by the changing environment into opportunities in order to avoid 'strategic drift'. Marks and Spencer is a prime example of a company that has not adapted to the changing customer demands and as a result has lost many of its loyal customer base.

Case history

Drivers of change

Greenhalgh (2001) identifies the following drivers of change that have created challenges for companies over the last few years:

o   Domestic businesses of any significance have become rare. They are now global, drawing on supply chains that transcend national boundaries and serving customers worldwide.

o   Both workforces and customers are becoming more heterogeneous. Therefore, a key task of any company is to benefit from this diversity and to market to the full spectrum of customers.

o   Industries have shifted from making products to providing services. For example, computer manufacturers are not just selling computers; they are selling the services that they provide such as word processing.

o   Start-up companies play an important role in introducing innovative products and new ideas to the marketplace. Young, technologically competent workers are drawn to these vibrant workplaces, making it harder for other companies to recruit and retain them.

o   Laws and public opinion now protect employee rights once protected by unions only.

o   Customer expectations of quality have increased and are now applied to all goods and services, rather than just luxury goods.

o   Concern for the environment has become a major item on companies' agenda. They now have to consider their environmental responsibility as well as their profits.

o   Employees who used to be valued for their skills are now valued for their knowledge. Knowledge workers have different ties to organizations – sometimes none – and need to be managed differently.

o   Large institutional investors are exerting their influence on how organizations are managed.

o   Free-standing organizations have given way to extended enterprises. These are boundary-less systems of networked companies, each contributing a distinctive competency. Lone companies no longer compete with other companies; instead, value-chain partnerships compete with each other.

Activity 1.4

Consider the drivers of change outlined above. Identify the impact of these factors on your own organization.

Case history

The Internet – new opportunities for Direct Line with jamjar.com venture

Direct Line, an established direct insurer and financial services provider, has entered into the Internet car retailing sector. There has been much publicity surrounding inflated UK car prices. Direct Line saw the opportunity to capitalize on this, and the increased interest in buying on-line, by launching their jamjar.com venture.

Jamjar.com is an Internet-based car retailing operation that claims to provide 15–30% discounts on UK-sourced cars as well as on imports from Europe. Customers can view and select from a wide range of both new and used cars and may trade in their existing car. Cars are delivered to the customer's home and there is a 7-day 'no questions asked' return policy if customers are not satisfied. Customers are even e-mailed a digital photograph of their car once it is loaded on to the car transporter to reassure them of their purchase!

Internet car sales are revolutionizing the way in which people buy cars and many car manufacturers are having to re-evaluate their distribution strategies and their relationships with their dealers. The Internet is the source of many new opportunities but it is also a threat to traditional ways of doing business.

Source: Griffiths (2000) www.Lexis-Nexis.com and www.jamjar.com

Exam hint

The Planning and Control examiners are looking for evidence that you can discuss the impact of changes on marketing strategy and provide applied examples. The following exam question was included in the June 1997 exam paper.

Societies are changing in a wide variety of ways. Identify the nature and significance of two such changes that are taking place within your own society and discuss their implications for the marketing planning and control process.

In the *FT Mastering Marketing* (1998) series, Kotler predicted that the following trends will be shaping marketing by the year 2005:

- o Disintermediation of wholesalers and retailers owing to electronic commerce. B2B purchasing over the Internet has increased even faster than consumer on-line buying.
- o Reduction in the number of customers visiting traditional shop-based retailers. Retailers will offer customers an 'experience' in addition to a product assortment in the form of entertainment, coffee shops, etc.
- o Customer databases containing rich information of individual customer preferences will be used to mass-customize products.
- o Companies will develop strategies to retain customers to a greater extent, and attracting customers from competitors will become more difficult. Companies will concentrate on increasing the value of existing customers.
- o Companies will develop ways of accounting that can measure individual customer profitability so that they will be able to target customers.
- o Many companies will have moved towards a loyalty building strategy and away from a transactional approach.
- o Companies will become much leaner by outsourcing their non-core activities.
- o Field salespeople will become franchisees rather than company employees.
- o Importance of mass TV advertising will diminish, as there is a proliferation of specialized on-line magazine and TV channels.
- o Companies will find it difficult to sustain competitive advantages and the only sustainable advantage lies in an ability to learn and change faster than competitors.

It is apparent that monitoring the external environment and developing a view of the future is a key element in developing a successful future strategy. The external environment will be discussed further in Unit 2 and developing a vision of the future in Unit 5.

The strategic marketing process

Up to this point we have focused primarily on marketing strategy. However, it is impossible to discuss marketing strategy without looking at it in the context of overall corporate strategy. There is often much confusion as to the similarities and differences of marketing and corporate strategy. This may partly be due to the fact that in a market-oriented organization, where the customer is at the heart of the organization, it is likely that marketing is the largest contributor to corporate planning. This section will highlight the relationship between marketing and corporate strategy, discuss the planning framework and clarify the different types of planning.

What is strategy?

The term strategy is probably one of the most used and often misunderstood terms in business. There is no universal definition of strategy and yet it is used extensively. Strategy has the same meaning, whether we are discussing corporate, marketing, promotional or even advertising strategy: it is concerned with how we might achieve our objectives. The difference between each type of strategy relates to the level at which the strategy is being developed. Corporate strategy according to Johnson and Scholes (1999), is:

> *concerned with what types of business the company as a whole should be in and is therefore concerned with decisions of scope*

whereas *marketing strategy* aims to transform corporate objectives into a competitive market position.

13

The main role of marketing strategy is to differentiate products/services from those of competitors by meeting the needs of customers more effectively. Therefore, according to Drummond and Ensor (2001) marketing strategy can be characterized by:

1. Analysing the business environment and defining customer needs
2. Matching activities to customer needs
3. Implementing programmes to achieve a competitive position relative to competitors.

In the 1970s and 1980s, a great deal of emphasis was placed on strategic planning and developing corporation-wide plans, often in a centralized manner. This produced detailed plans but often problems occurred at implementation because insufficient attention was given to how the plans were going to be executed. Today in business more attention is being given to strategic management (as opposed to strategic planning). This concerns both the formulation of strategy and how the strategy may be implemented. It is increasingly recognized that organizations need to be able to manage change in light of a dynamic environment. Figure 1.4 illustrates the elements of strategic management.

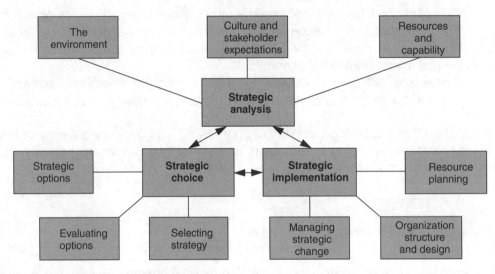

Figure 1.4 Elements of strategic management
Johnson and Scholes, 1999

It can be seen that strategic management consists of three elements:

o *Strategic analysis* – concerned with answering the question 'where are we now?' This involves analysing the external environment, internal resources and capabilities, and stakeholder expectations
o *Strategic choice* – what are the options available and which is the most attractive?
o *Strategic implementation* – often the most overlooked of strategy. It is concerned with allocating resources and turning the plans into action.

This process can be as equally well applied to marketing strategy.

The corporate strategy/marketing interface

It is impossible to discuss marketing strategy without first putting it into the context of corporate planning. The relationship between corporate planning and marketing planning can best be explained by Figure 1.5. It is helpful to think of these decisions sitting in a hierarchy with corporate planning at the top and marketing planning below it. The diagram also illustrates that, alongside marketing planning, plans should be developed for other functional areas of the business such as human resources management (HRM), logistics and operations. The vision and mission will drive the overall direction of the company and the functional areas of business will all work towards achieving the corporate objectives. The vision and mission will be discussed in Unit 6 – Strategic intent.

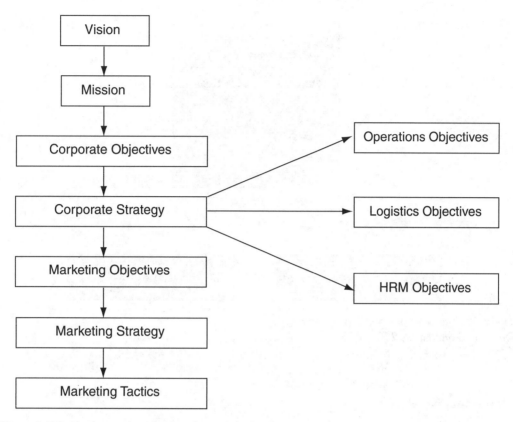

Figure 1.5 Corporate and marketing planning hierarchy

Marketing strategy is concerned with three elements – customers, competitors and internal corporate issues as illustrated in Figure 1.6. Strategic marketing management has three major phases: firstly, strategic analysis in order to answer the question where are we now? This will include external analysis of customers, competitors and the macro-environment, and internal analysis of corporate capabilities; secondly, formulation of strategy in terms of creating and evaluating alternative options and thirdly implementation where the strategies are translated into action. The three stages are not mutually exclusive and are not necessarily linear, in fact it is expected that there will be some feedback and amendments as the process progresses.

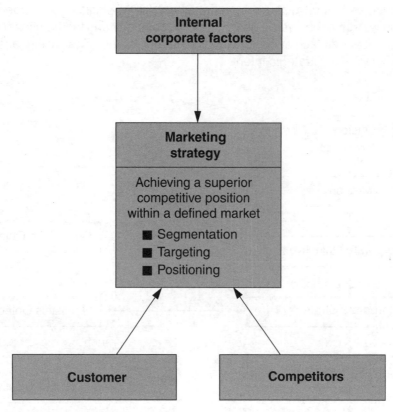

Figure 1.6 The basis of marketing strategy
Drummond and Ensor, 2001, p. 8

Extended knowledge

Chapter 1 of Drummond and Ensor's *Strategic Marketing Planning and Control* (2001) provides a useful discussion of strategic marketing management.

The basis of planning and control

In order to develop a successful marketing strategy, many organizations adopt a structured approach to planning and control.

Planning is a fundamental part of a manager's role. The purpose of planning is to allocate and co-ordinate resources to help achieve predetermined objectives. In a continually changing environment, planning encourages managers to consider the future, to try to anticipate the likely outcomes and to develop strategies that will capitalize on these changes. The plan itself also acts as a means of communicating the plan to others. Figure 1.7 illustrates the typical planning and control cycle that organizations may use to develop plans. This framework can be applied at both a corporate and a marketing level. The process will be similar although the focus of the plan will differ.

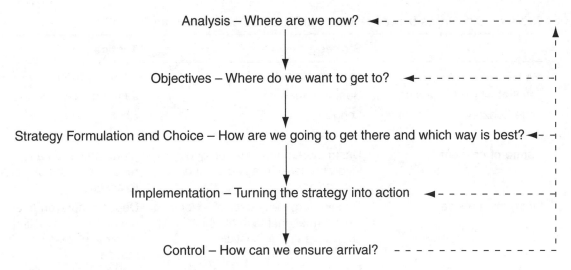

Figure 1.7 The basis of planning and control

This planning framework encourages managers to develop quantified goals and then identify alternative strategies that might lead to these objectives being met. Plans force managers to consider the future, because they may concentrate too much on the present and ignore the important issues. The implementation and control stages are essential components of the planning process but are often not given the attention they deserve. Too often, plans are developed with little thought as to how they may actually be put into practice. Relevant control mechanisms need to be developed to measure the success of the plan against the initial objectives. Control measures are often bolted on at the end but this may be too late. It may be necessary to develop intermediary control measures to act as early warning signals so that corrective action can be taken if necessary. The information generated from the control measures is then fed back into the planning and control cycle to inform future plans.

Types of planning

There is often much confusion regarding the terminology associated with strategy – objectives, strategy, tactics, contingency planning. Objectives, corporate, marketing or advertising are concerned with what is to be achieved and should be SMART (Specific, Measurable, Actionable, Realistic and Time bound). Both strategy and tactics are concerned with how to achieve the objectives and the difference between them depends on the level from which you are looking. For example, what is regarded as a tactic by the marketing director (such as a money-off coupon) may be regarded as a strategy by a marketing assistant. The difference between a strategy and a tactic is not clear-cut and will vary from organization to organization. Table 1.1 highlights some of the differences between strategy and tactics.

Table 1.1 Differences between strategy and tactics (Weitz and Wensley, 1988)

	Strategy	Tactics
Importance	More important	Less important
Level at which conducted	Senior managers	Junior management
Time horizons	Long	Short
Regularity	Continuous	Periodic
Nature of problem	Unstructured and often unique, involving considerable risk and uncertainty	More structured and repetitive, with risks easier to assess
Information needed	Require large amounts of external information, much of which is subjective and futuristic	Depend more on internally generated accounting and marketing research information
Detail	Broad	Narrow and specific
Ease of evaluation	Decisions are more difficult to make and evaluate	Decisions are easier to make and evaluate

Exam hint

At the Diploma level the CIM is expecting students to be concerned with strategic rather than tactical issues. Too many candidates confuse strategy and tactics and provide detailed discussion of tactical marketing programmes rather than focusing on the strategic issues. Make sure you understand the differences between strategy and tactics and you reflect this understanding in your answers.

Contingency planning is concerned with developing plans to deal with events that may occur but that are not addressed in the main plan. For example, companies involved in exporting their goods may develop contingency plans to deal with fluctuations in exchange rates.

Definitions

Objective – A statement of what an organization is trying to achieve. Ideally objectives should be SMART (Specific, Measurable, Actionable, Realistic and Time bound).

Strategy – A broad statement of the way in which objectives are to be met.

Tactics – Represents the details of the plan – who, what, when and how.

Contingency planning – Planning for uncontrollable events.

Activity 1.5

Planning in action

Consider your own organization and its planning and control cycle. What types of planning are evident? How effective are the plans? How are they controlled? To what extent do you think the planning process could be improved?

Planning in the real world

Strategic planning was once heralded as the only way to devise and implement strategies that would gain competitive advantage. A great deal of time and energy was put into developing frameworks that facilitated planning. The planning function was often separated from the rest of the organization and staffed by specialists. Planning models such as the one illustrated in Figure 1.7 continue to provide a useful framework; however, it is increasingly being recognized that strategic planning is not strategic thinking, and in some cases strategic planning actually gets in the way of strategic thinking. Many organizations have rigid planning cycles that have to be adhered to, whereas creative strategies do not necessarily conform to these timescales.

Extended knowledge

Henry Mintzberg provides an excellent discussion of the difference between strategic planning and strategic thinking. Refer to Mintzberg's article 'The Fall and Rise of Strategic Planning' in *The Harvard Business Review* January–February 1994, pp. 107–114.

Barriers to planning

Many plans fail, not because they are based on inappropriate strategies, but for other reasons that often relate to the human aspects of organizations. Drummond and Ensor (2001) identify the following barriers to successful planning:

- ○ *Culture* – if organizations are not market-oriented, staff may receive plans with much resistance and be reluctant to change their work practices.
- ○ *Power and politics* – all organizations are subject to internal politics. Far too often people have their own agendas that can lead to internal conflict.
- ○ *Analysis, not action* – much time can be wasted by analysing vast amounts of data without actually taking any action. This is a criticism often directed at students sitting the Analysis and Decision case study; they spend far too long analysing the data and fail to give adequate attention to the key issue of developing a future strategy.
- ○ *Resource issues* – there may be insufficient resources available to implement the plan.
- ○ *Skills* – in some cases managers do not have the skills necessary to make best use of the planning process. Too often planning becomes a ritualistic task that often results in an extrapolation of the previous year's activities.

Other barriers to successful planning include perceived lack of time, resentment of imposed plans, a reluctance to commit to targets and in some cases lack of knowledge or interest. Many plans fail at the implementation stage, and it is therefore suggested that the planning process must focus on this critical stage. Implementation will be discussed further in the unit 'Implementation and control'. Piercy (2001) advocates a multi-dimensional model of planning, which is illustrated in Figure 1.8. This model emphasizes that the planning process is concerned not only with the techniques associated with planning but also with the behavioural aspects and organizational dimension of the planning process.

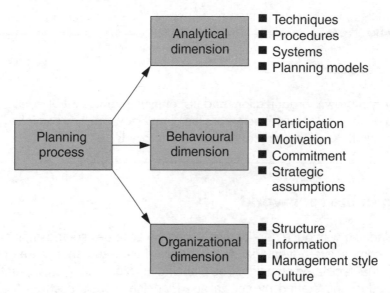

Figure 1.8 A multi-dimensional model of marketing planning
Piercy, 2000

It is clear that, for successful planning, not only has the plan got to be appropriate but also commitment from staff must be gained, and the structure and culture of the organization must facilitate and encourage change.

Organizational structures and culture

The way in which an organization is structured and the style of culture it exhibits will influence organizational effectiveness and efficiency. This text is not going to discuss in detail the various alternatives in terms of how organizations may be structured, but will provide a brief discussion of the alternatives and highlight the implications for marketing planning. Figure 1.9 identifies the three main approaches to organizational structures.

Organization by:	*Advantages*	*Disadvantages*

1. Function	Logical
	Allows for a clear
	  division of work
	  on the basis of
	  specialisms
		Poor communication
		Tends to inhibit
		  creativity
		Limits the
		  development of
		  cross-functional teams

2. Product/brand	Direct accountability
	  for the performance
	  of inidividual products
	  and brands
	Cross-functional
	  activities can be
	  integrated
	Levels of specialism
	  can be increased
		Costs tend to be
		  higher than for 1
		Levels of complexity
		  increase

*3. Territory or
    market sector*
	More focused market
	  decision making
	Better local knowledge
	Stronger links and
	  relationships with customers
		Higher overheads
		Possible duplication
		  of effort

Figure 1.9 The advantages and disadvantages of different organizational structures

Some organizations have developed matrix structures to overcome some of the shortfalls of these various structures. Matrix structures are designed to encourage a multidisciplinary approach, a higher degree of flexibility, better teamwork and to facilitate organizational learning and innovation. Figure 1.10 illustrates an example of a matrix structure for a manufacturing company.

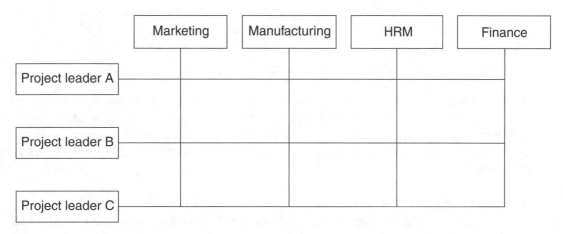

Figure 1.10 Matrix organization for a manufacturing company

Within organizations there is also an informal structure that exists alongside the formal one. This consists of social networks and relationships that have developed and may cut across department boundaries. The informal network should not be ignored when considering how to implement plans because it can often be a powerful means of getting things done (however, it can also create obstacles).

Case history

Panasonic – reshaping its organization

Until recently, electronics maker Panasonic operated its 13 US strategic business units as separate divisions. Panasonic was accused of being 'stuck in a marketing time warp', with each of its divisions operating in silos and making their own decisions on how their products should be marketed. The result being that too many different messages were being created and customers were confused as to the positioning of the Panasonic brand.

Customer research revealed that Panasonic was a well-respected brand but was not thought of as an innovative market leader. Customers were surprised that Panasonic operated in such diverse markets selling everything from DVD players to broadcast studio equipment to robot welding machines. The 'old-style' structure failed to capitalize on the synergy that could have been created had uniform marketing messages been communicated.

To solve these problems, Panasonic integrated its 13 divisions into one marketing voice. A key part of this strategy involved the development of a single brand message which was encapsulated in the tagline 'Ideas for life'.

Source: Van Camp (2002)

Global company structures

Global companies can have several advantages over their local competitors. Their sheer size gives them greater economies of scale in manufacturing, product sourcing, market coverage and product development. Their presence in many countries allows them to tap into new ideas and opportunities as well as giving them bargaining power over local governments.

However, in reality many global companies are perceived as being highly bureaucratic and slow to adapt. According to Birkinshaw (2000), 'the challenge for top managers lies in minimizing these liabilities, while retaining the benefits of size'. As Sir Martin Sorrell, Chief Executive of advertising group WPP, commented, 'Every CEO wants the power of a global company with the heart and soul of an entrepreneurial company'. This can be partly achieved through reward systems, by working on organizational culture and also through organizational structure. There is no one ideal way of organizing global companies. The organization will be influenced by a number of factors such as type of industry, number of businesses and countries in which it operates, location of customers and history. Birkinshaw (2000) proposed four global structures:

The international division

A separate international division is set up to deal with all sales outside the home market. Many medium-sized companies with limited international sales are set up in this way. However, few large global companies adopt this structure.

The global product division

In some companies product managers have responsibility for their product globally. The main advantage being that it facilitates the co-ordination of activities worldwide. However, this standardized approach can hinder the ability to respond to country-specific differences. The global product division is probably the most common structure among global companies such as BP, BT, 3M and Ericsson.

The area division

The main line of authority lies with the country or regional manager. This enables companies to respond to individual country needs. However, the co-ordination across countries suffers and it is difficult to achieve economies of scale. Ten years ago this was a common approach however, it is rare to find it today.

The global matrix

A business manager would report to two managers – a global business unit manager and a country manager. The country manager ensures that local market conditions are considered whilst the global business unit manager ensures activities are co-ordinated worldwide. This in theory appears ideal, however, the reality is often very different. In many cases business managers find themselves pulled in different directions by the two managers. To try and overcome this problem some companies have adopted an 'unbalanced' matrix where they report directly to the product division but then have a 'dotted line' to the country manager.

Case history

Network organization – Volvo cars

Network organizations are not an alternative to the four global structures described above. Instead they are best seen as an informal overlay that cuts across whatever formal structure is chosen. Volvo cars describes itself as a network organization because it has strong project groups that cut across functions, as well as cross-country teams. The networking concept is useful because it moves away from strict chains of command and can aid faster and informed decision-making. Networking organizations utilize tools such as cross-functional teams, global business teams, dotted line reporting and project groups. Underlying and supporting these strategies are IT systems, employee transfer and rotation policies.

Extended knowledge

For a comprehensive discussion of organizational structures, see Chapter 22 of Kotler's *Marketing Management, The Millennium Edition*, 2000.

Activity 1.6

Organizational structure

Draw an outline of your organization/SBU structure.

What impact does the structure have on:

- Planning
- Communication
- Culture

within your organization?

Definition

Culture – Aaker (1998) suggested that organizational culture involves three elements: (1) a set of shared values or dominant beliefs that define an organization's priorities; (2) a set of norms of behaviour; (3) symbols and symbolic activities used to develop and nurture those shared values and norms.

Culture

The culture of an organization often develops over many years and is influenced by a whole range of factors such as management style, organizational structure, the organization's history, chief executive leadership style, type of market, number and intensity of competition, location, PEST factors, union involvement and the nature of the business (i.e. traditional or based on new technologies). All these factors will develop a culture that is unique to a particular organization. However, it is possible to identify various organizational cultures. Deal and Kennedy (2000) identify four different cultures according to their attitude to risk (see Figure 1.11).

Speed of feedback

	Slow feedback	Fast feedback
Hard risk	"Bet your company culture"	"Hard Macho culture"
Attitude to risk		
Low risk	"Process culture"	"Work hard/play hard culture"

Figure 1.11 Corporate cultures

The company's corporate culture will have a major impact on the successful implementation of plans. It will influence the extent to which staff are prepared to change, adapt and accept new ways of working, will have an impact on staff motivation and will affect the image of the organization.

Case history

A clash of two cultures

Mergers, partnerships and strategic alliances are becoming commonplace in the industrial landscape and yet research has shown that many of these relationships do not reap the promised benefits. According to a KPMG study, just 17 per cent of cross-border mergers and acquisitions from 1996 to the end of 1998 added to shareholder value. What so many acquirers forget is that while finance might propel the deal, its lack of marketing synergy that will undo it. 'The hard stuff is relatively easy to calculate. But they usually haven't done their homework on the soft stuff, and so the integration fails because of a culture clash' says Anita Hoffman, Business Development Director at management consultancy Accenture. 'There is little discussion about how the two cultures will fit together in terms of how they go to market, how they sell and how they treat the customer' says Helena Rubenstein, Managing Director of branding consultancy The Lab .

The potential for a culture clash was enormous when Unilever acquired Ben and Jerry's ice-cream. Ben and Jerry's distinctive ethically oriented culture and brand values are in stark contrast to the vast conglomerate's culture. There was a danger that Ben and Jerry's would be submerged in Unilever's culture and lose its uniqueness. In an attempt to retain its unique culture and the brand's ethical stance, a clause that stated that 8 per cent of pre-tax profits should continue to go to charity was incorporated into the buyout agreement.

A major challenge for all parties involved in mergers, acquisitions or partnerships is how to effectively integrate disparate cultures. The importance of culture cannot be overemphasized and companies should seek out partners that they believe will prove to be complementary and synergistic.

Source: Mazur (2001), www.Lexis-Nexis.com

Extended knowledge

Johnson and Scholes provide a comprehensive discussion of organizational culture and its impact on strategy in their text *Exploring Corporate Strategy*, 5th Edition, Chapter 5, 1999, pp. 233–241.

Strategic marketing plans

This section will focus on the structure of the strategic marketing plan. Planning and plans are two very different concepts. Planning is concerned with the process of developing a coherent plan whilst the plan relates to the output (often the physical plan). The plan is the means by which the strategy is communicated within the organization. The structure and content of a strategic marketing plan will vary considerably between organizations. Numerous books written on marketing planning propose slightly different formats. However, many contain common components, including:

- o Current situation – external and internal analysis
- o Objective setting
- o Strategy formulation
- o Marketing programmes
- o Implementation issues
- o Control measures.

There is no one best format for a marketing plan and organizations will develop their own frameworks that match the needs of their company. However, Figure 1.12 illustrates the approach adopted by Drummond and Ensor (2001).

	1. Executive Summary
	1.1 Current position
	1.2 Key issues
Provides link to the overall strategy and illustrates marketing's contribution to achieving corporate goals.	**2. Corporate Strategy**
	2.1 Corporate mission/objectives
	2.2 Summary of overall position and corporate strategy

Improves communication and staff involvement by summarizing key aspects of the plan.

Provides link to the overall strategy and illustrates marketing's contribution to achieving corporate goals.

1. Executive Summary

1.1 Current position
1.2 Key issues

2. Corporate Strategy

2.1 Corporate mission/objectives
2.2 Summary of overall position and corporate strategy

3. External and Internal Analysis

3.1 Overview of market
3.2 Competitor analysis
3.3 Future trends
3.4 SWOT

A picture of the competitive environment is developed. Internal factors (strengths and weaknesses) need to address external factors (opportunities and threats).

There is a need to define financial targets and translate these into specific, measurable marketing objectives (e.g. market share, sales volume, customer retention).

4. Marketing Objectives

4.1 Financial objectives
4.2 Marketing objectives

5. Marketing Strategy

5.1 Market segmentation
5.2 Competitive advantage
5.3 Marketing strategy
5.4 Specific marketing programmes
 ■ product
 ■ place
 ■ promotion
 ■ price

The overall strategic direction of marketing policy is defined. The strategy may vary according to market segment.

Decisions are made relating to specific aspects of the mix. These may generate additional plans for each element of the mix.

6. Implementation

6.1 Schedule of key tasks
6.2 Resource allocation
6.3 Budgets
6.4 Contingency

Specific programmes are broken down into lists of activities. These are scheduled and given a time scale. Responsibility is assigned for each activity. A contingency (e.g. funds or time) may be set to cover any unforeseen problems.

7. Control and Forecasting

7.1 Assumptions made
7.2 Critical success factors
 ■ Benchmarks established
 ■ How measured
7.3 Financial forecasts
 ■ Costs
 ■ Revenue

A clear understanding of the assumptions underpinning the control process is required (e.g. projected market growth). The benchmarks measuring success must be assigned to critical activities. Profit and loss accounts may be forecast for the planning period.

Figure 1.12 Illustrative example of a strategic marketing plan

Alternatively refer to Malcolm McDonald's book – *Marketing Plans* – which provides a step by step guide to marketing planning (see Extended knowledge given below). In reality no two marketing plans are, or should be the same. However, the available frameworks can act as a starting point for many organizations.

Exam hint

On recent Planning and Control exam papers, students have not been asked to produce a full marketing plan. Too many students provide detailed marketing plans for the mini-cases which are not required and fail to answer the questions set. However, it is essential that you are familiar with the contents of a marketing plan and could develop one if asked. It is expected that you will prepare detailed marketing plans in preparation for the Analysis and Decision exam.

Despite the varying formats and structures of marketing plans they should all have one thing in common – they should generate action. It has been known for marketing executives to slave over the development of a marketing plan only to find that it never sees the light of day and is shelved because it is no longer appropriate. Marketing plans should be sufficiently flexible to take into account the changing environment.

Extended knowledge

You should already be familiar with the components of a marketing plan. However, it would be helpful for you to revisit this area. The following are useful sources that you would be advised to read.

Drummond and Ensor (2001). Chapter 12.

McDonald (2002). This text is particularly useful because it provides a step by step marketing planning system.

Kotler P (2000). Chapter 3.

Marketing plans are covered in the CIM Advanced Certificate module Marketing Operations. It may be worthwhile revisiting this module to refresh your memory.

Summary

- Marketing is not only concerned with functional activities such as promotion, pricing and market research. It is a business philosophy that seeks to put the customer at the centre of an organization's activities.

- Many companies are increasingly recognizing the importance of the societal marketing concept. This concept suggests that organizations not only have a responsibility to their customers and stakeholders, but also have a responsibility to society in general.

- The key components of a market orientation include having a customer orientation, a competitor orientation, interfunctional co-ordination, a supportive organizational culture and a long-term perspective.

- Market-led strategic change refers to the process of 'going to market' where firms should concentrate on understanding customers, segmentation, targeting and positioning, and importantly the means by which strategies are implemented.

o Organizations operate in a dynamic environment and therefore they have to take into consideration those external influences that will impact on their business. These influences are often referred to as drivers of change.

o In market-oriented organizations it is likely that marketing will be the largest contributor to corporate strategy. Corporate strategy is concerned with what types of business the company as a whole should be in, i.e. the scope of the business. Marketing strategy is concerned with transforming corporate objectives into a competitive market position.

o Planning is a fundamental part of a manager's role. It is concerned with the allocation and coordination of resources to help achieve predetermined objectives. The planning framework encourages managers to develop a systematic approach to developing objectives and then developing strategies to achieve these objectives.

o Strategy and tactics are often confused. They are both concerned with achieving objectives but the difference depends on the level within an organization from which you are looking.

o There are many barriers to planning within organizations that marketers must learn to overcome such as power and politics, lack of skills, lack of time and an organizational culture that resists change.

o Organizational structures and culture can have a major impact on organizational effectiveness and efficiency.

o A strategic marketing plan is the vehicle by which the marketing strategy is communicated within the organization. The structure and format of a strategic marketing plan will vary considerably between organizations. There is no one 'best' structure.

Further study and examination preparation

Extended knowledge

Bibliography and links

Aaker D (1998). *Strategic Market Management*, 5th Ed., John Wiley & Sons.

Birkinshaw J (2000). The structures behind global companies, *Financial Times Mastering Management* Series, 30 November.

Carpenter G (1998). Changing the rules of the marketing game, *Financial Times Mastering Marketing* Series, 14 September.

Crosier K (1975). What Exactly is Marketing? *Quarterly Review of Marketing*, Winter.

Deal T and Kennedy A (2000). *The New Corporate Cultures*, Texere Publishing.

Drummond G and Ensor J (2001). *Strategic Marketing Planning and Control*, Butterworth-Heinemann.

Greenhalgh L (2001). Managers face up to the new era, *Financial Times Mastering Management Series*, 23 January.

Griffiths J (2000). Direct Line enters market, *Financial Times*, 12 July p. 4.

Hooley GJ, Saunders JA and Piercy NF (1998). *Marketing Strategy and Competitive Positioning*, 2nd Ed., Prentice-Hall.

Johnson G and Scholes K (1999). *Exploring Corporate Strategy*, 5th Ed., Prentice-Hall.

Kohli AK and Jaworski BJ (1990), cited in Hooley GJ, Saunders JA and Piercy NF (1998), *Marketing Strategy and Competitive positioning*, 2nd Ed., Prentice-Hall.

Kotler P (2000). *Marketing Management, The Millennium Edition*, Prentice-Hall.

Mason T (2000). The Importance of Being Ethical – A New Breed of Caring Consumerism Means Companies Need to Consider Ethical Issues, *Marketing*, 26 October, p. 27.

Mazur L (2001). Acquisition Activity is on a High, but in most Cases the Deals Fail to Deliver, *Marketing*, 8 February, p. 26.

Meehan S and Barwise P (1998). Do you Value Customer Value? *Financial Times Mastering Marketing* Series, 14 September.

McDonald M (2002). *Marketing Plans: How to Prepare Them, How to Use Them*, 5th Ed., Butterworth-Heinemann.

Mintzberg H (1994). The Fall and Rise of Strategic Planning, *Harvard Business Review*, January–February, pp. 107–114.

Narver JC and Slater SF (1990), cited in Hooley GJ, Saunders JA and Piercy NF (1998), *Marketing Strategy and Competitive Positioning*, 2nd Ed., Prentice-Hall.

Piercy N (2001). *Market-led Strategic Change*, 2nd Ed., Butterworth-Heinemann.

Sorrell M (2000), cited in Birkinshaw J (2000), The Structures Behind Global Companies, *Financial Times Mastering Management Series*, 30 November.

Van Camp S (2002). Panasonic Brushes off Cobwebs, *Adweek*, vol. 22, p. 6.

Weitz BA and Wensley R (1988). *Readings in Strategic Marketing*, Dryden.

www.co-operativebank.co.uk

www.jamjar.com

unit 2 external analysis

By the end of this unit you will:

o Be aware of, and understand the importance of the external environment in developing strategy

o Be able to discuss various factors that are acting as drivers of change, and be able to provide examples of them

o Understand the dimensions of an environmental monitoring system

o Be able to describe, apply and critically evaluate Porter's model of industry analysis

o Understand the importance of competitor analysis and be able to undertake a detailed analysis of competitors

o Know the components of a market analysis

o Appreciate the importance of customer analysis, and be able to undertake a detailed analysis of both organizational and consumer customers.

Study Guide

o This unit will take you about 4 hours to work through

o We suggest that you take a further 3 hours to do the various activities and questions in this unit.

Key definitions

Environmental scanning – The process of monitoring and analysing the marketing environment of a company (Jobber, 2001, p. 142).

Marketing environment – Consists of the actors and forces that affect a company's capability to operate effectively in providing products and services to its customers.

Microenvironment – Consists of the actors in the firm's immediate environment that affect its capabilities to operate effectively in its chosen market. The key actors are suppliers, distributors, customers and competitors.

Macroenvironment – Consists of a number of broader forces that affect not only the company but also other actors in the microenvironment. These can be grouped under economic, social, legal, physical and technological forces. These shape the character of the opportunities and threats facing a company, and yet are largely uncontrollable (Jobber, 2001, p. 120).

Strategic group analysis – This aims to identify organizations with similar strategic characteristics following similar strategies or competing on similar bases (Johnson and Scholes, 1999, p. 127).

Organizational buying behaviour – The decision-making process by which formal organizations establish the need for purchased products and services, and identify, evaluate and choose among alternative brands and suppliers (Webster and Wind, 1972).

Introduction

An important part of the strategic development process is that of strategic analysis, i.e. answering the question 'Where are we now?'. Without first understanding this question it is impossible for organizations to decide where they want to go. Strategic analysis consists of undertaking an audit of both the external environment and the internal corporate environment. This unit is concerned with the external environment in the form of the macro-environment (PEST) and micro-environment (industry, market, competitors and customers). The next unit will address the issues relating to internal corporate analysis. Organizations do not exist in a vacuum and when developing their marketing strategy it is essential they take into account the changing external environment. Undertaking a strategic analysis will enable organizations to identify potential opportunities and threats that may arise from the changing environment and allow them to exploit potential opportunities and reduce the impact of threats.

Porter (1985) stressed the importance of analysing the external environment:

> *The essence of formulating strategy is relating a company to its environment. Every industry has an underlying structure or set of fundamental economic and technical characteristics. The strategist must learn what makes the environment tick.*

Activity 2.1

Contemporary examples

The Planning and Control Examiner is looking for evidence that students can apply theoretical concepts to practical situations. Scan the quality press such as the *Financial Times* and journals such as *Marketing, Marketing Week* and the *Economist* and search for articles that relate to the external environment, both macro and micro. Classify articles according to the type of external analysis they demonstrate. For example, an article on the impact of the Internet would be classified under the macroenvironment as a technological influence.

This portfolio of articles will provide you with a set of contemporary examples that you can use in the exam.

Environmental scanning

The environment is dynamic and it is often commented that the speed of change is increasing. This creates problems of uncertainty for managers and therefore, the need to monitor these changes is of paramount importance to all organizations. The means by which information is gathered about the environment is often referred to as environmental scanning.

Definition

Environmental scanning – The process of monitoring and analysing the marketing environment of a company (Jobber, 2001, p. 142).

Fahey and Narayanan (1986) identify three basic goals for environmental analysis:

1. The analysis should provide an understanding of current and potential changes taking place in the environment
2. Environmental analysis should provide important intelligence for strategic decision-makers
3. Environmental analysis should facilitate and foster strategic thinking in organizations.

Many organizations find it difficult to develop effective methods for scanning the environment. Probably more challenging is the task of converting this information into action. Information is basically a tool to reduce risk in decision-making. Too many organizations collect information religiously without actually using it to help make decisions. Organizations must develop scanning processes that not only collect the data but also convert these data into useful information that can aid decision-making. Information must then be transmitted to the right people, at the right time, and in the right format. Scanning includes both directed and undirected searching as well as informal and formal processes. On the one hand, scanning may involve formal analysis of the economic environment including interviews with industry experts; on the other hand, it may include browsing the national newspapers at the weekend. Both forms of scanning can be of equal value.

Case history

Effective scanning leads to new opportunities for Iceland (or does it?)

Iceland, the frozen foods specialist, was thought to have effectively identified an environmental change on which they were able to capitalize. Iceland correctly predicted that there would be a growth in the market for both organic foods and genetically modified (GM)-free foods. They used their stance on GM foods as a key differentiating factor. The growth in organic and GM-free foods has been fuelled by consumers' concerns over food safety and many organizations, including Iceland, saw this as a great opportunity.

Iceland positioned itself as a 'wholesome' retailer, by removing all artificial colours and flavourings from its own-brand products and being the first supermarket to ban GM foods. It purchased 40% of the world's supply of organic vegetables and attempted to widen the market for organic products by removing the traditional price differential between organic and inorganic foods. They sold their own-label organic frozen vegetables at the same price as other supermarkets' inorganic frozen vegetables.

On the surface this seemed to be an inspired strategy that capitalized on changes in the external environment. However, in reality Iceland's core customers were not interested in GM-free foods and in fact complained that they could not get their 'normal products'. This example illustrates that it is not enough to identify market opportunities but these must then be matched with a company's core competencies.

Source: Adapted from Mutel (2000), www.Lexis-Nexis.com

Environmental monitoring system

For environmental scanning to be effective it is important that organizations develop effective systems for managing the information generated from the process. Johnson and Scholes (1999) propose a framework for undertaking an environmental analysis (Figure 2.1). This model provides companies with a more formal approach to monitor the environment.

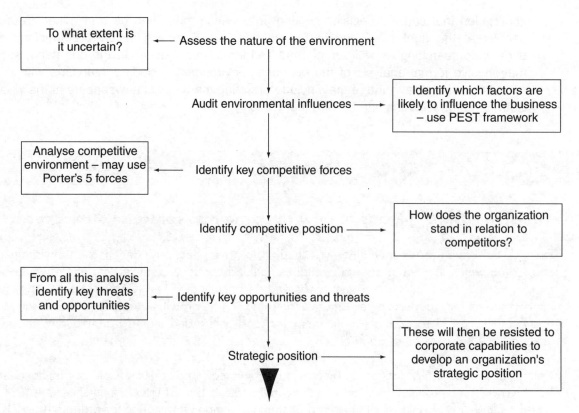

Figure 2.1 Steps in environmental analysis
Johnson and Scholes, 1999, p. 99

There is almost unlimited information available, and organizations cannot hope to scan all of it. Therefore, organizations have to look at the return on investment of their efforts in terms of the contribution the information makes to the marketing decision-making process. Aguilar (1967) suggests that managers search for information in five broad categories:

1. Market intelligence (market potential, competitors, customers, etc.)
2. Technical intelligence (licensing and patents, new products and processes, etc.)
3. Acquisition intelligence (information on mergers, partnerships and acquisitions)
4. Broad issues (PEST factors)
5. Other intelligence (resource availability, miscellaneous).

Extended knowledge

Read pp. 20–22 of Drummond and Ensor (2001), which provides a good summary of Aguilar's five categories of information.

See Chapter 5 (pp. 142–145) of Jobber (2001) for an interesting discussion of environmental scanning.

The process of environmental scanning is of paramount importance when organizations are trying to identify the 'drivers of change' for their industry. Too often, companies fail to even identify major 'drivers of change' because they are looking backwards instead of looking forwards.

Activity 2.2

Environmental scanning

With reference to your own organization identify types of:

o formal systematic scanning
o informal scanning

that your organization undertakes.

How effective do you think the process is? What is missing from the process? Think of an example where:

o the scanning process was successful in identifying a threat
o your organization failed to detect a threat because of weaknesses in their scanning process.

What recommendations would you make to improve the scanning process within your organization?

Macroenvironmental analysis (PEST framework)

You should already be familiar with the concept of PEST (Political and legal, Economic, Social and Technological factors) or you may use another acronym (such as PESTLE, STEP or SLEPT). Whichever acronym you prefer, the purpose is the same. To provide a useful framework for structuring thinking about the macroenvironmental factors that impact on organizations and facilitating subsequent analysis.

The purpose of this text is not to provide a detailed discussion of all the various PEST factors. These are all well documented (see Extending knowledge, below) and it is expected that you are already familiar with the framework from previous studies such as Marketing Operations. It is also important that you can describe these influences, and are able to discuss the implications of them on marketing planning. Figure 2.2 identifies some of the major factors that constitute the PEST framework. This text will highlight three key factors and provide illustrative examples of each: Information Communication Technology (the Internet), Globalization and Ethical Concerns.

Definitions

Marketing environment – Consists of the actors and forces that affect a company's capability to operate effectively in providing products and services to its customers.

Microenvironment – Consists of the actors in the firm's immediate environment that affect its capabilities to operate effectively in its chosen market. The key actors are suppliers, distributors, customers and competitors.

Macroenvironment – Consists of a number of broader forces that affect not only the company but also the other actors in the microenvironment. These can be grouped under economic, social, legal, physical and technological forces. These shape the character of the opportunities and threats facing a company, and yet are largely uncontrollable (Jobber, 2001).

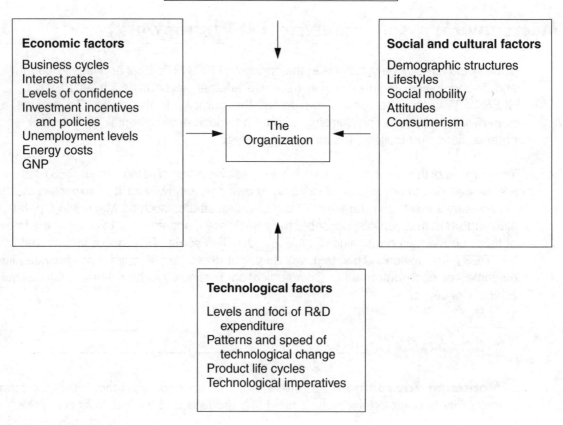

Political/legal factors

Legislative structures
Political structures
Government stability
Political orientations
Taxation policies
Employment legislation
Pressure groups
Trades union power
Relationships with foreign governments
Foreign trade regulations
Competitive behaviour legislation

Economic factors

Business cycles
Interest rates
Levels of confidence
Investment incentives
    and policies
Unemployment levels
Energy costs
GNP

The Organization

Social and cultural factors

Demographic structures
Lifestyles
Social mobility
Attitudes
Consumerism

Technological factors

Levels and foci of R&D
    expenditure
Patterns and speed of
    technological change
Product life cycles
Technological imperatives

Figure 2.2 The PEST framework
Johnson and Scholes, 1999, p. 99

Extended knowledge

To gain a good understanding of the PEST framework, and to refresh your memory, it is essential that you read Chapter 5 of Jobber (2001).

Alternatively you can refer to any other relevant text such as Kotler (2000) or Dibb et al. (2000).

Drummond and Ensor (2001) provide a good summary of the major PEST factors in Chapter 2, pp. 22–24.

Exam hint

The analysis of macroenvironmental influences is a key theme in all the CIM Diploma modules. For example, it is a key aspect when developing integrated marketing communications and has major implications for organizations involved in international marketing. In the Analysis and Decision major case study you will be expected to undertake an extensive PEST analysis and out of this you will develop future plans. Do not think of each module in a separate box – use the knowledge you have gained from all modules to help you in all the exams.

Activity 2.3

PEST analysis

For your own organization examine the macroenvironmental factors, using the PEST framework, that have impacted on your business over the last 5 years.

How has your organization responded to these threats/opportunities?

Information communication technology (ICT) – a key driver of change

ICT has revolutionized the ways in which companies do business. For example, the Internet has produced new distribution channels, has enabled companies to enter new geographical markets with greater ease and has improved, if not replaced in some cases, ordering systems, customer service and purchasing. Intranets are increasingly being used to improve internal communications and the impact of digital technology will be immense. The case history below provides three very different examples of companies that have seen the development of the Internet as an opportunity and have successfully capitalized on its increased use.

Case history

EMI records

Many music companies, particularly retailers, have felt threatened by the onset of the Internet for two reasons. Firstly, there is a trend towards on-line buying, where fans no longer need to visit a store to buy CDs. Market Tracking International predicts that the global value of the on-line music market (including CDs sold over the Internet) will be $5.2 billion in 2005 (11.3% of a forecasted $46 billion music market). Secondly, the main challenge facing the music publishing business is that more fans are downloading music directly from the Internet, sometimes illegally. These trends are a significant threat to record companies, which face the loss of their very healthy profit margins on CDs. The combined force of consumers empowered by this new technology and artists keen to use the Internet to sell directly to fans has led the record companies to realize that they will have to act quickly.

EMI has joined forces with Time-Warner and AOL in an attempt to develop their Internet business. Two main strategies are to sell their music on-line using free downloads as a promotional tool. EMI has taken equity in musicmaker.com, a site that allows consumers to custom-make their own CDs from a selection of 100,000 tracks. The concept is proving popular – unusually for e-commerce sites it is making money! EMI is also digitizing its entire catalogue of music, making it possible to sell all its 'artists' music over the Internet.

Possibly one of the greatest opportunities arising from the Internet is the ability to target and develop stronger relationships with key customers through e-mail and the use of special promotional offers.

The Internet is changing the face of the music business and many believe that the record companies will have to concentrate on the skills of creating acts and marketing them, and leave the distribution to others.

Source: Adapted from Murphy (2000).

Case history

Totalbet

Totalbet (www.totalbet.com) is the Tote's on-line betting site. It was set up as a joint venture with the sports news site PA Sporting Life, which itself a joint venture between the Mirror Group and the Press Association. Totalbet went live on 10 April 1999, to coincide with the Grand National.

'We realized a long time ago that the Internet was a medium that had a fairly major future and we wanted to have a major presence', says Rob Hartnett, Public Relations Director. 'We wanted to do it in partnership with someone who had Internet capability, and the site set up by PA Sporting Life was by far the most popular in Europe'.

When it was launched, the site was able to take bets only for the Grand National – but the range has since been extended. 'In the interim we've added other events and sports – soccer, rugby league and union, motor racing, golf and cricket', says Hartnett. Totalbet also carries editorial content from the *Sporting Life* site.

'The site has built up 5000 registrations in its first three months', Hartnett adds. 'To put that in context, our telephone betting operation has 50,000 accounts and its one of the biggest in Europe'. The level of on-line business per bet is higher than that for the Tote's telephone betting service, which is in turn higher than it is in shops. Hartnett says this reflects the fact that Internet users still tend to be relatively affluent.

To promote the site, the Tote initially relied heavily on its link with *Sporting Life*. An on-line and print advertising campaign was launched at the end of July, targeting sports sites and newspaper sports sections. Totalbet also sponsored three horse races. The introduction of pool betting to the site is also scheduled for the autumn. The Tote has the exclusive UK licence for pool betting on horse racing.

Because this form of betting requires less human intervention than bookmaking, which involves complex risk assessment, it is expected to be well suited to the Internet.

Source: Reed (1999).

Case history

Berry Bros. & Rudd

Berry Bros. & Rudd is a privately owned specialist wine retailer that can trace its origins back to 1698. In 1995, it became the first UK wine merchant to have a Web site, according to John-Paul Cockain, Berry's Internet shop manager.

Initially the site, at www.bbr.co.uk, acted as a shop window, but in November 1998 it became a shop in its own right. 'With Internet shopping expected to explode, it just seemed to us that the time was right', explains Cockain. The site is regularly reworked to improve navigation. It focuses on Berry's 300-year history to build trust in on-line shopping, and features special offers and J-P's Wine Surgery, which explains wine mysteries.

The Internet shop now accounts for 5% of Berry's London-based sales, with 60% of Internet purchases made by new customers. About 40% of sales are to customers outside the UK. 'The Internet has certainly opened us up to a much broader audience in the UK and overseas', says Cockain. Berry also supplies international shoppers through its duty free shop at Heathrow Terminal 3, which opened in 1994.

The company used print advertising and Internet banner ads to promote its on-line operations. The bulk of its on-line advertising is focused on sites where visitors are likely to be comfortable with on-line shopping.

Source: Reed (1999).

All these cases were sourced using www.lexis-nexis.com

ICT – managing customer relationships

ICT has revolutionized the ways in which customers communicate with companies. In the past, customers were limited to face to face, post or the telephone. Today's customers can interact with the companies via multiple channels – e-mail, company Web site, SMS, WAP and with the growth of interactive digital television, these channels are only set to increase further.

Companies are finding it increasingly difficult to manage these numerous points of contact. It is essential that they develop customer relationship management strategies that enable individual customer's behaviour to be tracked across multiple channels. At present, most companies do not have systems in place to take a unified approach to their customers. If done successfully, this will have several benefits: provides increased information on customers and identifies high-value customers, allows companies to tailor their marketing for different types of customers and provides opportunities for upselling and cross-selling. This in turn should lead to better customer retention and hopefully increased profitability.

Globalization – a key driver of change

Globalization is the tendency for organizations to operate on a global level. The term should not be taken literally, as frequently 'global' organizations focus on supply bases and customers in the major centres of economic activity of North America, Europe, Japan, China and south-east Asia and more recently India. The engine driving globalization is economies of scale. The size of global organizations gives them enormous economies of scale in manufacturing, in new product development and in market coverage. Global reach allows them to tap into new ideas and opportunities wherever they may occur. However, a major dilemma for global organizations is the extent to which local markets require adaptation of products and services, and/or marketing strategy and tactics, in order to meet the requirements of local consumers. For example, Hindus don't want to eat beef burgers, clothes for the American market must be adapted for the slighter Asian figure, and European and American cars must be adapted to meet stringent pollution limits in the Japanese market.

Exam tip

The Analysis and Decision major case study frequently selects an international context for students to apply their understanding of marketing. Consequently, students should be comfortable with applying marketing strategy to international business environments. Students will also find it useful to refer to the International Marketing Strategy diploma module for a more detailed discussion of this topic.

The three case histories below show examples of companies operating internationally.

Case history

Wal-Mart – conquering the World?

Wal-Mart was founded in 1962; it now has sales of £150 billion, 3400 American stores, 1200 international stores in nine countries and employs more than 1.3 million people. It is the world's largest retailer and has got an ambitious goal of doubling its sales in just 5 years. In order to achieve this goal, Wal-Mart will have to enter new overseas markets. Last year, 16% of the firm's total sales were generated by their international stores. However, Wal-Mart encounters many challenges when entering new markets. In Europe and Asia transport systems are not as refined as in the US. This has made it more difficult to keep down supply chain and inventory costs.

Entry into China and Korea has been successful, but Argentina and Brazil continue to be difficult markets. In Mexico they are now the largest retailer. The acquisition of the Asda brand in Britain is regarded as a success. The German market has proved more difficult primarily due to the cultural differences. For example, Wal-Mart employs 'greeters' to welcome customers to the store. German customers viewed the friendly door greeters with some suspicion and in some cases found them sickening. Wal-Mart also faced stiff competition from German chains.

Source: Adapted from Rossingh, D, Wal-Mart: A Retail Titan, http://news.bbc.co.uk/1/hi/business/2657089.stm, 14 January 2003.

Case history

Uniqlo

The path to globalization begins with entering the first non-domestic market. Uniqlo, the Japanese clothing retailer entered its first overseas market in 2001, by opening four stores in the UK. Consumer tastes are very similar in large parts of the clothing retailing market in many advanced industrial economies. Closely modelled on rival chains such as Gap and M&S, the retailer, owned by Fast Retailing in Japan, has already demonstrated an ability to compete successfully with overseas competition. As the store group expanded in Japan, the US rival 'Gap' found profits to be affected significantly by the opening of a Uniqlo outlet in the neighbourhood. Its success is due to the broad range of cheap but well-made, highly popular casual clothes offered such as jeans, chinos and polo shirts. They have been described as not particularly fashionable but simple and stylish. In addition they are offered at very low prices, with supplies sourced from China. Unlike most of the competition, the company controls all aspects of the business, from fabric dying, design, manufacture as well as retailing. This effective value offer is presented with embellishment such as a free trouser alteration service, which is normally only provided by more upmarket retailers.

Case history

Global marketing, local adaptation – international media

International media owners have generally been unable to acquire controlling interests in many media outlets in Asia. Few governments in this region will allow foreign ownership, especially of national television and newspapers. The main outlets for any media expansion are with cable and satellite television, consumer and business magazines and regional newspapers that have a multi-country audience.

International media groups must balance the need to achieve economies of scale through standardization with demands of local consumers for media to be directly relevant to them. Only a few titles have been successful with global standardization, e.g. the *Economist* and *USA Today*. Competing in local markets, international media groups must decide to what extent they are to attune the content to local interests and thereby reduce the potential cost savings from economies of scale. The compromise that has been common is to operate pan regional titles that have some local focus, e.g. AOL Time Warner's *Asiaweek* and Dow Jones' *Far Eastern Economic Review*. This is similar in approach to locally branded versions of international titles such as Star TV, the Asian version of Sky/Fox.

At the other end of the scale of adaptation are the fully local products. However, international media groups tend to be uncomfortable with this strategy and have avoided collecting a selection of single country, media titles. The general exception to this approach is in eastern Asia, where for example CNBC has five local products covering markets such as Japan, Hong Kong and Singapore, as well as the main CNBC Asia channel.

Extended knowledge

For a good overview of international marketing, see Chapter 21 of Jobber (2001).

Question 2.1

Answer Question 6 from the June 2002 Planning and Control paper on globalization. Go to www.cimeduhub.com to access specimen answers for this question.

Ethical concerns – a key driver of change

The concept of societal marketing suggests that marketing should be concerned not only with satisfying customers and achieving organizational goals but that companies should have a responsibility to society in general. Increasingly companies are coming under pressure to operate in an ethical manner. Issues such as environmental concern, human rights and fair-trading are increasing in importance in the political arena. This is a key driver of change in the current external environment and one that many companies are having to take into account. In fact, many companies are regarding the increased interest in ethical marketing as an opportunity rather than as a threat. As Vernon Ellis, International Chairman of Accenture, said at the New Statesman lecture last year, 'Global business is not something apart from society; its health and even its long-term survival depend on the global environment in which it operates' (Mason, 2002). Those companies that have not embraced ethical marketing are those that have yet to realize that it makes good business sense and can gain them a competitive advantage. Consumers are also becoming increasingly concerned about ethical issues. Research by Business in the Community shows that, where price is equal, more than 80% of Western consumers would change brands and have a better perception of a company that does something to make the world a better place (Mason, 2002). The Co-operative bank is a good example of a company that has positioned itself on their ethical banking practices (see Unit 1).

The following examples illustrate how two companies, keen to develop ethical business practices, have gained a competitive advantage.

Case history

The Day Chocolate company

An increasing number of businesses are winning the Fair Trade Logo for their products. This logo shows that the producers are receiving a fair price for their products. One such business is the Day Chocolate company which is partly owned by a co-operative of cocoa farmers formed in Ghana nine years ago. Originally the co-operative helped its members by organizing trading and ensuring that beans were weighed fairly, that they were paid promptly and they were offered credit facilities if they were in financial difficulties. However, the farmers only earned approximately £300 a year selling cocoa and they realized that they had to do more than just grow beans. They decided to make chocolate and so the Day Chocolate company was formed. The company manufactures chocolate bars under the brand name 'Divine'. Profits from the business are given back to the farmers in the form of cash bonuses and development grants for water wells and schools.

There are several ways in which the co-operative's members benefit. Producers receive a guaranteed price for their goods and the security of long-term standing contracts. Minimum health and safety conditions are established and there are training opportunities for the producers, especially for women and children. However, just being a fair trade product does not guarantee commercial success. Divine is competing with some of the world's biggest companies. Customers will not necessarily buy the chocolate just because it is a fair trade product, it must be of at least equal quality. The Co-op was one of the first stores to stock Divine and they have reported that sales have been very strong. The Day Chocolate Company is not only satisfying its customers, but also helping to improve the lives of people in more deprived areas of the world.

Source: Adapted from www.bbc.co.uk/workinglunch

Case history

Tesco

Tesco have been involved in 'cause-related marketing' initiatives for several years. One of the most well known is the 'computers for schools' scheme which has been running for 10 years. This is where customers collect vouchers and give these to schools, who exchange them for computers. The programme has been very successful from Tesco's perspective, 538,000 of its 9 million shoppers showed a substantial increase in spend during the programme. Schools have also been able to purchase computer equipment that otherwise they would be unable to afford.

A further initiative by Tesco has raised substantial funds for the I-CAN charity for children with speech and language difficulties. Tesco is hoping to raise £125,000 to help fund 20 early years centres offering education and therapy to children and their families. I-CAN believe that the deal is important financially but also that the programme helps to raise awareness of the charity, due to the 5 million parents with children under 5 visiting Tesco stores each day.

These types of schemes are sometimes criticized because the sponsors are often seen to benefit substantially more than the causes they support. However, many of these schemes are supporting causes that would otherwise struggle financially. They have also been criticized for impacting on traditional ways of giving to charity. Research suggests that this is not the case and that 'cause-related marketing' programmes reach people that do not traditionally give to charity.

Source: Adapted from Mason (2002).

Activity 2.4

Business in the Community

Business in the Community is an independent Charity that 'creates a public benefit by working with companies to improve the positive impact of business in society'. They are involved in numerous projects. Visit their Web site to collect examples of ways in which companies are implementing strategies that benefit wider society,

www.bitc.org.uk

Question 2.2

PEST

Answer Question 6 from the December 2000 Planning and Control paper.
Go to www.cimeduhub.com to access specimen answers for this question.

Industry analysis

Once an organization has undertaken an analysis of the macroenvironment they can move on to analyse the microenvironment. A key component of this is the industry within which an organization is operating. It is important that marketing managers have a good understanding of the industry dynamics and the relationships that exist within it. A useful framework for undertaking this type of analysis is Porter's five forces model (Figure 2.3), which enables companies to gain greater insight into the level of competition and where the balance of power lies within a particular industry.

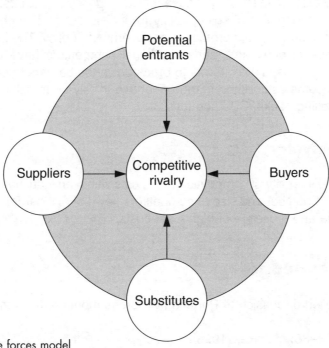

Figure 2.3 The five forces model
Adapted from Porter, 1980

This is a very brief overview of the five forces model. For more detailed coverage of this model, refer to the reading in the extended knowledge below.

Buyers

Buyer power relates to the bargaining power of a firm's customers. If customers have relatively more power than sellers they can put pressure on companies to reduce prices. Buyer power will be greater in situations where a few buyers hold a large proportion of the market or where there are many small suppliers. This is the situation in the UK, where multiple grocers such as Tesco and Sainsburys dominate the food retail market. They put great pressure on their suppliers, such as farmers and vegetable growers, to reduce prices.

Suppliers

This is concerned with the bargaining power of suppliers. Supplier power will be stronger when there are few suppliers that sell to a range of customers in diverse markets. For example, oil production is concentrated in the hands of a few powerful companies.

Substitutes

Substitutes are concerned with the products that compete indirectly with an organization's product offering. The intensity with which substitute products compete is generally less intense that for direct competitors. However, the impact of substitutes can be significant and have major implications for a firm. For example, the increased use of e-mail could threaten traditional mailing systems.

Potential entrants

The extent to which new players may enter the market is determined by the number of barriers to entry that may exist in an industry. These may include level of capital investment required to enter the market, economies of scale, ability to access distribution channels, brand strength and other factors such as patent protection or government policy. The Internet has had a major impact on barriers to entry and many traditional competitors have been attacked by new competitors that have used the Internet to break down the barriers to entry. For example, new retailers have become established that do not have to rely on traditional distribution channels such as those selling books, CDs and toys.

Competitive rivalry

This relates to the intensity of competition that exists within an industry. This will be determined by factors such as number and size of competitors, level of exit barriers, ability to differentiate, industry life-cycle and presence of high fixed costs.

Extended knowledge

For a more detailed discussion of Porter's five forces model refer to the following texts:

Chapter 5 (pp. 84–86) of Aaker (1998).

and/or

Chapter 2 (pp. 24–27) of Drummond and Ensor (2001).

Case history

Supermarket power

By applying the five forces model to the UK retail supermarket sector, it is evident that the balance of power lies with the supermarkets. So much so that the Competition Commission decided to investigate a number of key aspects of supermarkets' pricing strategies and their relationship with suppliers. Overall, the enquiry concluded that the multiple grocery industry was broadly competitive. However, the Commission found that some of the larger supermarkets had sufficient power that '30 of their practices adversely affected the competitiveness of some of their suppliers and distorted competition in the supply market'. For example, selling frequently bought items at below cost and varying prices according to local competition. The five major supermarkets had substantial advantages over smaller retailers, such as the ability to buy in bulk at discount from leading manufacturers.

Source: Adapted from Competition Commission: Findings on Supermarkets, 10 October 2000, http://news.bbc.co.uk/1/hi/business/965773.stm

Exam hint

The five forces model can often be helpful in analysing the industry in the mini-case of the Planning and Control exam. However, it is insufficient to just draw and describe the model; you must also be able to apply it to the industry in question.

Activity 2.5

Porter's five forces model

Undertake a five forces analysis of one of your organization's strategic business units.

What conclusions can you draw regarding the balance of power?

Competitor analysis

The industry analysis provides a broad understanding of the microenvironment in which an organization is operating; however, it is necessary to undertake a more detailed analysis of competitors within that industry. In order to gain a sustainable competitive advantage, it is essential that companies know their competitors and develop effective competitor information systems to monitor their activity. There is a wealth of information available on competitor analysis and therefore this text will highlight the key issues. For a more detailed discussion, please refer to the Extended knowledge at the end of this section.

Kotler (2000) suggests that in order to evaluate competitors organizations need to answer the following questions:

- ○ Who are our competitors?
- ○ What are their objectives?
- ○ What are their strategies (past and current)?
- ○ What are their strengths and weaknesses (capabilities)?
- ○ How are they likely to react?

Who are our competitors?

This may seem to be an obvious question. Many companies will have a number of competitors with which they compete directly, and which are visible and easily identifiable. For example, Ford obviously competes with companies such as Vauxhall, Nissan and Toyota. However, one can take a much broader perspective of competition and look at companies that are indirect or potential competitors. For example, it could be argued that Ford, in the widest sense, is competing with any company that produces a product/service that competes for the same disposable income as a car – a conservatory, holiday or house extension. It is impossible for companies to monitor all the different levels of competitors and therefore in the medium term they should concentrate on companies within the same strategic group. However, in the long-term companies should be monitoring the threat of new entrants or indirect competitors.

Strategic groups

According to Aaker (1998), a strategic group is a group of firms that:

o   Over time pursue similar competitive strategies (e.g. similar promotional and pricing strategies)
o   Have similar characteristics (e.g. size, attitudes)
o   Have similar assets and competencies (e.g. strong brand).

The strategic group framework is useful for identifying the companies with which a firm is in most direct competition. It also helps an organization to understand the basis on which competitive rivalry is taking place. There are many different criteria with which to identify strategic groups. According to Drummond and Ensor (2001) these may include:

o   Size of the company
o   Assets and skills
o   Scope of the operation
o   Breadth of the product range
o   Choice of distribution channel
o   Relative product quality
o   Brand image.

 Definition

> **Strategic group analysis** – This aims to identify organizations with similar strategic characteristics following similar strategies or competing on similar bases (Johnson and Scholes, 1999, p. 127).

In the financial services industry it is possible to identify a number of different strategic groups as illustrated in Figure 2.4.

o   Group 1 – local building societies (e.g. Cumberland Building Society)
o   Group 2 – national building societies (e.g. Nationwide)
o   Group 3 – multi-national financial service institution (e.g. HSBC).

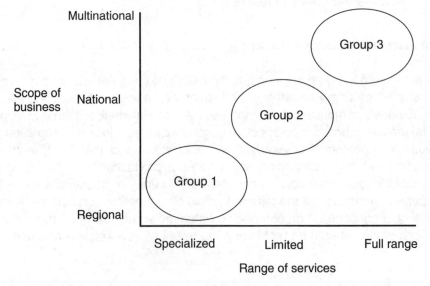

Figure 2.4 Strategic groups in the financial services industry (Meek and Meek, 2000)

Activity 2.6

Strategic groups

For an industry of your choice identify:

o   The attributes that would be most appropriate in identifying the various strategic groups
o   The various strategic groups that exist within the industry
o   Plot these on a matrix similar to the one presented in Figure 2.4.

Problems associated with identifying competitors

There are a number of problems that can arise when trying to identify a firm's competitors. It is often too easy to concentrate on large visible competitors whilst ignoring smaller competitors, which may be equally dangerous. There is also a possibility that attention will be given to existing competitors rather than potential new entrants. This has been the case for high-street banks in the UK. Many established traditional banks have been monitoring the direct competition within their strategic group. However, whilst they have been preoccupied by their direct competitors, the threat has in fact come from new entrants such as Virgin Financial Services. International competitors are in some cases also overlooked.

What are their objectives?

Once competitors have been identified it is necessary to identify their objectives in order to try and predict their future direction. Objectives may include market share domination, survival, short-term profits, long-term growth, etc.

What are their strategies?

In order to analyse strategies, both current and past, it is necessary to identify current markets and segments. A comparison of past and current strategies can provide useful insight into the possible direction in which the competitor is moving.

What are their strengths and weaknesses?

A strengths and weaknesses analysis will reveal the extent to which a firm is in a position to compete within the industry. It will help to identify competitors' capabilities such as their assets and resources, management ability, marketing capabilities, ability to innovate, production capabilities and financial standing. Porter's value chain (1980) can be a useful framework for analysing competitor's strengths and weaknesses. This model is discussed in Unit 4 – Auditing tools.

How are they likely to react?

A key element of competitor analysis is trying to predict how competitors may react when faced with competitor activity. Kotler (1999) identifies four types of competitor response:

o   Laid back – unlikely to respond to any initiative
o   Selective – will only react to certain types of attack
o   Tiger – will respond to any type of attack aggressively
o   Stochastic – their response is largely unpredictable.

From this analysis it will be possible to identify those competitors to attack and which to avoid.

Activity 2.7

Competitor analysis

Undertake a review of your three main competitors, either for an SBU or an individual product/service, by completing Table 2.1. What conclusions can you draw about which competitors to attack and which to avoid?

Table 2.1 Competitive analysis

	Competitor 1	Competitor 2	Competitor 3
What are their objectives?			
What are their strategies (past and current)?			
What are their strengths?			
What are their weaknesses?			
How may they react?			

Competitive intelligence system (CIS) and sources of competitive information

Gathering information to answer the questions posed above is often not easy. Some types of information will be readily available (such as annual reports, articles gleaned from the press, government statistics) and it is also possible to collect information using observational techniques (e.g. evaluating competitors advertising strategies, pricing policies and distribution management). Other types of information may be gathered using more ad hoc and informal methods, such as conversations with customers who also buy from your competitors, mutual suppliers, etc. The key to an effective CIS is that it is flexible enough to deal with data gleaned from a variety of sources ranging from formal systematic research to ad hoc informal conversations. The lengths to which some competitors will go to gather competitive intelligence sometimes push the boundaries of legality. For example, there have been instances where companies have stolen their competitors' rubbish in the hope of finding useful information. On another occasion bogus job interviews were held with competitors' employees, the purpose being to elicit information about their competitors. Companies can develop creative means of gathering competitive intelligence but they should ensure they are working within the law. Table 2.2 outlines an approach to categorizing competitive intelligence.

Table 2.2 An approach to the classification of competitor information

Recorded	Published information available either freely in the public domain or provided by a commercial research organization	• Government reports • Market research reports • General press • Trade press • Annual reports
Marketing activity and organizational activity[1]	Observable organization behaviour in the market	• Products and services in the market • Pricing • Approaches to distribution and service provision (including in-house and franchised) • Planning activity, building renovation and refurbishment • Advertising
Ad hoc – opportunistic	Information obtained from dialogue with people who have valuable information on competitors. These people may not realize that they have valuable information and may also not have any particular allegiance to various organizations within the industry	• Suppliers, e.g. of office equipment, including computer systems. Such diverse suppliers ranging from caterers to bankers can provide valuable information • Recruitment agencies • Trade/specialist shows and events • External seminars • Distributors, e.g. institutions offering courses and exams • Knowledgeable contacts in the business community • Government personnel with responsibility in the relevant markets • People who have worked for competitors or currently also work for competitors

[1]There is some overlap between information classified as recorded and marketing behaviour, i.e. some categories are not mutually exclusive. Of greater importance is the use of these three categories in organizing the collection and assessment of competitor intelligence.

According to Drummond and Ensor (2001, p. 36) competitive intelligence is useful for the following:

- o Anticipating competitor's activities
- o Analysing industry trends
- o Learning and innovation
- o Improved communication.

Activity 2.8

Competitor intelligence sources

Using the three main competitors identified in Activity 2.6, consider the relevant sources of competitor intelligence that are:

1. currently used in your organization
2. additional sources that would enhance your knowledge of your competitors.

How could this information be used by your organization?

Competitive intelligence cycle

The collection of competitive intelligence is not a one-off activity. It is a continuous cycle of data collection, analysis and decision-making. Figure 2.5 illustrates the concept of the competitive intelligence cycle and consists of four stages:

○ Planning and direction – outline information needs and sources
○ Collection – a strategy for collecting the data is developed
○ Analysis – concerned with converting data into useful information
○ Dissemination – tailoring information to meet user needs.

The firms that were once competitors may no longer be a threat and new competitors may enter the market at any time. It is essential that firms develop systems that not only collect data on existing competitors but also identify new ones.

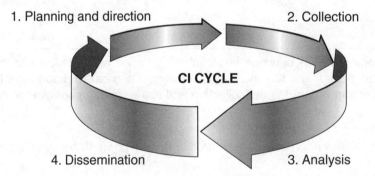

Figure 2.5 Competitive intelligence cycle
Adapted from Kahaner, 1997

Extended knowledge

Competitor analysis is well documented in a variety of texts. For a detailed discussion, please refer to the following:

For a useful discussion of competition, see Chapter 2 of Drummond and Ensor (2001), Chapter 3 provides a succinct overview of competitive intelligence.

Chapter 17 of Jobber (2001).

Chapter 7 of Hooley et al. (1998).

and/ or Chapter 4 of Aaker (1998).

For a practical discussion of competitive analysis, refer to Chapter 5 (pp. 203–211) of Davidson (1997).

Case history

Sources of competitor information

One of the most valuable services the Internet can offer is a short cut to information about millions of companies – whether potential collaborators, suppliers or competitors. In addition to initiating investigations using a search engine, e.g. www.google.com, more direct sources of information, especially on competitors, may be obtained from the following sites.

The Society of Competitive Intelligence professionals (www.scip.org) is dedicated to helping professionals develop expertise in creating, collecting, analysing and disseminating competitive intelligence.

To check the identity, reliability or credit-worthiness of another organization, try Dun and Bradstreet's site (www.uk.dnb.com). Its Globalseek service provides one-off information on companies. Detailed data for USA companies cost between $20 and $90.

For more detailed UK information, turn to UK Data (www.ukdata.com), which provides reports on every company registered with Companies House in UK. Costs range from £6 for a simple company overview to £24 for a comprehensive report.

For a more analytical edge, Business Credit Management UK (www.creditman.co.uk) provides International Chamber of Commerce information on 5 million UK businesses, live and defunct. A full report, at £42, includes the ICC/Juniper risk score.

For tailored competitor analysis – in both on-line and off-line markets – you may wish to try outsourcing your research. Smarterwork (www.smarterwork.com) links its users with an expanding pool of more than 3000 accredited 'experts' who will bid for, among other things, market research contracts. Smarterwork acts as a mediator, ensuring prompt payment and quality control by testing researchers before allowing them on its books.

This is a powerful opportunity to cut costs and save time. The site gathers researchers from throughout the world. Offers from outside the European Union or North America consistently undercut those from inside – a truly global marketplace.

Question 2.3

Competitor analysis

Answer Question 4 from the December 2002 Planning and Control paper on competitor analysis. Go to www.cimeduhub.com to access specimen answers for this question.

Question 3 from the December 2000 paper was also concerned with competitor analysis.

Market analysis

Once an analysis of the macroenvironment, the industry and competitors has been undertaken, it is appropriate to start analysing the market itself in greater detail. According to Drummond and Ensor (2001) market analysis would normally include the following:

- o Actual and potential market size (total market sales and growth potential)
- o Trends (analysing general trends that may highlight important market developments)
- o Customers (this will address questions such as 'who buys?' 'How do they buy?' 'Where and when do they buy?') This issue will be dealt with in the next section
- o Customer segments (identifying current, and possible, market segments and establishing the benefits they seek)
- o Distribution channels (analysing changes in distribution channels).

Extending knowledge

For further information on market analysis, see the following sources:

Chapter 4 of Aaker (1998).

and/or

Chapter 2 (p. 33) of Drummond and Ensor (2001).

Customer analysis

This section is concerned with analysing customers and trying to understand them. This information will help organizations in developing their segmentation, targeting and positioning strategies (this will be discussed in detail in Unit 8 – Developing a specific competitive position). Understanding customers is probably one of the most challenging activities that a firm will engage in. Many companies commit large sums of money every year in an attempt to predict the behaviour of their often elusive customers. Companies are increasingly recognizing that their customers are not a homogenous mass with similar needs and wants and similar profit potential. Thus the need for relevant and timely information is a key aspect of the auditing process. Customer analysis is well documented in many texts. Therefore, the purpose here is to highlight the key topics with which you should be familiar and direct you to further reading to gain greater insight into these core concepts. You should already be familiar with many of these concepts from previous studies, such as Marketing Operations and the Marketing Customer Interface.

Exam hint

Planning and Control exam questions may not always relate to the consumer market. There are many occasions when students are examined on B2B markets and therefore it is essential that you are familiar with both consumer and organizational buyers and the influences upon them.

Consumer markets

There are a number of key questions that must be answered when analysing consumer buyers:

o What factors influence their behaviour?
o Does behaviour vary according to the type of product/service purchased?
o What process of decision-making do they go through?
o Who is involved in the decision-making process?

A useful framework in helping to understand the relationship between these key questions is the 'black box model' illustrated in Figure 2.6. The black box model suggests that we can observe the inputs (i.e. the external environmental influences and the controllable marketing stimuli) in the form of the marketing mix. We can also observe the outputs in terms of whether buyers purchase our product or not, or their levels of brand loyalty. What we cannot observe is what is going on in the mind of the customer. The aim of customer analysis is to try and understand what is going on inside this black box (i.e. try to answer the above questions).

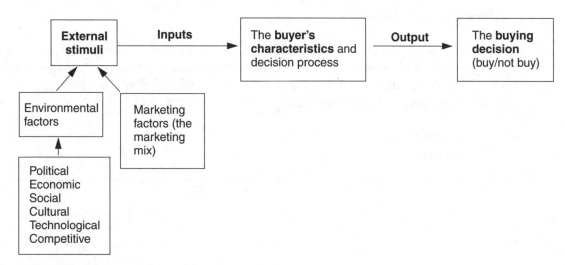

Figure 2.6 A black box model of the buying process

What influences consumer buying behaviour?

Most authors agree that there are four main influences on consumers, beginning with general factors and moving to increasingly specific factors:

1. Cultural factors such as:

   o culture
   o sub-cultures (e.g. religious groups, ethnic groups)
   o social class.

2. Social factors such as:

   o reference groups
   o family
   o roles and statuses.

3. Personal influences such as:

   o age and life-cycle stage
   o occupation
   o economic circumstances
   o lifestyle
   o personality and self-concept.

4. Psychological aspects such as:

   o motivation
   o perception
   o learning
   o beliefs and values.

Extending knowledge

For a detailed discussion of these factors, refer to Jobber (2001), Chapter 3, pp. 71–83.

Activity 2.9

Influences on behaviour

For the following two products outline how an understanding of cultural, social, personal and psychological influences can aid our understanding of consumer buying behaviour. Which influences do you think are the most important? What are the implications for a marketing manager of these products?

o Beer or Lager
o Financial services.

Does behaviour vary according to the type of product /service purchased?

The same individual may behave differently depending on the type of purchase they are making. It is important for marketers to understand the various types of buying behaviour. Two important criteria that can be used to identify types of buying behaviour:

- o the level of involvement that the customer has with the product
- o the extent to which the customer perceives differences between the various product offerings.

Using these two criteria, it is possible to develop a matrix that highlights four different types of buying behaviour as shown in Figure 2.7.

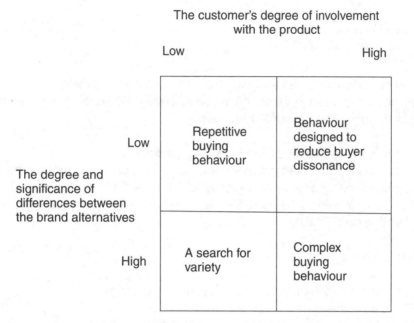

Figure 2.7 The four types of buying behaviour
Adapted from Assael, 1987, p. 87

Activity 2.10

Types of buying behaviour

Identify at least one example of products/services that would fit into each quadrant of the matrix illustrated in Figure 2.7. What are the implications for marketing managers?

What process of decision-making do they go through?

The buyer is going to be influenced by the factors that have already been outlined and the type of purchase situation. However, the process through which the buyer progresses when purchasing is also going to be an important consideration. Marketers need to have a good understanding of this process in order to tailor their marketing offering. Buyers typically go through the following stages, which are illustrated in Figure 2.8.

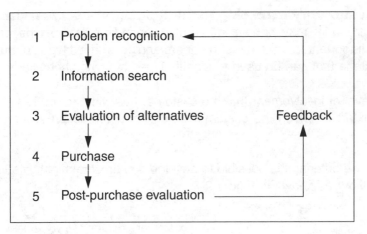

Figure 2.8 The five stages of the buying process
Adapted from Assael, 1987, p. 87

This model has been criticized for being too simplistic and for failing to acknowledge that many buyers do not move through these stages sequentially. However, it is useful in highlighting the key stages through which a buyer progresses.

Who is involved in the decision-making process?

On many occasions, purchase decisions are made by a group rather than by an individual. For example, when a new car is being purchased it is rare that the decision will be made by one individual. Those individuals involved in the purchase decision have been referred to as the decision-making unit (DMU).

The DMU consists of:

o   The initiator – the person who suggests the purchase
o   The user – the consumer of the product
o   The influencer – anybody that may affect the decision
o   The decider – the person ultimately responsible for making the decision
o   The purchaser – the person who actually buys the product.

These roles may all be performed by one person, or more than one person may perform each role. However, it is important that marketers understand the various roles involved and are in a position to identify to whom they should be targeting their marketing activity.

Case history

Consumer shopping habits

Consumer buying behaviour is changing due to the increased usage of technology.

Traditionally, consumers had little choice but to shop in the high street. However, consumers can now buy what they need from the Internet, catalogues or interactive TV. Although home shopping accounts for only 5% of retail sales, this still amounts to £10 billion lost revenue by the high street (Knight Frank Retail Review, 1999). Price WaterhouseCoopers estimate that this will grow from 1% of retail sales today to 6% by 2003. The high street is no longer a necessity but an option and retailers are now having to respond to the increased competition from the Internet. Shopping on the Internet is undeniably convenient and in many cases cheaper than the high street, but it is a very limited experience compared with the three-dimensional branded environment of the store. This is the competitive advantage that high-street retailers have over Internet retailers and many are beginning to capitalize on this unique selling point (USP).

One of the most prominent expressions of this trend in the UK so far is Niketown in Oxford Circus. Visitors can join running clubs, attend sports clinics, meet athletes and play with any number of interactive displays. It is as much an entertainment centre as a shop and is one of 14 Nike has built around the world.

The Waterstone's store in London's Piccadilly Circus has six floors, all themed around the books on display. The children's floor, for example, features a juice bar and a play area, while the art, architecture and design top floor has a trendy cocktail bar. The basement is a cafe, with newspapers, magazines and Sky TV.

Boots has launched healthcare and beauty services. For example, it is offering dental services and homeopathy treatments. It has also opened a walk-in medical centre at a Birmingham store, offering basic nurse-led services.

In London, Ford has been working with Imagination to open its first site, called Capital Ford, which is allegedly the largest dealership in Europe. Outside, it features a specially landscaped off-road driving area for testing 4×4 models, while inside the environment is similar to a motor show. There is a cafe, Internet stations, interactive CD-ROM terminals, a merchandising display and staff trained in communicating the wider aspects of Ford's brand.

Girl Heaven is the ultimate little girls' store. Situated in the Bluewater complex, it is targeted at 2- to 12-year-old girls who may want to have their picture taken in a princess costume, braid their hair or experiment with make-up.

REI's, Seattle-based flagship outdoor equipment store features a rain-room to test out waterproof gear, a 65 ft climbing wall for rock climbers and an outdoor rough-terrain track for testing mountain bikes and hiking boots.

Source: Adapted from Curtis (1999), www.Lexis-Nexis.com

Extended knowledge

For a detailed discussion of the types of consumer buyer behaviour, the decision-making process and the decision-making unit, refer to Jobber (2001), Chapter 3.

See Drummond and Ensor (2001), Chapter 4, pp. 45–52.

Question 2.4

Consumer buying behaviour

Answer the Question from the June 1996 Planning and Control paper on consumer buying behaviour.

Organizational buying behaviour

Organizational buying behaviour can be more complex than consumer buying behaviour because not only do organizational purchasers still have their own individual characteristics, but they are also influenced by organizational factors. In addition, there are generally more people involved in the purchase decision.

Definition

Organizational buying behaviour – The decision-making process by which formal organizations establish the need for purchased products and services, and identify, evaluate and choose among alternative brands and suppliers (Webster and Wind, 1972).

Influences on organizational buyers
There are a number of influences on organizational buyers:

- Environmental
- Organizational
- Interpersonal
- Individual.

These are illustrated in Figure 2.9 in the Webster–Wind framework. It has traditionally been thought that organizational buyers are wholly rational in their purchase behaviour. However, it is now becoming apparent that this is far from true and that organizational buyers are still human beings at work, susceptible to the same influences as consumer buyers.

Figure 2.9 The Webster–Wind framework
Adapted from Webster and Wind, 1972

The decision-making Unit (DMU)

The DMU exists in an organizational context in the same way as it exists in consumer markets, but to a greater extent. In many instances there are large DMUs and more formal processes for purchasing products. There is often the presence of a 'gatekeeper' who filters information. A key task of industrial marketers is to identify the members of the DMU and to target the most influential members or those that make the final decision. Drummond and Ensor (2001, p. 70) suggest that individuals will play six main roles:

- ○ Initiator
- ○ User
- ○ Buyer
- ○ Influencer
- ○ Decider
- ○ Gatekeeper.

The size of the DMU will be influenced by the type of purchase decision being made.

Types of purchases

As in consumer markets the buying situation or type of purchase will influence the decision-making process.

Jobber (2001) identifies three types of purchase situations:

- ○ Straight rebuy – routine orders such as stationery reordering
- ○ Modified rebuy – a situation in which the buyer wants to modify product specifications, prices, delivery, etc.
- ○ New task – appointing a new advertising agency.

Each of these types of purchase holds different challenges for marketers. For example, for an established supplier of a straight rebuy product their main task would be to provide a good level of service so that customers are satisfied and do not seek new suppliers. Non-established suppliers would concentrate their efforts on offering something new and trying to get small orders that with time would grow into larger orders.

The decision-making process

Organizational buyers move through a number of stages from initial problem identification to purchase, in a similar manner to consumer markets. However, it has been suggested that there are a further three steps in the organizational decision-making process. Figure 2.10 illustrates the decision-making process with reference to the differences that exist for each of the three types of purchase behaviour.

	Buy classes		
Buy phases	*Straight re-buy*	*Modified re-buy*	*New task*
1 The recognition of the problem	N	Possibly	Y
2 The determination of the general need	N	Possibly	Y
3 The specific description of the required product	Y	Y	Y
4 The search for potential suppliers	N	Possibly	Y
5 The detailed evaluation of suppliers	N	Possibly	Y
6 The selection of a supplier	N	Possibly	Y
7 The establishment of an order routine	N	Possibly	Y
8 Performance review and feedback	Y	Y	Y

Figure 2.10 The buy grid matrix
Adapted from Robinson et al. 1967

Many of these models that have been discussed in relation to buying behaviour suggest that customers are rational creatures that look to maximize the utility of their purchase. This is a feature of 'economic man', a term developed by Marshall, an economist. However, as we all know in reality customers can be fickle and unpredictable. This does not, however, diminish the efforts of marketing managers to try and understand their customers. Understanding customers and trying to predict their changing tastes and preferences are the essence of marketing.

Extending knowledge

For a detailed discussion of organizational buying behaviour refer to Chapter 4 of Jobber (2001).

See Drummond and Ensor (2001), Chapter 4, pp. 69–78.

Activity 2.11

Select an example of a new task or modified rebuy purchase made recently within your organization. Identify the members of the decision-making unit. How could a company selling this product use this knowledge to help market their product/service?

Summary

o The external environment consists of the macroenvironment (PEST) and the microenvironment (industry, market, competitors and customers).

o The macroenvironment is continually changing and marketers need to monitor these changes via environmental scanning in order to identify threats and opportunities that may arise.

o Organizations must develop effective environmental monitoring systems that collect relevant information, translate this information into a usable format and disseminate it to the right people at the right time to aid decision-making.

o Porter's five forces model provides a useful framework for analysing industry structure and for identifying where the balance of power is located.

o Companies need to know whom they are competing against in order to gain a sustainable competitive advantage. They should be able to answer the following questions. 'Who are our competitors?' 'What are their objectives?' 'What are their strategies?' 'What are their strengths and weaknesses?' 'How are they likely to react?'

o Organizations must develop effective systems for gathering and managing competitor information.

o It is essential that firms have a good understanding of the market in which they are operating. A market analysis would include information such as actual and potential market size, market trends, customer buying behaviour, distribution channels.

- A great deal of time and effort is spent trying to understand customer behaviour and attempting to predict their behaviour. Customers can be classified into consumer buyers and organizational buyers.

- Consumer behaviour is influenced by a wide variety of factors – cultural, social, personal and psychological factors. The type of purchase will also influence behaviour, as will the buying process.

- Purchases are often not made independently, and in many cases will be made by a decision-making unit including the initiator, the user, the influencer, the decider and the purchaser.

- Organizational buyers are influenced by environmental, organizational, interpersonal and individual factors. The type of purchase whether it is a straight rebuy, a modified rebuy or a new task purchase will also influence buying behaviour, as will the decision-making process.

Further study and examination preparation

Extending knowledge

Bibliography and links

Aaker D (1998). *Strategic Market Management*, 5th Ed. John Wiley & Sons.

Aguilar FJ (1967). *Scanning the Business Environment*, Macmillan.

Assael H (1987). *Consumer Behaviour and Marketing Action*, Wadsworth Publishing.

Curtis J (1999). What is the Future of UK Shopping? *Marketing*, 4 November.

Davidson H (1997). *More Offensive Marketing*, Penguin.

Dibb S, Simkin L, Pride W and Ferrel OC (2000). *Marketing: Concepts and Strategies*, 4th Ed., Houghton Mifflin.

Drummond G and Ensor J (2001). *Strategic Marketing Planning and Control*, 2nd Ed. Butterworth-Heinemann.

Fahey L and Narayanan VK (1986). *Macroenvironmental Analysis for Strategic Management*, West Publishing.

Hooley GJ, Saunders JA and Piercy NF (1998). *Marketing Strategy and Competitive Positioning*, 2nd Ed. Prentice-Hall.

Jobber D (2001). *Principles and Practice of Marketing*, 3rd Ed. McGraw-Hill.

Johnson G and Scholes J (1999). *Exploring Corporate Strategy*, 5th Ed. Prentice-Hall.

Kotler P (2000). *Marketing Management, The Millenium Edition*, Prentice-Hall.

Mason T (2002). Good Causes Deliver for Brands, *Marketing*, p. 11, 4 January.

Meek and Meek H (2001). *Marketing Management*, Financial World Publishing.

Murphy C (2000). Brit pop wakes up to net revolution – The web is the new rock and roll – and music companies are trying to figure out how best to protect themselves in an age of direct downloads, *Marketing*, 16 March.

Mutel G (2000). Do Upmarket stores 'own' organic? – Organic food is becoming a big part of supermarkets' strategies, *Marketing*, 14 September.

Porter ME (1980). *Competitive Strategy*, Free Press.

Porter ME (1985). *Competitive Advantage: Creating and Sustaining Superior Performance*, Free Press.

Reed M (1999). Real-world outfits make most of net – A wide range of businesses are taking steps to benefit from the explosion of e-commerce, *Marketing*, 26 August.

Robinson PJ, Faris CW and Wind Y (1967). *Industrial Buying and Creative Marketing*, Allyn & Bacon.

Webster FE and Wind T (1972). A General Model of Organizational Buying Behaviour, *Journal of Marketing*, 26 April, pp. 12–17.

unit 3
internal analysis

By the end of this unit you will:

o Appreciate the importance of internal analysis in helping to identify the internal assets, capabilities and competencies that can be used to create competitive advantage

o Understand and be able to critically evaluate the following approaches to internal analysis:

  o Resource-based approach (organizational assets, capabilities and competencies):

    o Technical resources

    o Financial standing

    o Managerial skills

    o Organization

    o Information systems.

  o Asset-based approach to marketing:

    o Customer-based assets

    o Distribution-based assets

    o Alliance-based assets

    o Internal assets.

  o Marketing activities audit:

    o Marketing strategy audit

    o Marketing structures audit

    o Marketing systems audit

    o Productivity audit

    o Marketing functions audit.

o   Understand, and be able to critically evaluate, an innovation audit

o   Be able to undertake an innovation audit consisting of:

    o   The organization's current performance in delivering innovation

    o   The organization's policies and practices supporting innovation

    o   The organizational climate

    o   The balance of cognitive styles of the senior management team.

Key definitions

Resource-based view of the firm – Emphasizes the need for an organization to exploit its distinctive capabilities. An organization's capabilities are based upon the assets and competencies over which it has either access or control (Drummond and Ensor, 2001).

Organizational assets and capabilities – Organizational assets are the endowments a business has accumulated, such as those resulting from investments in scale, plant, location and brand equity, while capabilities reflect the synergy between these assets and enable them to be deployed to the company's advantage (Day, 1994, cited in Hooley et al., 1998).

Organizational competencies – The abilities and skills available to the company to marshal the effective exploitation of the company's assets (Drummond and Ensor, 2001).

Marketing audit – Is a systematic examination of a business's marketing environment, objectives, strategies and activities with a view to identify key strategic issues, problem areas and opportunities. The marketing audit is therefore the basis upon which a plan of action to improve marketing performance can be built (Jobber, 2001).

Innovation audit – Reviews how effectively the organization is able to deliver the level of innovation necessary to create new products, new services and new ways of undertaking activities (Drummond and Ensor, 2001).

Study Guide

o   This unit will take you about 2 hours to work through
o   We suggest that you take a further 3 hours to do the various activities and questions in this unit.

Introduction

A key task for organizations undertaking a strategic analysis is a review of both the external and internal corporate environments. The previous unit was concerned with analysing the external (macro and micro) environment. This unit focuses on the approaches that can be used to help undertake an internal analysis. In turn this will help to identify the firm's core assets and competencies that can form the basis of competitive advantage. A company's competitive position arises out of, not only identifying market opportunities, but also with matching these with organizational capabilities (see Figure 3.1). A number of different approaches can be adopted in order to identify a firm's core competencies and this unit will explore the nature of these: resource-based approach, asset-based approach and the marketing activities audit. The ability to innovate is becoming an increasingly important requirement for successful companies. Therefore, it is important that organizations can evaluate the extent to which they are innovative. This can be achieved by undertaking an innovation audit. This unit will explain the concept of, and discuss the key components of, an innovation audit.

Figure 3.1 Product and service innovation performance measures
Adapted from Davidson, 1997

Resource-based approach

A key task for organizations undertaking an internal analysis is to conduct an audit of the resources available to the firm, both tangible and intangible. Resources are all the assets and competencies/capabilities to which a company has access. Assets can be regarded as the tangible and intangible capital of the company such as physical assets in the form of land etc., marketing, e.g. brands, legal, e.g. patents, etc. Competencies refer to the firm's ability to be able to convert assets to achieve particular goals. (N.B. The terms competencies and capabilities are often used interchangeably.)

Definition

Resource-based view of the firm – A resource-based view of the firm emphasizes the need for an organization to exploit its distinctive capabilities. An organization's capabilities are based upon the assets and competencies over which it has either access or control (Drummond and Ensor, 2001).

According to Hooley et al. (1998), resources and capabilities can be simplified into the following:

- o **Technical resources**: These relate to the technical skills possessed by the organization such as the ability to develop new products and processes. This resource is particularly relevant given the pace at which technology is developing and the world is changing.
- o **Financial standing**: Financial resources will determine to a large extent the ability for companies to develop their business.
- o **Managerial skills**: Management experience, skills and their ability to motivate staff can be a valuable resource.
- o **Organization**: Particular types of organizational structures can inhibit successful strategy development, whereas others can be a valuable resource in helping to facilitate effective communication and the implementation of successful strategies.
- o **Information systems**: Companies with powerful and effective information systems have access to a powerful resource. For example, customer databases can be a very valuable asset.

Day (1994) suggested that resources can be broken down into:

- o Assets
- o Company capabilities.

Asset-based approach

The asset-based approach to marketing can be contrasted with a purely marketing approach. The product concept suggests that companies take an inside-out approach and focus very much on the product rather than customer needs. In contrast, the marketing concept is concerned with identifying and satisfying customer needs, i.e. an outside-in approach. The asset-based approach recognizes that it is not sufficient just to be able to identify customer needs but that an organization must have the capabilities to meet these needs.

Definition

Organizational assets and capabilities – Organizational assets are the endowments a business has accumulated, such as those resulting from investments in scale, plant, location and brand equity, while capabilities reflect the synergy between these assets and enable them to be deployed to the company's advantage (Day, 1994).

Organizational assets can be either tangible or intangible and may include the following (Hooley et al., 1998):

- o **Physical** – These assets include land, factories, premises, etc.
- o **Financial** – Tangibles such as cash and intangibles such as credit worthiness
- o **Operations** – Tangibles such as plant and machinery, and intangibles such as processes and systems
- o **Human** – The people are the tangible resources but their skills and experience are intangible
- o **Legal** – These assets include patents and copyrights
- o **Systems** – Customer databases are examples of tangible assets whereas decision support is intangible.

     ° **Marketing assets**: These are mainly intangible assets and can be categorized into four main groups, according to Hooley et al. (1998):

        1. **Customer-based assets** – often one of the most defensible assets a company may have, despite being often highly intangible. They relate to the customers and what they regard to be important. These include:

          ° *Image and reputation* – for example, Virgin has a reputation as being a brand 'for the people'

          ° *Brand franchises* – Heinz has come under increasing pressure from own label brands. However, they continue to be able to charge a premium price because people value the Heinz brand

          ° *Unique products and services* – such as Morgan cars

          ° *Country of origin* – for example, Audi is synonymous with high-quality German engineering.

        2. **Distribution-based assets** – these relate to the manner in which products are distributed to customers. These can include: the distribution network, distribution control, pockets of strength, distribution uniqueness, delivery time and security of supply, and the supplier network. For example, the distribution network of cars in the UK is currently an important asset because it is controlled by the car manufacturers. However, with the removal of the block exemption this asset will be eroded. Avon cosmetics has a unique distribution channel selling through a network of representatives calling at customer's houses.

        3. **Internally based marketing assets** – these include: cost advantages, customer base, technological skills, production expertise, copyrights and patents, franchises and licences, and partnerships and corporate culture. For example, the patented cyclone in Dyson vacuum cleaners is an important asset. Organizations that can produce goods/services for less than competitors have a cost advantage. This can be converted into a marketing asset in the form of either a low price, e.g. the low-cost airlines such as easyjet and Ryannair, or alternatively the cost saving can be used to increase profitability. Amazon.com has a major asset in the form of their customer base. They have a great deal of knowledge and information about their existing customer base and this can be used effectively to target them with relevant future offers.

        4. **Alliance-based marketing assets** – many organizations have realized that an effective way to expand their assets and capabilities is through partnerships with other firms. These assets could include: market access, management skills, shared technology and exclusivity. For example, the strategic alliance between MG Rover and China Brilliance Holdings has provided both parties with access to new geographical markets.

Extended knowledge

For a more detailed discussion of marketing assets, see pp. 115–128 in Hooley et al. (1998).

Case history

BAE Systems and Thales Partnership

In January 2003, a £2.8 billion contract to build two new aircraft carriers for the Royal Navy was awarded to a partnership between the British BAE Systems and its French arch-rival Thales. This partnership highlights the potential benefits of a co-operative arrangement where each company has different core competencies and by working together these can be fully exploited. The deal made BAE the prime contractor with Thales providing the design and undertaking about one-third of the work. Geoff Hoon, the Defence Secretary, stated 'the innovative partnership arrangement would maximize the strengths of both competing bids, as well as the Ministry of Defence's own expertise'.

This partnership builds on Thales' core competencies which lie in their design ability and BAE's expertise in military systems. Both risks and rewards will be shared by both parties and so it is in the interest of everybody for the programme to be successful.

Company capabilities/competencies

Definition

Organizational competencies – The abilities and skills available to the company to marshal the effective exploitation of the company's assets (Drummond and Ensor, 2001).

The second group of resources relate to company capabilities. According to Hooley et al. (1997), capabilities can exist at three levels within an organization: strategic, functional and operational. In addition, at each of these levels they can be located within individual people, certain groups or can exist at a corporate level. For example, the ability of a company to learn is a strategic capability but it could be based at either an individual level, a team level or throughout the organization.

Not all capabilities lie within the organization. As many companies are now downsizing and focusing on their core business they are increasingly relying on external organizations to help deliver goods/services. For example, airlines subcontract many aspects of their business to external organizations such as catering, cleaning, checking in, etc. The ability to manage these external relationships can be an important capability.

Extended knowledge

For succinct coverage of organizational capabilities, see the table in p. 106 and the explanation in p. 107 of Hooley et al. (1998).

Case Study

Merging of core competencies

In 2001 McDonald's, the global hamburger giant, acquired a third of Prêt a Manger, the luxury sandwich chain. The rationale behind the move was to build on the core competencies of both brands in order to enter the US market with the Prêt a Manger brand. McDonald's' core competencies of franchising, global operations, marketing and managing real estate were key to the successful entry of this new market.

Entering the US market, initially in New York, proved to be a difficult task for Prêt a Manger. A great deal of red tape stood in their way. The acquisition by McDonald's meant that Prêt a Manger could tap into McDonald's' knowledge of local legislation, unique labour issues and other complexities associated with starting up a new venture.

The relationship is symbiotic in that McDonald's also needs Prêt a Manger. McDonald's has been under pressure to boost its flagging sales. Many of its core customers, the baby boomers, are growing up and looking for more than just burgers. In addition, McDonald's' sales have been hit by bad publicity regarding health scares. Therefore, this acquisition has helped McDonald's to enter into other potentially lucrative segments.

Extended knowledge

For further reading on assessing corporate capabilities, see:

Drummond and Ensor (2001), Chapter 5.

Hooley et al. (1998), Chapter 5.

The internal analysis will identify a firm's assets and competencies. However, some of these will be far more important than others. It is possible to chart the relationships between assets and competencies in the hope that a firm can uncover the critical links. This will help reveal the key factors that contribute to the success of the company and which they can exploit further.

Extended knowledge

For further reading on the linkages between assets and competencies, see Johnson and Scholes (1999), pp. 160–179.

Activity 3.1

Activity briefing

Using your own organization as an example. Identify the core assets and capabilities using the framework in p. 106 of Hooley et al. (1998) to help structure your answers. Compare and contrast these with another firm in the same strategic group. Can you identify any unique capabilities?

Question 3.1

Core capabilities

Answer Question 1a from the December 1999 Planning and Control exam paper on core capabilities. Go to www.cimeduhub.com to access specimen answers for this question.

Exam hint

Internal analysis has been the focus of several questions on the Planning and Control Paper. Many of which have been compulsory questions relating to the mini-case. You will be expected not only to be able to identify the organizational assets but also to demonstrate how they can be employed in developing the future strategy of the company. There have also been a number of other questions, often in Section B, that relate partly to internal analysis.

Marketing activities audit

 ## Definition

Marketing audit – The marketing audit is a systematic examination of a business's marketing environment, objectives, strategies and activities with a view to identify key strategic issues, problem areas and opportunities. The marketing audit is therefore the basis upon which a plan of action to improve marketing performance can be built (Jobber, 2001).

A key aspect of internal analysis is the evaluation of marketing activities. Kotler et al. (2001) suggests a framework for the **internal** marketing audit that would include analysing the following five areas.

Marketing strategy audit

This is concerned with reviewing corporate and marketing objectives and strategy to ensure they are relevant, realistic and successful. A key part of this audit is concerned with identifying if adequate resources are available.

Marketing structures audit

This analyses the way in which the marketing function is organized and how it relates to other business functions.

Marketing systems audit

This examines various systems such as the planning process, new product development process, marketing information systems and control processes.

Productivity audit

This is concerned with financial criteria such as profitability and cost effectiveness of various products, markets and distribution channels.

Marketing functions audit

This involves detailed analysis of the marketing mix: products/services, pricing strategy, distribution policy, promotional strategy, etc.

Extended knowledge

For further reading on the marketing audit, see pp. 99–101 in Kotler (2001).

Activity 3.2

Consider your own organization. To what extent does your organization undertake a full and regular review of your company's internal marketing activities?

Who is responsible for this analysis and how often is it undertaken?

Give examples of the types of actions that have taken place as a result of the internal marketing audit?

What, if any, recommendations would you make to improve the internal marketing audit process?

Innovation audit

Peter Drucker once wrote 'The business has two – and only these two – basic functions: marketing and innovation. Marketing and innovation produce results; all the rest are costs'. Firms are under increasing pressure to stay ahead of their competitors and in order to do this they have to cultivate a climate of innovation and creativity within the organization. This is becoming increasingly important given the rapid speed at which technology is developing and subsequently markets are changing. It is, therefore, imperative that any internal analysis includes a review of a firm's performance in relation to innovation, in order to identify whether the necessary assets and capabilities are present.

Extended knowledge

For further reading on the importance of creativity and innovation, see:

Kay (1993)

Higgins (1996)

Martensen and Dahlgaard (1999).

Definition

Innovation audit – The innovation audit reviews how effectively the organization is able to deliver the level of innovation necessary to create new products, new services and new ways of undertaking activities (Drummond and Ensor, 2001).

According to Drummond and Ensor (2001), the innovation audit examines four key areas:

o   Organizational climate
o   Current performance
o   Review of policies and practices to support innovation
o   Balance of cognitive styles.

Each of these is examined in more detail below.

Organizational climate

For an organization to be successful at innovation there needs to be a climate that fosters creativity and innovation. Drummond and Ensor (2001) suggest that there are two approaches that can be taken to investigate an organization's climate: an attitude survey and metaphorical analysis.

Attitude survey

The objective of this is to conduct an audit of the current attitudes of staff about the organizational climate with regard to innovation and creativity. Burnside (1990) suggests there are eight enablers that support innovation and four factors that act as disablers. Enablers include:

o   **Teamwork** – level of trust and commitment within the teams
o   **Resources** – extent to which sufficient resources are available in the form of staff, facilities, finance and information
o   **Challenge** – to what extent is the work interesting and challenging?
o   **Freedom** – how much freedom do individuals have to explore their own ideas?
o   **Supervisor** – to what extent does the management support and facilitate innovation and provide clear goals and objectives
o   **Creativity infrastructure** – how does the organization encourage and facilitate innovation, e.g. in terms of cross-functional teams, etc.

- ○ **Recognition** – this relates to the extent to which staff are recognized and rewarded for their efforts
- ○ **Unity and co-operation** – an organizational climate that encourages an environment of collaboration and values creativity is clearly one that will encourage innovativeness.

Disablers that act as constraints on the ability to innovate include:

- ○ **Insufficient time** – too often people have too little time to devote to developing long-term ideas because they are too busy managing their day to day tasks
- ○ **Status quo** – fear of change from the existing ways of doing things
- ○ **Political problems** – internal conflicts between different areas of the business
- ○ **Evaluation pressure** – rigid control systems have been criticized for stifling creativity and innovation.

Metaphors

The second means of auditing the organizational climate relates to the use of metaphorical descriptions that is a proven creativity tool (Morgan, 1993). Rather than asking individuals directly to describe their feelings about their organization they are asked to describe their organization in terms of a metaphor. For example 'This organization is like a steam train – makes a lot of noise, attracts a lot of interest but is not really relevant today'. These metaphors can then be analysed in terms of negative and positive views of the following:

- ○ Managerial skills
- ○ Organizational structure
- ○ Operations
- ○ Organizational life-cycle
- ○ Strategic orientation
- ○ People orientation
- ○ Power orientation.

This method overcomes the limitations of literal language, provides deeper insights than direct questioning and allows a more rounded perspective of the organization to be developed.

Case history

BMW 7 series – driven by innovation?

The launch of their new BMW 7 series sedan has created great controversy in the car world. It has been suggested that it is the most controversial model that any German carmaker has ever launched. BMW designers realized that modern luxury cars had so many controls and gadgets that drivers were becoming overwhelmed. They decided to replace all these controls with one system – I-Drive, that is operated by a single mouse-like device and a computer screen positioned on the dashboard. It is perhaps the most revolutionary development in car manufacturing in recent years.

The control panel is located where the traditional gear stick used to be. I-Drive can be used to set everything, from the radio, the air conditioning, the heated seats, suspension, the telephone to the position of your seat, sounds simple enough – all the controls at the click of a mouse.

BMW have been accused of creating a 'solution looking for a problem' when they invented I-Drive. Some test drivers find sorting through the 700 options on the menu a touch difficult! Many of the functions can also be controlled using a voice command system but with 270 different voice commands to choose from this can also be a minefield. Alternatively you can resort to good old switches. However, buyers spending over £40 000 may be unhappy about relinquishing the use of the car's unique selling point and a key part of its technology.

Despite the complex control system and the fact that some critics have described the car as ugly, it is regarded by many as a dream to drive.

The car must be appealing to some customers because sales are 17% higher than those for previous 7-series during the same early months of its life.

Is this an example of a 'solution looking for a problem' or great insight and innovativeness on the part of BMW?

Current performance

There are a number of hard measures that can be used in order to assess the effectiveness of the organization's current performance in relation to innovation. Drummond and Ensor (2001) suggest the following hard measures that can be employed:

- Rate of new product/service development in the last *x* years.
- Customer satisfaction ratings
- Staff turnover
- An innovation/value portfolio (see Figure 3.2) can be applied to a firm's strategic business units or products to identify whether they are:
  - Settlers – provide me-too value
  - Migrators – offer greater benefits than competitors
  - Pioneers – represent significant innovations such as the BMW new 7 series (see Case history)

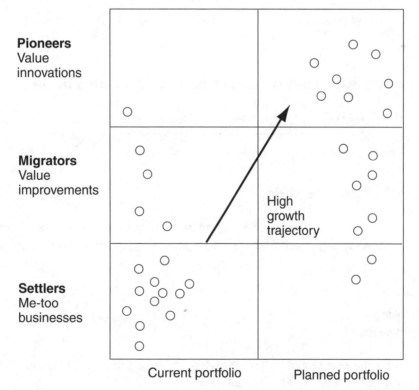

Figure 3.2 The innovation/value matrix
Kim and Mauborgne, 1998

The results from this type of analysis can be very revealing. For example, if an organization discovers that most of their products are in the settlers category it could be concluded that they are paying insufficient attention to innovation.

Activity 3.3

Activity briefing

Study the table in Figure 3.3 What conclusions can you draw about the current performance of the organization in relation to innovation from these innovation measures?

Innovation criteria	3 years ago	This year
Number of significant innovations in past 5 years	14	7
Number successful	4	4
% Success rule	29%	57%
% Total sales in product/ services launched in past 5 years	18%	30%
% Incremental sales	11%	13.5%
Average annual sales per new product/service (£m)	5	8
Incremental payback per new product/service (years)	3	4

Figure 3.3 Product and service innovation performance measures
Adapted from Davidson, 1997

Review of policies and practices to support innovation

This would involve analysing the current policies and structures that are in place to facilitate creativity and innovation. For example, what processes are in place to ensure that promising new ideas see the light of day.

Balance of cognitive styles

The fourth element of the innovation audit is to evaluate the cognitive preferences and behaviours of the management team. Four cognitive styles have been identified:

- o Intuition
- o Feeling
- o Thinking
- o Sensation.

It is important to have a mix of cognitive styles because these will influence the organization's orientation towards creativity and innovation.

Extended knowledge

For further discussion on the innovation audit, see Drummond and Ensor (2001), Chapter 5, pp. 90–96.

Question 3.2

Innovation audit – mini-case Weetabix

Refer to the mini-case study from the June 2000 Planning and control paper – Weetabix. Answer Question 1b only. Go to www.cimeduhub.com to access specimen answers.

Activity 3.4

Measuring innovation success

Undertaking a full innovation audit is a time-consuming process and not feasible for a student to conduct as an activity as part of their studies. Therefore, this activity asks you to carry out a limited analysis of your organization's innovation success.

Undertake an analysis of your organization's current performance in delivering innovation. See Figure 3.3 and produce a similar table for your own organization.

What conclusions can you draw from this analysis?

Summary

o   Internal analysis is a key part of the situation analysis and refers to the internal auditing process that will identify a firm's core resources. Resources can either be in the form of assets or capabilities. These can then be used as the basis of creating competitive advantage when matched with opportunities in the marketplace.

o   The internal analysis is concerned with identifying a firm's strengths and weaknesses. The resource-based approach to marketing suggests that the first stage in assessing strengths and weaknesses should be to conduct an audit of the resources available to the company, including both tangible and intangible resources. Resources can be grouped into the following: technical resources, financial standing, managerial skills, organization and information systems.

o   The asset-based approach to marketing recognizes that it is insufficient to identify opportunities in the marketplace. These must be matched with internal assets in order for the strategy to be successful, i.e. in terms of resources, skills and capabilities.

○ Assets can be classified as: physical, financial, operations, human, legal, systems, and marketing (consisting of customer-based assets, distribution-based assets, alliance-based assets, internal assets).

○ The terms capabilities and competencies are often used interchangeably. They refer to the abilities and skills available to the company to marshal the effective exploitation of the company's assets.

○ Capabilities can exist at all levels within an organization – strategic, functional and operational. They can also be present within the whole organization, or within particular teams or even just within individual people.

○ The internal marketing audit consists of a review of the marketing activities of an organization and is split into five key areas: marketing strategy audit, marketing structures audit, marketing systems audit, productivity audit and marketing functions audit.

○ The ability to innovate is becoming an increasingly important requirement for organizations. Markets are changing rapidly due to changes in the external environment such as new technologies. Therefore, any audit of a firm's internal environment should include a review of their performance with regard to innovation.

○ The innovation audit reviews four key areas of the organization: current performance in delivering innovation, policies and practices that are currently used to support innovation, organizational climate with regard to innovation and the balance of cognitive skills of the senior management team.

Further study and examination preparation

Extending knowledge

Bibliography

Burnside R (1990). Improving corporate climates for creativity, in West MA and Farr JL (Eds) *Innovation and Creativity at Work*, Wiley.

Davidson H (1997). *Even More Offensive Marketing*, Chapter 2, Penguin Books.

Day GS (1994). The capabilities of market-driven organizations. *Journal of Marketing*, 58 (3), 37–52.

Drummond G and Ensor J (2001). *Strategic Marketing Planning and Control*, 2nd Ed. Butterworth-Heinemann.

Higgins JM (1996). Innovate or evaporate: creative techniques for strategists, *Long Range Planning*, 29(3), 370–380.

Hooley GH, Saunders JA and Piercy NF (1998). *Marketing Strategy and Competitive Positioning*, 2nd Ed. Prentice-Hall.

Jobber D (2001). *Principles and Practices of Marketing*, 3rd Ed. McGraw-Hill.

Johnson G and Scholes K (1999). *Exploring Corporate Strategy*, 5th Ed. Prentice-Hall.

Kay J (1993). *Foundations of Corporate Success*, Oxford University Press.

Kim CW and Mauborgne R (1998). Pioneers strike it rich, *Financial Times*, 11 August.

Kotler K, Armstrong G, Saunders J and Wong V (2001). *Principles of Marketing*, 3rd European Edition, Prentice-Hall.

Martensen A and Dahlgaard JJ (1999). Strategy and planning for innovation management – supported by creative and learning organizations, *International Journal of Quality and Reliability Management*, 16(9) 878–891.

Morgan G (1993). *Imagination, the Art of Creative Management*, Sage Publications.

unit 4 auditing tools

Learning objectives

By the end of this unit you will:

o Be able to describe, apply and critically evaluate a range of auditing tools:

1. Product life-cycle

2. The diffusion of innovation process

3. Experience curves and the role of market share

4. Profit impact of marketing strategies (PIMS)

5. Portfolio analysis

6. Value chain

7. Gap analysis.

o Know the key components of, and be able to undertake, a marketing audit and SWOT analysis.

Key definitions

Value chain – It is one of the most useful tools for analysing utility and cost drivers and the relationship between both . . . . The value chain describes how the activities of the business contribute to its task of designing, producing, delivering, communicating and supporting its product (Doyle, 2002, p. 82).

Product life-cycle – A useful tool for conceptualizing the changes that take place during the time that a product is on the market (Jobber, 2001, p. 248).

Diffusion of innovation – The diffusion of innovation process describes how a new product (innovation) spreads throughout a market over time (Jobber, 2001, p. 294).

Portfolio analysis – A tool by which management identifies and evaluates the various businesses that make up the company (Jobber, 2001, p. 253).

Gap analysis – The difference between a company's current forecast of how the company will perform in the future and where they would like to be, i.e. their objectives.

Marketing audit – An audit is a systematic, critical and unbiased review and appraisal of the environment and of the company's operations. A marketing audit is part of the larger management audit and is concerned with the marketing environment and marketing operations (McDonald, 1999).

SWOT – A SWOT analysis is a structured approach to evaluate the strategic position of a business by identifying its strengths, weaknesses, opportunities and threats. It is a simple method of synthesizing the results of the marketing audit (Jobber, 2001, p. 42).

Study Guide

- o This unit will take you about 4 hours to work through
- o We suggest that you take a further 4 hours to do the various activities and questions in this unit.

Introduction

The last two units have focused on the current situation in terms of external and internal analyses. There are many tools that can be used to help interpret the current situation. These are often referred to as auditing tools. These models cannot only be used for auditing the current situation but can also play an important role in helping to develop future strategy (i.e. can be used for identifying both 'where are we now?' and also 'where do we want to be?' questions). This unit will outline the various models and frameworks that can be used for both strategic analysis and strategy development. For example, portfolio analysis tools such as the General Electric matrix can be used to identify the current location of strategic business units or products but can be equally valid in determining future strategies.

You will have already been introduced to many of these models in previous CIM modules such as Marketing Operations where you will have encountered the product life-cycle. It is expected that at Diploma level students will not only be able to describe each of the models but that you will also be able to apply them and provide a critical evaluation of their uses and limitations.

Exam hint

On each of the recent Planning and Control exam papers there has been at least one question on techniques for analysis and strategy development. They have appeared in both Section A (compulsory question) and Section B (choice). For example, in the December 2002 paper there was a question on the product life-cycle and in the June 2002 paper there was a question on the PIMS studies and also the value chain.

Value chain

The value chain (Porter, 1980) can be a very valuable auditing tool as well as proving useful for identifying strategies to gain competitive advantage. This model shown in Figure 4.1 was originally developed for accounting purposes to identify the profitability of the various stages of the manufacturing process. More recently it has been acknowledged that the model can be applied to measures of competitive advantage rather than just profit. Porter (1985) suggests that competitive advantage is determined to a large extent by the way in which companies manage each element and the interactions between them. The value chain provides companies with a means of identifying ways of creating more customer value and analysing an organization's capabilities. The model was traditionally applied to manufacturing companies but more recently it has been recognized that it can be applied equally well to service organizations.

Definition

Value chain – It is one of the most useful tools for analysing utility and cost drivers and the relationship between both . . . . The value chain describes how the activities of the business contribute to its task of designing, producing, delivering, communicating and supporting its product (Doyle, 2002, p. 82).

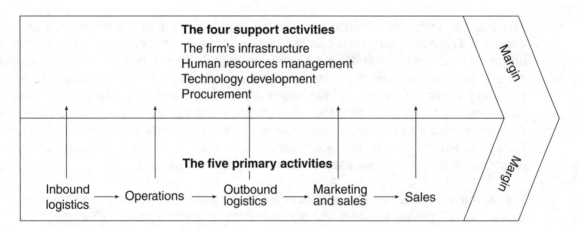

Figure 4.1 The value chain (Porter, 1985)

The model highlights nine interrelated value-creating activities that can help to create value. These are divided into primary and support activities.

Primary activities

- ○ **Inbound logistics** – activities concerned with receiving, storing and the internal distribution of raw materials
- ○ **Operations** – the means by which the raw materials are converted into the final product
- ○ **Outbound logistics** – activities that relate to the process of delivering the product to the customer such as storage, warehousing and transportation
- ○ **Marketing and sales** – involves making sure the customers are aware of the product
- ○ **Service** – includes activities such as customer service, after-sales service, installation and training.

Support activities

- ○ **Firm infrastructure** – this relates to the organizational structure, management style, culture and systems
- ○ **Human resource management** – recruitment, training and rewarding of staff
- ○ **Technology development** – includes research and development, IT and process improvements
- ○ **Procurement** – purchasing of various inputs.

By focusing on these various functions, companies can improve performance and effectiveness and identify areas in which they can add customer value. It not only provides a structured framework for examining costs and performance within organizations but also provides a sound basis for interfirm comparisons. The value chain can be extended to include suppliers, distributors and customers to analyse the relationships between companies and to identify ways of adding value in the supply chain such as Just-in-time delivery (JIT). It can also be a valuable tool for analysing competitors, e.g. for identifying cost advantages.

Extended knowledge

For further reading on the value chain, see Hooley et al. (1998), pp. 159–162.

Activity 4.1

The value chain

Apply the value chain to your own organization or an organization of your choice. To what extent does it help to identify sources of competitive advantage? Are there any limitations of the model?

Case history

Ikea

The value chain played a key role in helping Ikea, the Swedish furniture supplier, to analyse their business and identify their core competencies. Through an analysis of the industry's value chain, Ikea's management realized that a large proportion of their costs were in assembling and transporting the furniture. This analysis informed their strategy of developing a few very large sites in central locations to reduce distribution costs. They also decided to sell unassembled furniture, which led to dramatic cost reductions. This enabled Ikea to price themselves very competitively vis-a-vis competition and as a result they acquired a higher market share.

Exam hint

In the exam you will be expected not only to be able to outline and discuss the value chain but also to critically evaluate the model and even apply it to a particular scenario. In December 1999 students were asked to apply the value chain to easyJet as a means of identifying competitive advantage.

Limitations of the value chain

Despite being a valuable auditing tool the model does have limitations. It is very inwardly oriented, rather than being focused on the external environment (in particular the market and customers). It is also worth remembering that in most industries a single organization rarely undertakes all the value-creating activities and therefore any analysis should recognize the wider value system.

Question 4.1

Value chain

Answer Question 2 from the June 2002 Planning and Control paper on the value chain. Go to www.cimeduhub.com to access specimen answers for this question. Question 2 from the June 2000 paper was also on the value chain.

Product life-cycle

The product life-cycle (PLC) (see Figure 4.2) appears in almost every textbook on marketing and yet it is often described as the least understood marketing tool. This is because, although most marketers can describe the various stages of the PLC, few seem to take any real account of the concept when planning future strategies. The PLC recognizes that products, like humans, have a finite life and move through a variety of distinct stages from introduction to growth, maturity, decline and eventually death. Therefore, marketers need to modify their strategies and tactics to ensure that the maximum profit is generated from each stage. The PLC concept has many limitations (which will be discussed below); however, it does highlight a range of important considerations:

- Products have a finite life and will eventually die
- During their existence they will move through a variety of stages that will all require different strategies in order to try and extend the life and generate the maximum profit
- It also highlights that the profit potential from each stage will vary considerably.

Definition

Product life-cycle – A useful tool for conceptualizing the changes that take place during the time that a product is in the market (Jobber, 2001, p. 248).

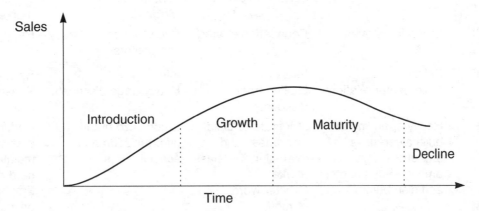

Figure 4.2 The classic S-shaped PLC curve

The product life-cycle can be applied at a number of levels:

o   Total industries – such as the motor industry
o   Product classes – such as cars, vans and lorries
o   Product forms – such as people movers, estate cars and sports cars
o   Brands – such as Renault Espace, VW Beetle and Ford Escort.

Rink and Swan (1979) believed that in order for managers to fully understand the context in which the brand is developing, it is essential they understand the distinction between the various categories of the PLC. The length of each stage will vary considerably depending on which category we are considering. For example, industry and product classes tend to have the longest PLCs. However, it is often difficult to judge the nature of the PLC for individual brands. For example, the Persil brand (washing product) has endured longer than each of the product classes – washing powder, liquid detergents and now tablets. Product forms tend to conform to the classic PLC curve to a greater extent than the other categories.

Table 4.1 summarizes the various marketing mix decisions for each stage of the PLC. It must be remembered that this table simplifies the decisions and provides guidance only. Each product must be viewed independently. For example, the table suggests that a low-price strategy should be adopted in the introductory stage. However, this may not always be the case. For example, organizations may choose to adopt a skimming strategy by setting a high initial price to cream off profits in the short-term. This is often used by new, innovatory products for which customers are prepared to pay a high price. The strategic use of the PLC will be focused on in this text. However, the decline stage will be discussed in some detail because this is a major strategic decision facing companies in deciding whether to rejuvenate or withdraw products.

Table 4.1

Marketing mix strategies	Introduction	Growth	Maturity	Decline
Product	Basic product, limited range	Develop product extensions and service levels	Modify and differentiate Develop next generation	Phase out weak brands Consider leaving market
Price	Low-price strategy	Penetration strategy	Price to meet or beat competitors	Reduce
Distribution	Selective Build dealer relations	Intensive Limited trade discounts	Intensive Heavy trade discounts	Selective Phase out weak outlets
Advertising	Heavy spending to build awareness and encourage trial among early adopters and distributors	Moderate to build awareness and interest in the mass market Greater word of mouth	Emphasize brand differentiation and special offers	Reduce to a level that maintains hard core loyalty Emphasize low prices to reduce stock
Sales promotion	Extensive to encourage trial	Reduce to a moderate level	Increase to encourage brand switching	Reduce or stop completely
Planning time frame	Short to medium	Long range	Medium range	Short

 ## Activity 4.2

Product life-cycle in practice

In the exam, it is essential that you illustrate your answers with current examples. Collect articles from current marketing press such as *Marketing Week, Marketing, Campaign* and national newspapers that illustrate the product life-cycle in practice. In particular, identify products or services that have reached maturity/decline and identify the strategies being used to either rejuvenate or delete these products/services.

Value of the PLC

The PLC can be a valuable tool for a number of reasons. Jobber (2001, p. 249) identifies a number of insights that the PLC provides:

○ **Product termination** – The PLC emphasizes that nothing lasts forever. There is a danger that marketers will fail to recognize this and become complacent, not developing new products to replace established ones.

○ **Growth projections** – The PLC warns against the dangers of assuming that growth will continue indefinitely. This is particularly critical when companies are facing major investment decisions based on existing products.

○ **Marketing objectives and strategies change during the PLC** – This emphasizes the need to review marketing objectives and strategies as the product/service moves through various stages. For example, promotional objectives may change from raising awareness (initial stages) to reminding customers (latter stages of the cycle).

○ **Product planning** – The PLC emphasizes the need to have a balanced portfolio of products, i.e. to have new products in the pipeline to replace those in maturity or decline. Companies should be using the cash generated by mature products to fund new product development. It is essential that this is managed effectively to avoid cash-flow problems when established products enter decline and there are no new products to fill the gap. This links in with the Boston Consulting Group matrix, which will be discussed later in the unit.

○ **Dangers of overpowering** – Companies that launch an innovatory new product ahead of competitors have the opportunity to charge a high price. However, unless they have patent protection competitors may enter the market and undercut them.

In addition, the PLC can be used as a control tool in that comparisons can be made with life-cycles of similar products.

Limitations of the PLC

Despite some of the insights the PLC provides it has many limitations. Jobber (2001, p. 252) provides a good overview of these:

○ **Fads and classics** – Many products do not follow the traditional S-shaped PLC. For example, there are those products (described as fads) that show a rapid growth but an equally rapid decline such as Buzz Light Year toys, cabbage patch dolls and various 'executive toys'. In contrast, some products (known as classics) seem to defy the PLC concept and live forever – some examples include Bisto and Coca Cola. Swan and Rink (1982) identified 17 different life-cycle curves, which question the validity of the traditional PLC S-shaped curve.

○ **Marketing effects** – The PLC is the *result* of marketing activity, not the cause, and therefore marketers have to be careful they do not fall into the self-fulfilling prophecy where they expect a product to decline, withdraw marketing support and the product declines.

○ **Unpredictability** – There is little indication of the timescale of the PLC. The duration of each stage varies considerably with the product and may range from weeks to years. Therefore the model is of limited use as a forecasting tool.

○ **Misleading objectives and strategy** – The model has been criticized for being too prescriptive in terms of the objectives and strategies that are appropriate for each stage. There is little scope for creativity.

There is also an additional problem in that it is often very difficult to identify where a product is located on the PLC (therefore management decisions may be based on incorrect assumptions). The model can also encourage marketers to be product-focused rather than market-focused. It is often very difficult to predict the shape and duration of the PLC due to external factors such as political, social, economic and technological and competitive activities.

Extended knowledge

For further discussion on the product life-cycle read Jobber (2001), pp. 248–253.

Case history

Marmite

Marmite has been a British Institution for 100 years. It is in the top 100 food brands and can be found in 25% of all UK households. Despite being 'hated' by a significant proportion of consumers it has continued to fight off challenges from Bovril and the Australian brand Vegemite. Marmite is an example of a product that has been in the maturity stage of the product life-cycle for a significant number of years.

Despite changing consumer tastes, the product has remained largely unchanged over the last century. Advertising has played a key role in maintaining its relevance to today's consumers. Marmite's advertising has always been memorable. The latest campaign builds on the nation's divided feelings about Marmite's distinctive taste 'you either love it or hate it'. Unilever Bestfoods, owner of Marmite, is experimenting with brand extensions in conjunction with Walkers with the launch of Marmite flavoured crisps.

The continuing success of Marmite has been attributed to its strong brand image and loyal customer base, often introduced to Marmite as babies and then continued to be eaten throughout their lives.

Source: Adapted from Grant (2002)

Managing products in the decline stage

It is worthwhile considering the latter stages of the PLC because these often prove to be the most challenging for marketers. Do we try to rejuvenate our product or do we accept it has reached the end of its useful life and withdraw it?

Case history

Dr Martens

The Dr Martens brand is a cultural icon and has been seen as an expression of youth culture for four decades. The brand is synonymous with hardwearing boots. However, Dr Martens (DMs) is falling out of favour with today's youth. Instead, they are turning to designer sportswear and the ubiquitous trainers that support that image. Dr Martens has been accused of falling behind the times, failing to innovate and of losing any relevance for today's youth. The great challenge facing Dr Martens is how to rejuvenate the brand, revive sales and re-establish itself as 'a desired expression of youth culture'.

Source: Adapted from Chandiramani (2002)

Activity 4.3

Activity briefing

Read the case history on Dr Martens and suggest the alternative strategies that could be pursued by Dr Martens.

There are a number of options available to companies facing products in the decline stage of the PLC. Wilson and Gilligan (1997) identify four alternatives:

○ **Non-deletion** – This option involves attempting to rejuvenate the product to extend the life-cycle. This strategy has been successfully employed by companies such as the VW Beetle, Tango and Fairy Liquid.

○ **Eliminate overnight** – Some organizations may decide to divest immediately and withdraw the product from the market. This strategy is most relevant where the organization does not intend to commit resources to develop the product or service. Where products at the decline stage damage corporate image, or other products and services marketed by the organization, then the decision can be reformulated to ask: 'Can the business afford not to eliminate the product immediately?'. This can be a risky strategy because it can have repercussions for the company in terms of negative publicity and may have a knock-on effect on other products they offer.

○ **Increase price or reduce promotion** – This strategy relies on products fading away naturally because marketing support is withdrawn. This option is often pursued by financial service providers that may have old savings products that have been superseded by more modern accounts. Rather than closing down all these accounts, they stop promoting them and hope they will naturally fade away.

○ **Stay to attract competitors' customers** – This may be an attractive option when many players have withdrawn from the market and there is still demand for a particular product. This strategy has been successfully employed by Electronic Data Services (EDS) who have invested in large-scale automated cheque clearance facilities to gain economies of scale in this overall declining market. Many financial service organizations have started to contract out this function, which was traditionally undertaken in-house, to EDS.

An alternative strategy may be to look for new markets to extend the life of existing products – new segments or new geographical markets. For example, tobacco manufacturers have extended the life of tobacco products by marketing the product in countries that are less well-regulated than Europe or USA (such as African countries).

There are a number of factors, both financial and non-financial, that companies must consider when deciding how to deal with declining products. These include:

- o   Budget implications of each option
- o   Estimated future profitability of each strategy
- o   Future market potential
- o   Customer/distribution expectations
- o   Any opportunity to launch in other markets?
- o   Is a replacement product available?
- o   What effect will deletion have on customer perceptions?
- o   Any impact on provision of spare parts?
- o   Will there be any impact on other products within the portfolio?
- o   Does the product contribute to the sale of other products?

Activity 4.4

Managing products in decline

Identify one product/service that is, or has been thought to be in the decline phase of the PLC. Outline the strategies adopted to manage this product during this phase, i.e. deletion, rejuvenation, etc. How successful has this strategy been?

Question 4.2

Product life-cycle – decline phase

Answer the Question from the June 1996 Planning and Control paper on product life-cycle – decline phase.

Concluding thoughts

The PLC is a useful model in prompting marketers to consider the possible fate of their products and provides some useful insights into the various stages a product may pass through and strategies that may prove useful. However, in reality it is often too simplistic and generalized to be used in isolation, and it cannot replace management expertise and judgement. It may prove to be more useful as a control technique rather than as a forecasting technique. The PLC is not the marketer's panacea but it can be useful if used in combination with other models and frameworks and alongside good management judgement.

Question 4.3

Product life-cycle

Answer Question 6 from the December 2002 Planning and Control paper on product life-cycle. Go to www.cimeduhub.com to access specimen answers for this question. Question 7 June 2001 and Question 7 December 1998 were both questions on the PLC.

Exam hint

Exam questions on the PLC have been popular among students and yet many answers are disappointing. In the exam it is not sufficient to just draw the PLC and describe the various stages. It is important that you answer the question set rather than regurgitating everything you know about the PLC. In many cases questions have focused on a specific stage of the PLC and students have been asked to discuss the implications for marketing strategy. The Senior Examiner is looking for a critical evaluation of the model and its uses and limitations, at a strategic rather than a tactical level.

Diffusion of innovation

The PLC provides an indicator of the various stages through which a product passes but provides little indication of the timescale. The rate at which new products will be adopted varies considerably but Rogers (1983) developed a model which is shown in Figure 4.3. Rogers' model illustrates the pattern of adoption that is often evident following the launch of a new product. This model is not explicitly stated in the Planning and Control syllabus but it usefully links in with new product development and the PLC and has therefore been included in this section.

Definition

Diffusion of innovation – The diffusion of innovation process describes how a new product (innovation) spreads throughout a market over time (Jobber, 2001, p. 294).

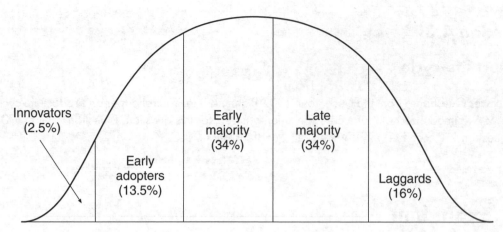

Figure 4.3 Diffusion of innovation
Rogers, 1983

Rogers' model identifies the various types of individuals and the rate at which they will be likely to purchase new products. This model is useful in helping to identify potential target markets for new products and for tailoring the marketing mix to meet the needs of each group of customers. For example, a different pricing strategy may be necessary when targeting the early majority rather than innovators. The innovators may be prepared to pay a high price for an innovative new product and yet this price may have to be reduced to appeal to other target groups. It can be a useful tool for segmenting the market. However, the difficulty lies in a marketer's ability to identify these segments and to reach them effectively (e.g. those individuals that are innovators in the consumer electronics market may not be innovators in the golf equipment market). This poses a challenge for marketers when they are developing their marketing campaigns. The characteristics of each category of adopters are outlined below.

o **Innovators** – These customers embrace new ideas and new products readily and are often prepared to pay high initial prices to be the first in the market. They are often regarded as opinion leaders and are seen as key targets for new products. Innovators are people who currently purchase 'smart homes', where, for example, household appliances communicate with control devices by phone or via the Internet.

o **Early adopters** – This group is also willing to adopt new ideas, but not at the same speed as the innovators. They are more likely to seek information before purchasing than the innovators.

o **Early majority** – Accounts for approximately one-third of customers. In general they are more conservative than the innovators and early adopters and more likely to be risk averse. For example, people who would consider making a purchase on the Internet.

o **Late majority** – Another third of customers, including people that are often cautious about new products. Mobile phones are probably appealing to this group currently.

o **Laggards** – This group tends to be very traditional and averse to change. They may be very price-sensitive and wait for prices to reduce. In fact they may change only when their current product becomes obsolete. For example, people may be forced to buy a CD player when they can no longer buy vinyl records or a record player.

The rate at which new products are adopted can also vary considerably. A number of factors will influence the speed at which the products are adopted:

o **Newness** – The extent to which the new product challenges or supports existing behaviour. For example, mobile phones were adopted rapidly because they fitted in with existing behaviour, whereas television shopping challenges traditional shopping habits and the take-up has been slower.

o **Trialability** – How easy it is for customers to try the new product. For example, a person can easily visit a showroom and try out a CD player. In contrast the take-up of ISAs (individual savings accounts) has been slower because it is impossible to trial the product before purchase.

o **Relative cost** – For low-priced items such as confectionery, the rate of take-up may be faster than for more expensive items such as consumer electronic products.

o **Additional costs** – To what extent does the customer incur costs when purchasing? For example, for contact lenses these include 'cleaning-fluid' costs and 'time and trouble costs' associated with maintenance of contact lenses versus spectacles.

o **Complexity** – How easy is it to communicate the product and its benefits? The new stakeholder pensions launched in UK were complex and the Government invested a great deal of money in communicating the benefits to people.

Activity 4.5

Diffusion of innovation

Identify one new product/service that has been adopted rapidly by customers and one that has been very slowly adopted or not at all. Compare and contrast these two products and give reasons why one has been accepted rapidly whilst the other has not.

Extended knowledge

For further discussion on diffusion of innovation, read Jobber (2001), pp. 294–297.

Portfolio analysis

Much of the time in marketing we consider the management of products or strategic business units as separate entities. However, in reality many companies have multiple products servicing multiple segments and markets. Some of these products will require much investment; others will generate income. Companies need to devise a means of allocating their limited resources among products or strategic business units so as to achieve the best performance for the company as a whole. Decisions have to be made regarding which products or brands should be invested in, which to hold and which to remove support from. The process of managing groups of brands/products or strategic business units is called portfolio planning. In the same way that financial investors try to maintain a balanced portfolio of investments with different levels of risk, marketing managers strive to achieve a balanced portfolio of products.

Definition

> **Portfolio analysis** – A tool by which management identifies and evaluates various businesses that make up the company (Jobber, 2001, p. 253).

Portfolio analysis starts with historic data but can be used to project forwards to the future and possible future strategies. Portfolio analysis tools, like the PLC, are very flexible and can be applied to products, brands and strategic business units. The overall aim of a company should be to maintain a balanced portfolio and develop a sustainable competitive advantage.

There are a number of different portfolio planning tools. These are well documented in most marketing texts but we will focus on three of the most well-known models – the Boston Consulting Group Growth-Share Matrix and two multi-factor models (the General Electric Market Attractiveness-Competitive Position model and the Shell Directional Policy Matrix). Other multi-factor models such as the Arthur D. Little Strategic Conditions Matrix and the Abell and Hammons 3 × 3 Investment Opportunity Chart differ slightly from the GE matrix but the underlying principles are similar and will therefore not be discussed separately in this unit.

Extended knowledge

Three portfolio analysis tools will be discussed in this unit. For a more detailed discussion of the strengths and weaknesses of the various tools, refer to Chapter 3 of Hooley et al. (1998).

Boston Consulting Group growth share matrix (BCG)

What is the BCG?
The Boston Consulting Group, a leading management consultancy, developed a 2 × 2 matrix that allows the portfolio of products/SBU to be positioned on the matrix according to:

- market growth rate
- relative market share (i.e. relative to the leading competitor).

The underlying principle of the BCG is the generation and management of cash within a business. According to Drummond and Ensor (2001, p. 96), 'relative market share is seen as a predictor of the product's capacity to generate cash' and 'market growth is seen as a predictor of the product's need for cash'. This would suggest that products with high market share will achieve high sales, but will need relatively less investment than new brands and should have lower costs due to scale economies. Products in fast-growing markets require higher levels of investment than those in slower growing markets. Products in low-growth markets with a high market share will be generating cash, which can be used to help fund other products that require investment; cash flow is not the same as profitability.

Figure 4.4 outlines the BCG. Market growth rate indicates the growth rate of the market in which each product/SBU operates and is used as a proxy for market attractiveness. The scale on the axis will depend on the market and the general economic conditions. Relative market share refers to the market share of each product/SBU relative to the leading competitor. Market share acts as a proxy for competitive strength. The scale is a logarithmic one and the division between high and low market share is 1. For example, if our product had a market share of 50% and the next leading competitor had 25% this would be indicated as 2 on the horizontal axis. If our market share was 15% and the leading competitor is 30% our score would be 0.5. The products/SBUs are represented on the matrix by circles and fall into one of the four quadrants, as illustrated in the figure.

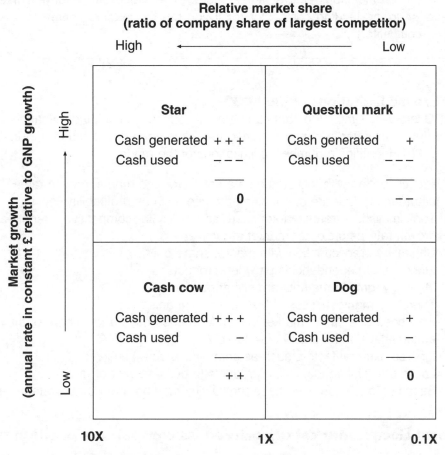

Figure 4.4 The Boston Consultancy Group's growth share matrix (BCG)

Table 4.2

Stars	Question marks
o Build strategies by increasing sales or market share	o Build selectively
o Invest to maintain leadership status	o Identify and focus on niche markets
	o Harvest and divest others
Cash cows	**Dogs**
o Hold strategies to maintain sales or market share	o Harvest or
o Defend position	o Divest or
o Use cash generated to sustain stars, invest in NPD and support a select number of question marks	o Identify profitable niche markets and focus on these

Once products have been plotted on the matrix, it is possible to identify the potential strategies for each type. (Table 4.2 outlines the options for each type of product.) It is also possible to identify the number of cash cows, stars, question marks and dogs present in the portfolio. If the portfolio is unbalanced, action should be taken to improve it.

Exam hint

A common mistake that students make when plotting the BCG is that they depict absolute market share rather than 'relative' market share. When calculating relative market share it is in relation to the leading competitor (or if you are the leading competitor then the next largest competitor).

What are the limitations of the BCG?

The BCG is a very simple tool that can be highly effective in helping managers to understand their portfolio. However, a number of criticisms have been directed at it. For instance, Jobber (2001, p. 257) identifies a number of limitations of the model:

- Preoccupation with focusing on market share and market growth rates. There may be other factors that are of equal importance such as profitability
- Too simplistic – treats market share as a proxy for competitive strength and marketing growth rate as proxy for market attractiveness
- Unhealthy preoccupation with market share gain
- Ignores interdependencies between products
- Many low-growth markets are still attractive
- There are many successful low-share companies
- How does one define market? Does Mercedes have a low share of the car market or a high share of the luxury car market?
- Ignores external factors such as competitive activity
- Lacks precision in identifying products to build/harvest or drop
- Based on cash flow – perhaps profitability may be a more accurate criterion?

General Electric market attractiveness competitive position model (GE)

What is the GE model?

The GE matrix was developed by McKinsey and Company in conjunction with General Electric in the USA, in response to some of the weaknesses of the BCG matrix. This model built on the success of the BCG but acknowledged that market growth rate alone was an insufficient measure of market attractiveness and market share in measuring competitive strength. A multi-factor matrix was developed that enabled managers to build in the measures that were relevant to their industry.

Market/industry attractiveness criteria could include measures such as:

- Market factors (size, growth rates, segment size, price sensitivity)
- Competition (types and strength)
- PEST factors
- Profit potential.

Competitive/business strength criteria could include measures such as:

- Market share (total market, segments)
- Bargaining power of suppliers and customers
- Reputation
- Patents
- Relationships/strategic alliances
- Distribution capabilities
- Ability to develop a competitive advantage or cost advantages.

Once the criteria have been selected, each factor should be given a weighting that recognizes their relative importance. Table 4.3 gives an example of the weighting (totals 10).

Table 4.3 Weighting the criteria

Market attractiveness	
Market growth rate	2
Market size	2.5
Strength of competition	1
Social factors	0.5
Profit opportunity	4
Total	**10**
Competitive strength	
Market share	2.5
Patents	1
Distribution capabilities	2
Relationships	2
Cost advantages	2.5
Total	**10**

Each market attractiveness factor and competitive strength is scored out of 10 (1 = very unattractive/weak and 10 = very attractive/strong) for each product/SBU. Each score is multiplied by the weighting to produce an overall score for market attractiveness and competitive strength for each product/SBU. These can then be plotted on the GE matrix.

Once the products have been plotted on the matrix it is possible to identify potential strategies for each portion of the matrix. This is illustrated in Figure 4.5.

The GE matrix provides managers with greater flexibility than the BCG and enables them to select the criteria that are most relevant to their particular situation.

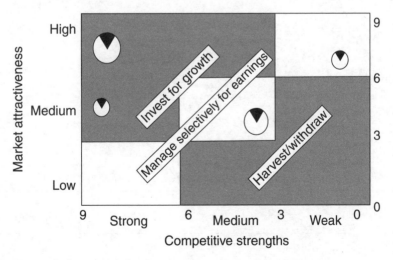

Figure 4.5 The General Electric multi-factor matrix Limitations of the GE matrix

The GE matrix allows a much richer analysis than the BCG; however, it does receive some criticism. It can be a difficult model to use due to the amount of information required and the need for managers to agree the criteria and weighting. There is also an additional problem in that, due to the flexibility of the model, there is opportunity for bias to enter the analysis. It has been suggested that to avoid this the analysis should be conducted at a managerial level higher than the one being analysed.

Activity 4.6

The GE matrix

Using your own company or an organization of your choice select three products or strategic business units on which to base a GE matrix. Complete the table.

- o Identify four relevant measures of market attractiveness and four measures of competitive strength
- o For each market attractiveness measure weight their importance out of 10. Repeat for competitive strength
- o For each product/strategic business unit give a score out of 10 for each of the measures (1 meaning very weak and 10 being very strong)
- o Calculate the rating for each factor by multiplying the score by the weighting and produce a total (out of 100) for each product/strategic business unit.

Plot the products/SBUs on the GE matrix.

	Product/SBU 1			Product/SBU 2			Product/SBU 3		
	Weighting	Score	Rating	Weighting	Score	Rating	Weighting	Score	Rating
Market Attractiveness									
1									
2									
3									
4									
Total	10			10			10		
Competitive Strength									
1									
2									
3									
4									
Total	10			10			10		

Shell directional policy matrix

The Shell directional policy matrix adopts an approach similar to that of the GE matrix, the main difference being the axes. The axes on the Shell directional policy matrix are Prospects for Sector Profitability and Enterprises' Competitive Capabilities (see Figure 4.6).

Prospects for sector profitability

		Unattractive	Average	Attractive
Enterprise's competitive capabilities	Weak	Disinvest	Phased withdrawal	Double or quit
	Average	Phased withdrawal	Custodial growth	Try harder
	Strong	Cash generation	Growth leader	Leader

Figure 4.6

Limitations of portfolio models

Portfolio models have value in helping managers to think more strategically about their business and resource allocation. However, they have not been free of criticism. Brownlie (1983) criticizes portfolio analysis for the following reasons:

- ○ It is over-simplified
- ○ Often offers a misleading representation of strategy options
- ○ Makes use of inappropriate and overly generous measures
- ○ Rests on an assumption that market leadership invariably offers benefits
- ○ Ignores the real benefits of market niching
- ○ Ignores a series of important and strategic factors in the competitive environment.

Concluding thoughts

Despite the limitations of the portfolio models they have made a significant contribution to portfolio planning. Jobber (2001, p. 259) identifies a number of ways in which portfolio analysis tools are of value to the strategic planner:

- ○ **Different products and different roles** – The models highlight that all products should not be treated equally and may have different roles such as cash generation or profitability.

- ○ **Different reward systems and types of managers** – Because different products should have different profitability objectives it is fair to say that managers may require different skills and reward systems. For example, new products that are being built may require marketing-led managers, whereas managers of harvested products may have to be more cost-orientated.

- ○ **Aid to managerial judgement** – Like any model portfolio planning provides guidelines for strategic thinking but the tools should not be seen as a replacement for management judgement.

Question 4.4

Portfolio analysis

Answer Question 3 from the December 2001 Planning and Control paper on portfolio models. Go to www.cimeduhub.com to access specimen answers for this question. Question 4 on the December 2000 paper was also on portfolio analysis.

Extended knowledge

Hooley et al. (1998) provide a good discussion of portfolio analysis in Chapter 3 in their article.

Case history

Unilever – Portfolio management

Unilever, a multinational company in fast moving consumer goods (FMCG) used to produce approximately 1600 consumer brands. The company realized that they could improve their economies of scale, and increase the efficiency of their supply chain, by reducing the number of products they manufactured. They undertook a portfolio exercise that revealed that only a quarter of their brands provided 90% of their turnover. Therefore, they decided to reduce their brands by 75% and to concentrate their marketing activity on 400 of their high-growth brands. The criteria used to identify the brands to maintain were that they should be in the top two sellers in their market segment such as Dove soap, Lipton tea and Calvin Klein perfume. In addition, highly successful local brands, such as Marmite and Persil, were also to be supported. The rest of the brands, such as Pears soap and Timotei shampoo, would either be sold off or harvested gradually. It is anticipated that this strategy will reduce costs by approximately £1 billion over 3 years and provide an additional £450 million to spend on marketing the surviving brands.

Experience curves and importance of market share

The experience curve

Many marketing strategies are based on the premise that market leadership is a desirable goal. It is important that we understand the rationale behind this premise. The experience curve suggests that as a firm accumulates experience of carrying out an activity or function there is evidence of decreasing costs, the result of this being that unit costs reduce as a company becomes more experienced (see Figure 4.7). The implication of this is that the first company to enter a market and attain a large market share will have cost advantages over those entering the market later.

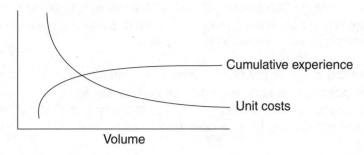

Figure 4.7 Experience curves

According to Aaker (1998), the experience curve may be based on:

○ **Economies of scale** – Scale economies can be derived from more efficient methods of production at higher volumes

○ **Learning** – People learn to undertake tasks faster and more efficiently simply by repetition

○ **Technological improvements in production/operations** – The use of new machinery/IT systems, etc. to improve production or operations can reduce costs dramatically, particularly in capital-intensive industries

○ **Product redesign** – Simplification of products can sharply reduce costs.

Aaker (1998) also acknowledges that there are several considerations when using the experience curve:

○ Multiple products can complicate the concept – there may be several experience curves to analyse

○ The experience curve does not apply in every situation

○ Technological developments may make the experience curve obsolete

○ Lowest costs do not have to equate to lowest prices.

It is essential that managers focus on the customer, not on the process. Sometimes preoccupation with economies of scale and the experience curve can detract from the customer and changing needs. Companies can fall into the trap of focusing on how to improve current processes and ignore the fact that the process is becoming obsolete.

Extended knowledge

For further discussion of the experience curve, read pp. 187–189 of Aaker (1998).

Importance of market share

Companies with higher market share gains have more experience than their competitors. This experience results in lower costs; lower costs mean that at a given market price the market leader in terms of market share will have the highest profits, and therefore will have more to spend on R&D, which in turn enables them to maintain their high market share. This partly explains why many companies strive to be market share leaders, but there are other reasons as to why achieving market share is desirable:

○ Economies of scale – explained above

○ Increased bargaining power – with suppliers, etc.

○ Security – for various stakeholders

o   Status – there is often a sense of status associated with being number 1 in the market
o   Measure of managerial performance – market share gain is often used as such a measure
o   Supported by PIMS research (see below).

However, there are a number of factors companies must take into account when deciding to pursue a share-gaining strategy – such as competitive reactions, cost of gaining market share, how long the strategy can be maintained, level of maturity in the market, effect on other areas of the company's activity and level of customer loyalty.

Profit impact of marketing strategy (PIMS)

The PIMS studies found a strong relationship between market share and return on investment. This research set out to identify the key factors influencing profitability by examining the performance of approximately 3000 strategic business units. The results of this study showed that market share was a key factor in profitability and in general terms there was a linear relationship between profits and relative market share, as shown in Figure 4.8. For example, the study found that organizations with a market share of 40% or more will achieve a return on investment of 30%, three times that of companies with a market share of under 10%. Organizations have been encouraged by this research to pursue market share gains, as this should lead to an increase in profitability.

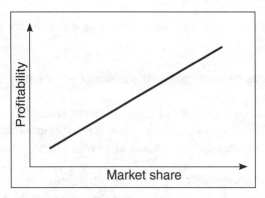

Figure 4.8 PIMS research – profit related to market share

Criticisms of PIMS

High market share will not automatically improve profitability and several criticisms have been directed at the PIMS research:

o   Definition of the market – Porter (1980) wrote: 'there is no single relationship between profitability and market share, unless one conveniently defines the market' and it has been suggested that research findings are more as a result of flexible definition than reality. For example, does easyJet have a large market share of the budget airline industry or small share of the total airline industry?
o   Evidence of many successful low share businesses
o   Evidence of V-shaped curve rather than a linear relationship between market share and profitability (see Figure 4.9). For example, in the June 1999 Analysis and Decision case study of Biocatalysts (an industrial enzyme manufacturer), there was evidence that small niche players and large dominant competitors were profitable but it was those medium-sized companies that were 'stuck in the middle' which did not see a good return on investment.

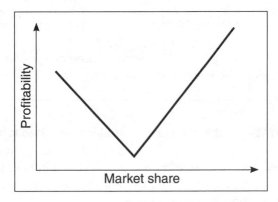

Figure 4.9 V-shaped profit/market share relationship

Extended knowledge

For further discussion of the PIMS research, see Wilson and Gilligan (1997), pp. 104–107 and 342–347.

Concluding thoughts

The PIMS research provides useful insights into the factors contributing to profitability. However, it must be used (as should all models) with some caution. A high market share does not always equate to high profits; these will also depend on a number of other factors such as the level of maturity of the market, level of customer loyalty, likely competitive reactions, PEST factors and the effect on other areas of the organization's activities. For example, market share gain may be at the expense of damaging a premium image.

Question 4.5

PIMS

Answer Question 3 from the June 2002 Planning and Control paper on PIMS.
Go to www.cimeduhub.com to access specimen answers for this question.

Gap analysis

Gap analysis is a fairly simple diagrammatical method of presenting 'where are we now?' and 'where do we want to be?' as illustrated in Figure 4.10.

Definition

Gap analysis – The difference between a company's current forecast of how the company will perform in the future and where they would like to be, i.e. their objectives.

The strategic analysis will identify the current situation and then forecasts can be made of how the company will perform in the future. It is then possible to identify the gap between the two and develop strategies to try to close this gap. Unit 7 – Creating strategic advantage and Unit 8 – Developing a specific competitive position – will discuss the ways in which companies can achieve their objectives and close this gap.

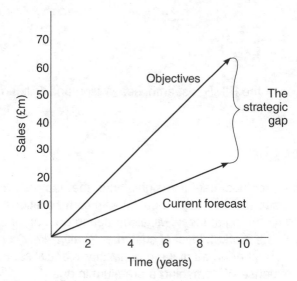

Figure 4.10 Gap analysis

Marketing audit

The marketing audit is a comprehensive framework for undertaking an analysis of the current situation.

Definition

Marketing audit – An audit is a systematic, critical and unbiased review and appraisal of the environment and of the company's operations. A marketing audit is part of the larger management audit and is concerned with the marketing environment and marketing operations (McDonald, 1999).

The marketing audit helps to identify:

- o The organization's environment and the nature of the environmental threats and opportunities
- o Its marketing systems (strengths and weaknesses)
- o Its marketing activities.

According to Kotler (1997), there are six elements to a marketing audit:

1. The marketing environment – both the macro- and microenvironments
2. The marketing strategy – appropriateness and success
3. The marketing organization – structure and staffing
4. The marketing systems – such as the planning process and the MkIS
5. Marketing productivity – cost effectiveness and profitability
6. The marketing functions – detailed evaluation of the marketing mix.

The aspects of the marketing audit relating to internal analysis were discussed in more detail in Unit 3 – Internal analysis. A key aspect of the marketing audit is that it should be independent. This is often difficult to achieve if it is conducted by internal staff with a vested interest in the results. Therefore, many companies elect to periodically employ external agencies such as marketing consultants to undertake the audit to ensure that the analysis is independent.

Extended knowledge

For a detailed discussion of the marketing audit, refer to Kotler (2000), pp. 708–711.

SWOT analysis

SWOT (strengths, weaknesses, opportunities and threats) is a well-known tool often used during the auditing process. This framework is a useful way of summarizing all the information gathered from the auditing process and should be used to identify the critical factors. Often too many SWOTs contain extensive lists of factors rather than focusing on the key aspects. It can be helpful to produce a weighted SWOT that identifies the critical factors and relates the internal strengths and weaknesses to the external threats and opportunities. The main purpose of the SWOT is to focus attention on the critical issues when developing strategies.

Definition

SWOT – A SWOT analysis is a structured approach to evaluate the strategic position of a business by identifying its strengths, weaknesses, opportunities and threats. It is a simple method of synthesizing the results of the marketing audit (Jobber, 2001, p. 42).

Extended knowledge

Refer to Jobber (2001, pp. 42–43) for further discussion of SWOT analysis.

Summary

o There are a number of models/tools that can be used for auditing the current situation and for developing future strategy – value chain, PLC, diffusion of innovation model, experience curves, PIMS, portfolio analysis and gap analysis.

o The value chain is a tool that helps marketers identify ways of creating more customer value and analysing company capabilities. The model identifies nine interrelated value-creating activities, divided into primary and secondary activities.

o The PLC is often described as the most familiar but least understood marketing tool. The model suggests that products and services have a finite life and will move through a series of different stages. Each stage will require different strategies in order to try to extend the product's life and generate maximum profit. The model is criticized for being over-simplistic.

o The rate at which consumers adopt products will vary depending on a number of factors such as level of newness, complexity of the product and trialability. The diffusion of innovation model helps to identify the various groups of customers in relation to the speed at which they will adopt a new product.

o Most companies do not just offer one product or service: many have multiple products serving multiple segments and they are faced with decisions relating to how to manage their portfolio (i.e. which products/SBUs to invest in and which to divest). Portfolio analysis tools can help marketers to manage their portfolios by categorizing their products/SBUs.

o The Boston Consulting Group (BCG) matrix is a simplistic model that categorizes products/SBUs according to market growth rate and relative market share. It is a useful starting point for many marketers but it has been criticized for being over-simplistic and for misleading managers because of its reliance on only two factors.

o To overcome some of the limitations of the BCG model multi-factor portfolio analysis techniques were developed such as the General Electric model, Shell directional policy matrix and the Arthur D. Little matrix. These models use a whole range of factors in addition to market growth rate and relative market share. They have also been criticized for being highly subjective.

o Many companies often regard market leadership as a desirable goal and market leadership is based on the experience curve. The experience curve suggests that as a firm accumulates experience of carrying out an activity its costs fall.

o The profit impact of marketing strategy (PIMS) research identified a strong relationship between market share and return on investment. This research has encouraged firms to pursue market share objectives.

o Gap analysis is a diagrammatical method of presenting 'where we are now and where do we want to be in the future?'

o The marketing audit is a framework for undertaking an analysis of the current situation, both internal and external. SWOT analysis is a tool for drawing together the information from the audit that highlights key strengths, weaknesses, opportunities and threats.

Further study and examination preparation

Extended knowledge

Bibliography

Aaker D (1998). *Strategic Market Management*, 5th Ed., John Wiley & Sons.

Brownlie DT (1983). Analytical frameworks for strategic market planning, cited in Baker MJ (Ed.) (1983), *Marketing Theory and Practice*, Macmillan.

Chandiramani R (2002). Can Dr Martens regain its relevance to youth? *Marketing*, p. 13, 7 November.

Drummond G and Ensor J (1999). *Strategic Marketing Planning and Control*, Butterworth-Heinemann.

Grant J (2002). How can Marmite build on its first century? *Marketing*, pp. 11, 31 January.

Hooley G, Saunders J and Piercy N (1998). *Marketing Strategy and Competitive Positioning*, Prentice-Hall.

Jobber D (2001). *Principles and Practice of Marketing*, 3rd Ed., McGraw-Hill.

Kotler P (2000). *Marketing Management, The Millenium Edition*, Prentice-Hall.

McDonald M. (1999). *Marketing Plans: How To Prepare Them, How to Use Them*, 4th Ed., Butterworth-Heinemann.

Porter M (1980). *Competitive Strategy: Techniques for analysing Industries and Competitors*, Free Press.

Porter (1985). *Competitive Advantage: Creating and Sustaining Superior Performance*, Free Press.

Rink DR and Swan JE (1979). Product life-cycle research: a literature review, *Journal of Business Research*, 78 (Sept), 219–242.

Rogers EM (1983). *Diffusion of Innovations*, Free Press.

Swan JE and Rink DR (1982). Variations on the Product life-cycle, *Business Horizons*, 25 (1), 72–76.

Wilson RMS and Gilligan CT (1997). *Strategic Marketing Management: Planning, Implementation and Control*, Butterworth-Heinemann.

unit 5

financial analysis and techniques for developing a view of the future

By the end of this unit you will:

o   Be familiar with a variety of tools for financial analysis, including:

1.   Balance sheets

2.   Profit and loss accounts

3.   Ratio analysis

4.   Productivity analysis

5.   Segmental analysis.

o   Be able to demonstrate an understanding of the financial implications of marketing planning

o   Be able to discuss a variety of techniques for forecasting the future, including:

1.   Trend extrapolation

2.   Modelling

3.   Individual forecasting

4. Intuitive forecasting

5. Consensus forecasting

   a. Jury forecasting

   b. Delphi forecasting

6. Scenario planning

7. War gaming

8. Synthesis reports.

o Understand the strategic use of information

o Understand, and be able to discuss market sensing and its role in marketing planning.

 ## Key definitions

Profit and loss account – Measures the operational performance of a company over a period of time. It does this by summarizing revenues and costs over a period of time, which allows profits, or losses, to be determined.

Balance sheets – Provide a snapshot of the financial position of an organization in terms of its assets, liabilities and capital at a particular moment in time.

Ratios – Represent a snapshot of the firm's financial/productivity position and fall into five general categories: profitability, gearing, liquidity, asset utilization and investment performance.

Trend extrapolation – Simply takes a historical trend over time and extrapolates where the trend line will be, if extended in the future (Drummond and Ensor, 2001, p. 107).

Modelling – Is to identify the key variables in a situation and to model how they interact with each other (Drummond and Ensor, 2001, p. 108).

Individual forecasting – Is where an organization seeks an individual's view of the future because they are regarded as an expert in a particular field. The organization does not want this person's view to be diluted by other less-expert individuals.

Jury forecasting – Involves bringing together a group of individuals, either internal staff or external experts, to discuss their views on the future and to ultimately come to a consensus decision.

Delphi forecasting – Involves seeking the views of experts on an individual basis. The 'experts' normally remain anonymous and have no communication with each other. Forecasts are collected from each expert and then the results are fed back to all participants. They are then asked to amend their forecasts until a consensus view is reached.

Scenario planning – Involves identifying a diverse range of potential futures that will help managers to identify and understand the key factors that may impact on the business in the future.

War gaming – Is a term that is taken from military planning, where actions and counter-actions of opponents are simulated, using either physical models in large dioramas or, more commonly, using computer models.

Study Guide

- ○ This unit will take you about 3 hours to work through
- ○ We suggest that you take a further 4 hours to do the various activities and questions in this unit.

Introduction

The last unit provided an overview of the various tools that can be used in the auditing process and to help develop future strategies. The first part of this unit will continue this discussion with reference to the role of financial analysis. Understanding the current situation is a vital part of developing a marketing strategy. However, in order to develop a strategy that is looking towards the future, it is essential that organizations utilize techniques for developing a view of the future. This unit will outline the various tools available to do so. The future is uncertain; however, it is essential that companies develop techniques to identify new trends, in the hope that they can capitalize on any new opportunities.

Financial auditing tools

These tools can support answers to major marketing planning questions:

1. 'Where are we now?', as the financial component of a marketing audit
2. 'Where do we want to be?', when used in the context of objective setting, from which planners must generate appropriate strategies
3. 'How do we know we have arrived?', used in the context of marketing control.

It is assumed that students have an understanding of profit and loss accounts, balance sheets and ratio analysis. You can revise these topics by reading the appropriate sections in the Advanced Certificate module 'Management Information for Marketing Decisions'. This unit will provide a brief overview of financial analysis and highlight the key issues in relation to the Planning and Control syllabus.

Profit and loss accounts

The profit and loss account measures the operational performance of a company over a period of time. It does this by summarizing revenues and costs over a period of time, which allows profits, or losses, to be determined. The Advanced Certificate module MIMD would have introduced you to profit and loss accounts. Activity 5.1 will also check your understanding of this concept.

Balance sheets

A balance sheet provides a snapshot of the financial position of an organization in terms of its assets, liabilities and capital at a particular moment in time. This is in contrast to a profit and loss account, which measures profits over a period, usually an accounting year. You should be familiar with the format and contents of a balance sheet from studying the CIM Advanced Certificate module Marketing Information for Marketing Decisions. To check your understanding undertake Activity 5.1.

Ratio analysis

In corporate and strategic planning, the focus tends to be on topline financial values. These are derived from the profit and loss account and from the balance sheet. The main categories of ratios, with some examples of each, are summarized in Table 5.1.

Definition

Ratios – Represent a snapshot of the firm's financial/productivity position and fall into five general categories: profitability, gearing, liquidity, asset utilization and investment performance.

Table 5.1 Classification of topline financial variables more commonly used in strategic planning

Type of ratio	Example topline ratios

Fundamental strength of the business	1. Profitability ratios
	  º Gross profit margin = (GP/Sales) × 100
	  º Net profit margin = (NP/Sales) × 100
	2. Capital structure ratios, also termed 'gearing' ratios
	  º debt ratio = total debt/total assets
	  Where;
	  º total debt = current liabilities + long-term liabilities
	  º total assets = fixed assets + current assets
	3. Liquidity
	  º current ratio = current assets/current liabilities
	  º liquid ratio = (current assets − stock)/current liabilities

Operational efficiency of the business	4. Asset utilization
	  º stock turnover ratio = cost of goods sold/stock at cost on balance sheet
	  º debtor turnover = sales turnover/debtors
	  º credit turnover ratios = cost of goods sold/trade creditors from the balance sheet

Investment performance ratios	5. Investment performance ratios º Price to earnings ratio (i.e. P/E ratio) = Market price per share[1]/earnings per share[2]

[1] From stock market.

[2] Declared annually or twice per year by the company.

Marketing planners consider ratios in monitoring their own organization, and in contrasting its financial strength with that of other organizations. Profitability ratios are most commonly used for this purpose. They also provide an insight into how efficiently and effectively an organization is managed and indicate the amount of resources a competitor may be accumulating for future competitive action. Investment performance ratios are used by financial stakeholders, especially potential financial stakeholders. In some organizations, the influence of these key stakeholders can even be translated into share price and P/E ratio targets for chief executive officers. Low and/or falling share prices are a clear sign of competitive weakness: they are a sign of poor past performance, a consensus market view (which includes many informed and important stakeholders and analysts) which anticipates weak future performance and, even more crucially, makes the organization vulnerable to takeover. While one organization may not wish to buy a particularly weak business with a low share price, a competitor may gain strategic advantage from an acquisition. Investment performance ratios may be viewed as summarizing the conclusions that may be drawn from profitability, capital structure, liquidity and asset utilization ratios.

Activity 5.1

Knowledge check on the use of ratios in the analysis of the balance sheet and of the profit and loss account

Use the profit and loss account and balance sheet for 'Pantronics Limited' to calculate the ratios presented in Table 5.1.

Profit and loss 'Pantronics Limited'

	£	£		
Sales		1,160,000	**A**	
Opening stock (1 January 20xx)	90,000			
Purchases	762,000			
B	852,000			
Less closing stock (31 December 20xx) **C**	100,000			
Cost of sales		752,000	**D**	D = B – C
Gross profit		408,000	**E**	E = A – D
Less overheads:				
Directors' remuneration	90,000			
Debenture interest	7,200			
Other overheads	270,000			
		367,200	**F**	F = Sum of overheads
Net profit for year before taxation		40,800	**G**	G = E – F
Less corporation tax		14,280		
Profit for year after taxation		26,520	**H**	
Less interim dividends paid:				
Ordinary shares	12,000			
Preference shares	2,000			
Final dividends paid				
Ordinary shares	22,000			
Preference shares	2,000			
		38,000	**I**	I = sum of all dividends
Retained profit for year		–11,480	**J**	J = H – I
Add balance of retained profits at beginning of year		82,000	**K**	Profits retained*
Balance of retained profits at end of year		70,520	**L**	L = J + K

*i.e. from last year.

Balance sheet – 'Pantronics Limited'

	COST £	DEP'N TO DATE £	NET		
Fixed assets					
Intangible					
Goodwill	90,000	36,000	54,000		
Tangible					
Freehold land and buildings	324,000	36,000	288,000		
Machinery	414,000	162,000	252,000		
Fixtures and fittings	180,000	45,000	135,000		
	1,008,000	279,000	729,000	**A**	Total fixed assets
Current assets					
Stock		85,000			
Debtors		64,600			
Bank		37,400			
Cash		3,400			
		190,400		**B**	Total current assets
Less current liabilities					
Creditors	51,000				
Proposed dividends	20,400				
Corporation tax	25,500	96,900		**C**	Total current liabilities
Working capital			93,500	**D**	D = B − C
			822,500	**E**	E = A + D
Less long-term liabilities					
10% Debentures			60,000	**F**	G = total assets less total liabilities
Net assets			762,500	**G**	G = (A + B)− (C + F)
Financed by					
Issue share capital					
40,000 10% preference shares of £1 each, fully paid			40,000		
630,000 ordinary shares of £1 each, fully paid			630,000		
			670,000	**H**	
Capital reserve					
Share premium account			21,980	**I**	
Revenue reserve					
Profit and loss account			70,520	**J**	
Shareholder funds			762,500	**K**	K = H + I + J

Also assume: Market share price = 165p.

Activity 5.2

Revision of accounts and financial ratios

If you would like to revise accounts and financial ratios visit the site: www.bized.ac.uk/dataserv/comrep.htm

If you feel comfortable with accounts and with ratios, use your own company accounts, or accounts of another business that you have access to, to assess performance. Try and link various measures of performance, through calculating business ratios, with the marketing activity of the organization. How has marketing strategy, tactics, and the marketing environment, influenced the financial performance of the organization?

Productivity analysis

Productivity analysis considers the relationship between inputs and outputs and is sometimes referred to as input–output analysis. Table 5.2 provides the general formula for this, along with two examples to illustrate the principle.

Table 5.2 Productivity analysis

General formula	Marketing outputs/ Marketing inputs	The general principle is that any output may be expressed as a ratio of any input. The particular variable selected depends on the reason for calculating the productivity ratio
Example 1	Change in sales turnover/ Change in communications expenditure	The assumption behind this ratio is that a communications campaign has been undertaken and that this is the sole, or main reason behind an increase in sales turnover. Additional information must be gathered at the time of collecting ratio data, in order to confirm that another factor has not been the cause of the change. For example, poor distribution by a competitor, or a competitor withdrawing from the market
Example 2	Increase in consumer awareness/Change in advertising expenditure	This provides a useful measure by which to judge, at least in part, the performance of the company. This example is to illustrate that the ratio need not always be purely of financial measures. It may be of a physical and financial measure (see real indices below)

Real indices

One note of caution in using productivity ratios must be taken when using a mixture of a financial measure and a physical measure to calculate a single ratio, e. g. sales turnover (£)/number of sales people. The danger arises from inflation of financial values such that any increase in the ratio could arise purely from a general rise in prices (i.e. inflation) rather than be caused by the influence of marketing activity. The solution to this problem is to remove the influence of inflation from any data expressed in monetary terms (in principle by dividing by an appropriate inflation index). The ratio that results is termed a 'real index' or measure.

Comparative analysis

In applying productivity ratios, organizations may monitor how the indices have changed over time, by comparing:

1. How individual ratios for the organization (i.e. internal ratios) have changed over time
2. Ratios for competitor organizations to assess how their productivity, as well as relative productivity, have changed. Assessments based on these types of ratios must in particular consider how data are compiled to ensure that correct inferences are made from using comparative data.

Segmental analysis

Segmental analysis forces the marketer to consider the market that is the focus of analysis. This, to some people, seems an excessively simple task, but is often ill-considered. It is at the core of much marketing analysis. Hours of marketing planning can be wasted if the market has not been defined correctly. Segmental analysis may consider three main areas: product areas, geographical areas and consumer segments.

For example, consider the market for pasta.

Product areas
1. Do you include fresh, tinned, atmosphere packaged and dry pasta?
2. Should pasta products be included which include some other processed product (e.g. cannelloni or tortellini?)
3. Should pasta be included in ready meals with a pasta component?

Geographical areas
If the European pasta market is being considered, is this defined as some or all member countries of the European Union? Should countries that are about to join the Union be considered? Should Switzerland and Norway be included, even though they are not members of the EU?

Consumer segments
There are many possible approaches when considering the segmentation of this market, e.g. income, lifestyle, household composition and measures that combine all or some of these segmentation criteria.

Defining the market, which is the foundation for much marketing analysis, is not always a simple process. Marketing strategists must be informed in this decision by a clear view of the markets they are in, which they wish to enter and who is defined as a 'competitor'.

Segments and organizational size
The analysis may generate very different results as the subject for analysis changes. The analysts may need to change the subject of analysis in order to understand its effect. Which definition is considered will depend on the marketing decision the analysis supports. For example, where an SME from Australia wishes to launch on the UK market, most of the analysis will be on the UK market. However, a multinational enterprise will be interested in as wide a definition of 'the market' as possible, probably starting with the EU, but undertaking particularly detailed studies in markets considered to be significant currently or with the potential to grow.

Combining the segments
Which products and sub-products to include, will depend on the view taken on the elasticity of demand and on the relative substitutability of different products. Analysts will start by considering the most substitutable products as most relevant for inclusion in their analysis. Time and

resources available as well as, for example, marketing research information on consumer perception of substitutes, will determine how wide the analytical net is spread. From a product market perspective low-cost tinned pasta, shaped into circles, in tomato sauce purchased for ease of eating by children (i.e. family life-cycle stage with dependent children) will have few highly substitutable competitors. Obviously from a consumer segment perspective pasta rings is only one solution to the 'quick, simple childrens' meal, for which there are many substitutes.

In contrast, from a product market perspective, high-income singles or 'empty nesters' with active lifestyles are likely to include 'quality and speed of preparation with minimal effort' as important product attributes. As long as a solution is presented to this problem, then quite a wide range of pasta offerings (in combination with other meal elements presented in the food outlet) is likely to be acceptable. From a consumer segment perspective, a multitude of non-pasta potential competitors exists.

Extended knowledge

For a detailed discussion of financial analysis refer to the MIMD module. There are several good articles which introduce finance to the non-finance specialist. For example, Cox and Fardon's (1997) *Management of Finance, a guide to business finance for the non-specialist*, Osborne Books.

Exam hint

The Planning and Control exam is not examining your detailed knowledge of financial accounts. However, you are expected to understand the financial implications of marketing planning. You will be expected to undertake detailed financial analysis when you sit the Analysis and Decision exam.

Techniques for developing a future orientation (forecasting)

Organizations operate in dynamic environments. In order to develop marketing plans that reflect these changes it is necessary to utilize techniques that can help forecast the future. Organizations that can effectively forecast future trends and developments will be well positioned to capitalize on the opportunities arising out of these changes. A variety of techniques can be used to develop a vision of the future.

A crucial initial decision, before selecting a particular analytical tool, is the perspective that will be taken of 'the market'. This perspective will be influenced by the size of firm conducting the analysis. These issues were discussed in segmental analysis, and Table 5.3 summarizes the three main perspectives.

Table 5.3 Main elements forecast

	Electronics industry example	**Airline industry example**
Industry	Mobile telecommunications	Inter-continental air traffic
Market sector	Consumer mobile phones	Trans-Atlantic (Europe-USA) business travel
Product	Text messaging mobile phones	Supersonic business travel

A variety of techniques are available to support analysis. Which technique is most appropriate will depend on the data that are available, the complexity and type of problem and the timescales involved.

Students naturally like to know which models to use in particular contexts. It is difficult to provide a simple guide as many models may be used in a variety of contexts. In addition, some of the syllabus 'techniques' are approaches rather than detailed, specific methods (e.g. 'individual forecasts', 'intuitive forecasts', 'scenario planning'). Perhaps the most simple classification approach is to consider techniques in relation to (a) forecasting horizon and (b) breadth of forecast. In the three-level 'breadth' classification of Table 5.3, 'product' is narrowest and 'industry' broadest. 'Trend' extrapolation, a type of statistical technique, is best suited to narrow, short-time horizons as the technique can take account of only a limited amount of 'narrowly defined' information. 'Individual forecasts', 'intuitive forecasts' and modelling may be used for all types of forecasting, from individual product sales forecasts for the next 3-month period to the outlook for the industry over the next 20 years. Techniques best suited to broad, long-range forecasts include consensus forecasting and scenario planning. The time-consuming nature of such forecasts, and their resource requirements, mean that they are mainly suited to decisions where the cost implication of success, and of failure, is relatively great. They are helpful where data are difficult to obtain, where numerical information is insufficient, or where long-run data sets do not allow the use of statistically based techniques.

Trend extrapolation

This technique uses information on the past to predict the future. The assumption is that the relationships between variables that held in the past will continue to hold in the future. If sales revenue growth averaged 3% in each of the last 4 years, trend extrapolation will predict that this will be the case in the future. In practice, data are more variable than this and extrapolation is likely to be based on a statistical 'best-fit' line. The principle is, however, the same.

 Definition

Trend extrapolation – This technique simply takes a historical trend over time and extrapolates where the trend line will be if extended in the future (Drummond and Ensor, 2001, p. 107).

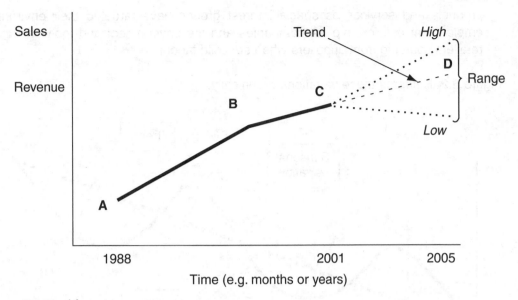

Figure 5.1 Trend forecast

Trend forecasting is conceptually quite simple but more difficult in practice. Even when a decision has been made to use the past as the basis for predicting the future, two main questions arise:

1. How far into the past should you go to calculate the trend?
2. How should you summarize the past in a way that can be extrapolated into the future?

Extended knowledge

See the Advanced Certificate module MIMD, where, e.g. data smoothing is discussed.

In Figure 5.1, the trend line C–D has been based on sales revenue data for the period B–C (i.e. the recent part is considered the most relevant basis on which to predict the future). If it were considered that the period B–C is somehow unusual then the whole period A–C would be used to develop a trend prediction. The decision must be taken based on specialist market knowledge.

When considering trends, forecasters must be clear about the underlying market forces that are influencing demand for individual products and services. These can be separated, or decomposed, into separate elements:

o   **Seasonal variation** during any single year. Many industries are influenced by this: frozen foods in the summer, consumer goods at Christmas, chocolate sales increase at gift-giving festivals (especially Christmas and Easter), etc. This has a knock-on effect in the associated business-to-business markets.

o   **Cyclical variation** due to changes in economic activity associated with business cycles. These can extend over periods from a few to over 15 years.

o   **Random variation** due to unpredictable events. Demand fell rapidly in the UK tourist sector in 2001 due to adverse publicity following the foot and mouth outbreak and the negative imagery presented to potential customers throughout the world. Perrier suffered a large reduction in demand due to temporary benzene contamination of their product in the early 1990s. Individual companies have suffered from random reductions in demand for their

121

products and services as special-interest groups have targeted their environmental or employment policies, e.g. oil companies and the environment and footwear and clothing retailers sourcing from suppliers who use 'child labour'.

Figure 5.2 Illustrates these variations graphically.

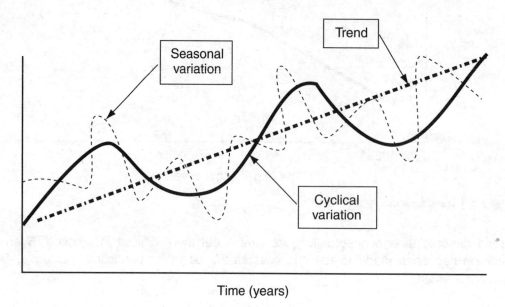

Time (years)

Figure 5.2 Decomposition of data

Modelling

Models are simplifications of the 'real world'. Much marketing theory may be described as models. For example, that successful marketing implementation will be achieved if each of the 7 'Ps' is managed effectively. However, the context in which 'models' are discussed here focuses on their application to forecasting. There are various approaches to classifying models. Here we consider models in terms of whether or not they describe the 'black box'. Figure 5.3 illustrates the 'black box' model.

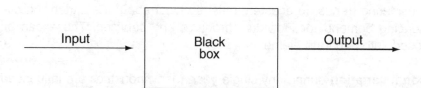

Figure 5.3 A conceptual representation of the 'black box' model

Definition

Modelling – The technique is to identify the key variables in a situation and to model how they interact with each other (Drummond and Ensor, 2001, p. 108).

The general approach to modelling is that, after analysis, it will be possible to predict outputs if a given level of inputs is known. Black box, or input–output, models attempt to establish a relationship between inputs and outputs (assuming all other factors remain constant). For example:

- £20,000 advertising expenditure will result in an increase in sales of £50,000
- A 20% price reduction over 4 weeks will result in 10% increase in sales revenue over the following year.

Such models, e.g. regression models, do not try to explain what takes place within the black box.

Case Study

Developing a pricing model for the Mercedes A-Class

Many companies base price setting on whim, or on anecdotal evidence gathered from a narrow selection of sales staff. Even Mercedes-Benz, prior to launching one of its A-class models in the German market in 2001, initially proposed a price tag of DM29,500 (£9000), based on little more than the belief that DM30,000 was psychologically important.

To confirm the company approach to price setting, a specialist agency was recruited. Their first task was to establish consumer perception of the new model. The agency's conclusion was that the new model was, 'A multifunction version, which appealed to only about a quarter of buyers, but that these buyers value it highly'. A video was prepared by the agency comparing the new A-class model with the BMW 3 series and the VW Golf, showing that it offered more space than either. The video was screened to 200 consumers who were then interviewed. This information was the foundation on which a computer model was built that described the sensitivity of consumers to the 'value offer' and to price.

The conclusion from the computer-pricing model was that for a particular segment, it was not as price elastic as the company had first thought. Consequently, the vehicle was launched in Germany at a price of DM31,000. It still hit its 200,000-volume target but Mercedes made an extra DM300 million a year.

Although it is acknowledged that consumers' intentions, as stated in research, can be misleading, that does not mean that consumer research should not be used to develop realistic pricing models.

In contrast to input–output models, simulation-type models attempt to explain what takes place within the box. Examples include models of consumer behaviour which attempt to explain each stage, in detail, of the decision-making process.

One application of simulation modelling has been implemented by food retailers. For example, a supermarket layout may be represented in a computer model, with customers arriving and leaving the store and moving around the store represented by queues or by individual dots (pixels on a computer screen). The management team wishes to know how to optimize:

- store layout (and their ability to influence customer flow around the store and to encourage unplanned purchasing behaviour)
- product shelf space allocation

123

     ◦ allocation of staff between shelf stacking and checkout duties
     ◦ location for merchandizing activity.

In working with this model, assumptions may be made about the numbers of customers arriving at the store each hour, time spent in the store, checkout processing time, purchases made in each type of shelf location (e.g. bottom, middle, top), etc. and these can be experimented within a store simulation model. Such modelling techniques enable managers to experiment with the influence of different parameters on the system and to understand the system more clearly.

Case history

An example of a retail store simulation

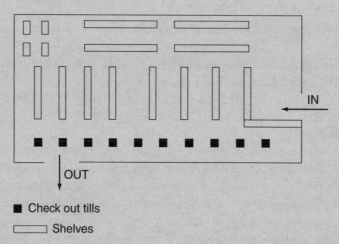

■ Check out tills

▭ Shelves

Figure 5.4 Simulating a retail outlet

Assumptions:

1. 120 shoppers arrive each hour
2. Each shopper spends on average £60
3. The average time in store is 15 minutes
4. Time to process a shopper at the checkout averages five minutes.

In this simulation (see Figure 5.4), the shopper moves around the store and arrives at the checkout. Queues develop at the checkouts and the supermarket manager must decide on the relative balance between shelf-stacking staff and checkout staff; too many shelf stackers and customer satisfaction declines rapidly at the checkout and the potential to lose repeat business rises; too many people on the checkout and the shelves start to run out of products. There are many other issues; for example, how to get the customer to stay in the store longer, to browse the shelves (i.e. move away from the narrow confines of the shopping list) and so spend more money. The simulation can be expanded to include the impact of changing store layout, inclusion of more merchandising activity and altering the marketing mix and outside the store. In addition to affecting movement around the store, the spread of arrival times over the day and the numbers arriving are likely also to be affected. By changing one single assumption of the simulation, the impact on queue development (and associated revenue flow) can be examined and assessed.

Case history

Building your own simulation model in-house

'ithink analyst' is a simulation software package (from High Performance Systems, Inc. of the USA) which allows the user to simulate complex business scenarios. The program simplifies the process of building simulation scenarios to explore the effects of business decisions. Model building proceeds in three parts:

1. The creation of a flowchart-type map of the process or pattern of influences that will be the subject of the simulation
2. Provision of detailed information specific to the business situation which you wish to simulate, to fine-tune the model for the user's specific requirements
3. Running the model and using the output generated, in the form of tables and charts, to support the analysis of the simulation.

The advantage of this approach is that it allows the user to understand the business situation in greater detail through experimenting with the model. However, as for many learning activities, some time must be invested in understanding how to construct models using this, or similar, tools before full advantage can be taken.

Extended knowledge

Download a demo version of 'ithink' from www.cognitus.co.uk. See the cognitus 'business services' button 'software'. At this point select the 'ithink' button to find out more about business dynamics modelling.

Econometrics

Econometric methods involve the application of mathematical modelling, mainly statistical, to the description of economic relationships, such as the level of consumer demand (in an industry sector or in the whole economy), inflation, the exchange rate and interest rates. The types of techniques employed include, e.g. correlation, regression and time series analyses. These may be used to estimate the factors that influence key variables of interest (known as the dependent variable). The complexity of the systems, which econometric techniques attempt to describe, generally requires multiple equations. The main benefits of such techniques are that they allow the sensitivity of the systems, described by the models, to be explored. For example, the effect of a 1% increase in inflation on the level of consumer demand for cars, or for the whole economy, may be estimated. Such techniques also generate estimation error ranges and certainty probabilities of the estimate being correct. Government economists, leading business schools and large corporations tend to be the main places where econometric analysis occurs. Results of such analysis are presented frequently in the business pages of broadsheet newspapers, as well as the specialist business press.

Individual forecasting

This is where an organization regards an individual's view of the future as especially significant. The organization does not want this particular individual's view to be diluted by coming to a consensus with other less expert individuals. Individual experts may be used for a wide range of forecasts, from the demand for individual products and services, to future scenarios of industry sectors or of economies. Arthur C. Clarke, for example, has been used by many organizations, including the National Aeronautics and Space Administration (NASA), to provide a view of the future of space technology and travel. Such future views allow planners to create more realistic business and marketing plans, in the case of NASA for lobbying government for funds. There is a line of debate which suggests that accounting for future views actually causes the future to happen. This is especially probable where experts are exceptional and have a track record of being right. For example, if significant experts, acting for each major automobile manufacturer, believe a breakthrough in fuelcell technology is imminent, then each company will fund this not to be left behind. This therefore increases the probability of the breakthrough happening.

It is difficult to deconstruct the processes that occur when experts provide a forecast. Often no specific technique is used: the forecast is based on a life's accretion of knowledge and experience. Such forecasts have been termed **intuitive**, but that has in the past stood for 'predictions' that have been little more than guesses. Expert 'intuition' is increasingly being modelled by computer scientists using complex models and principles such as neural networks, which try to replicate the functioning of a human brain. This is still some way off from practical marketing planning application.

Definition

Individual forecasting – Is where an organization seeks an individual's view of the future because they are regarded as an expert in a particular field. The organization does not want this person's view to be diluted by other less expert individuals.

Consensus forecasting

Rather than relying on the expertise of a particular individual, it is more common to use groups of people, especially where the forecast has a substantial influence on the success of the business. There are two approaches to group forecasting:

1. Where group members interact in person with each other (e.g. jury forecasts)
2. Where group members are in separate locations and interaction is purely through reporting group findings, usually in the form of written summary results (e.g. Delphi forecasts).

The aim of consensus (group) forecasting is to develop a forecast by reaching some form of consensus agreement. The general principle of jury forecasting was introduced to the Advanced Certificate in the module Marketing Information for Management Decisions, and particular reference is made in that module to Delphi forecasting.

Jury forecasting

Jury forecasting involves bringing together a group of individuals, either internal staff or external experts, to discuss their views on the future and to ultimately come to a consensus decision. The accuracy of the forecast will depend to a large extent on the quality of the individuals within the group. There can be problems with jury forecasting, mainly due to group dynamics. For example, long-established managers may dominate the group and junior members with valid suggestions may feel intimidated. There is also a tendency for 'groupthink' where the views of dissenting individuals are ignored. According to Drummond and Ensor (1998), there are four key factors that affect the level of 'groupthink':

- o   High cohesiveness
- o   Strong leadership
- o   Lack of objective search and evaluation
- o   Insulation of group.

Groupthink can result in a number of problems for jury forecasting according to Drummond and Ensor (2001):

- o   Illusions of invulnerability
- o   Collective rationalization
- o   Belief in the inherent morality of the group
- o   Pressure on dissenters
- o   The illusion of unanimity
- o   Self-appointed mind guards.

Jury forecasting can be a valuable forecasting technique as long as companies recognize the problems associated with groupthink.

Extended knowledge

For further amplification of groupthink, refer to:

Drummond and Ensor (2001). *Strategic Marketing Planning and Control*, Butterworth-Heinemann, Chapter 6, pp. 109–112.

Delphi forecasting

Delphi forecasting can help to overcome some of the problems associated with jury forecasting. Instead of the group meeting together the views of experts are sought independently. In most cases the 'experts' will remain anonymous and will have no communication with each other. The whole process is co-ordinated by somebody not involved in the forecast. The Delphi method has several stages:

1.   Forecasts are invited from a variety of experts
2.   The co-ordinator reviews these forecasts and may remove any spurious forecasts
3.   The experts are then sent the various forecasts and asked to comment or amend their own forecast in light of the other forecasts
4.   The co-ordinator reviews these forecasts and the process continues until a consensus opinion is arrived at.

Definition

Delphi forecasting – This type of forecasting involves seeking the views of experts on an individual basis. The 'experts' normally remain anonymous and have no communication with each other. Forecasts are collected from each expert and then the results are fed back to all participants. They are then asked to amend their forecasts until a consensus view is reached.

This method overcomes some of the problems of groupthink. However, it does have its own problems. For example, it is a very time-consuming process and the time delays may result in the participants becoming demotivated. *The FT Mastering Marketing* (1998) series included an interesting article on forecasting. This article suggested that the following principles should be followed when using Delphi forecasting techniques:

- ○ Structure the forecasting problem so that it makes good use of the experts knowledge (this may call for breaking the problem into a series of smaller problems)
- ○ Write out the problem and check that it is comprehensible
- ○ Prepare alternative written statements of the problem
- ○ Use at least five experts but no more than 20
- ○ Ensure that experts do not receive incentives that could compromise objectivity
- ○ Ask each expert to make an independent forecast
- ○ Choose experts who differ from one another
- ○ Choose experts with some expertise in the problem area (although high expertise is not necessary)
- ○ Allow the experts to revise their forecasts in light of information from other experts.

Source: *Financial Times Mastering Marketing* Series (1998).

Scenario planning

Scenario planning is planning for different futures. An implicit assumption of this technique is that the forecaster understands how the present has been determined, i.e. the external environmental factors which contribute to the present, and the external environmental factors that will be important in the future.

 Definition

Scenario planning – This involves identifying a diverse range of potential futures that will help managers to identify and understand the key factors that may impact on the business in the future.

Forecasters will construct different scenarios based on assumptions about changes in one or two variables, or influential factors:

1. Assumptions about how a key variable will change
2. Assumptions about likely combinations of a range of relatively important variables.

For example, critical in any scenario of the future of the airline industry are assumptions behind (1) the growth in demand for air travel, the particular routes that will grow fastest (short, medium and long haul), (2) the size (i.e. carrying capacity) and (3) speed of next-generation passenger aircraft. Scenario planning for a 20-year time horizon for the airline industry is likely to be based on several assumptions for each of these three key variables. According to Drummond and Ensor (2001), there are four main stages in the development of simple scenarios:

1. Identify critical variables – This involves establishing the factors that will act as drivers of change in the future. Once identified they should then be evaluated in terms of their importance to the organization and the extent to which they can be predicted.
2. Develop possible string of events – Using the important drivers of change it is then possible to develop a number of different scenarios.

3. Define the scenarios – Once a whole range of scenarios has been developed it is then necessary to evaluate the alternatives.
4. Identify the issues arising – The robust strategies produced from this process should then be reviewed, the objective being to assess whether any critical issues have been identified that may impact on the business.

Scenario planning is concerned with encouraging managers to think 'outside the box' and to identify possible future events that may have major implications for the organization. Drummond and Ensor (2001, p. 118) suggest three benefits of using scenario planning:

o   It helps managers to understand the critical issues that lie at the heart of the organization
o   It encourages managers to consider the future and the possibility of discontinuities in the external environment
o   It places strategic issues on the management agenda.

Scenario planning has several advantages over traditional econometric models. Econometric models contain few explanatory variables, most of which can be easily quantified. They do not take into account the development of new relationships or possible changes in trends. Scenario planning embraces and tries to anticipate the possibility of these changes happening.

Case history

Scenario planning and banking 'futures'

A major advantage of using scenario planning is that it encourages the creation of new mental maps of the consumer environment. Rather than considering only one possible outcome, the approach involves developing a selection of possible outcomes in a way that is meaningful to the organization.

A Danish bank wished to consider the future of banking in 10 years, the starting point on which the scenarios were to be based. Three possible scenarios were developed:

1. A 'systems bank' concept where the bank offered many computerized, standardized products
2. A 'segmented' banking scenario in which a combination of different levels of products and service were offered to specific target groups
3. An 'individualized' scenario where high levels of individual customer support were offered. In this scenario, the bank required a substantial number of staff to deliver the personalized service, in addition to computerized systems, to produce a high level of 'value-added' for its clients.

In this particular approach to scenario planning, the company selected the scenario that it regarded as providing the greatest competitive advantage, aligned with its current strengths. The bank in question actually selected the third scenario on the grounds that too many banks were competing in the first scenario, while the second scenario was not regarded as sufficiently different to the first. In this approach, the bank envisaged possible futures and selected the one that was considered to provide a long-term competitive advantage.

'If you want a unique strategy it is wise to start from a unique perspective' (Rolf Jensen, Director of the Copenhagen Institute). Scenario planning applied in this context enabled a 'proactive' rather than 'reactive' approach to be adopted.

Extended knowledge

For a further discussion of scenario planning, refer to:

Drummond and Ensor (2001), Chapter 6, pp. 115–119.

Mercer D (1998), Chapters 6–8.

Question 5.1

Scenario planning

Answer Question 6 from the December 2001 Planning and Control paper on scenario planning. Go to www.cimeduhub.com to access specimen answers for this question. Question 7 on the June 2000 paper was also on scenario planning.

War gaming

This is a term that is taken from military planning, where actions and counter-actions of opponents are simulated, using either physical models in large dioramas or, more commonly, using computer models. In marketing, war gaming may be enacted by individuals or teams, with the strategies and tactics of opponents represented. Where this is undertaken, simulation tends to be favoured as a technique. The advantage of this approach is that it allows multiple options to be investigated. Planners may then allocate probabilities to the occurrence of each simulated option, in order to generate most probable/least probable scenarios. Benefits accrue simply from the process of simulated planning and when this is undertaken by teams, the process additionally encourages team building. The strength of the conclusions resulting from the simulation is dependent on the accuracy of the data on which the simulation is based, and on the algorithms used to resolve strategy and tactics decisions.

Synthesis reports

This approach has its origins in clippings libraries where all newspaper articles on a given topic, e.g. fast food or a particular company, would be filed into a selected, common 'clippings' folder.

This approach is now undertaken electronically and is available as a themed electronic 'clippings' service that several publishers currently provide free on a trial basis. Subscription services also provide summaries (i.e. abstracts) of specified topics for worldwide publications. This also includes abstracts, in English, from non-English-language publications. In addition to these services, marketers have access to a growing number of electronic synthesis tools. For example, 'intelligent agents' are software programmes which can 'learn' the type of material the user requires and may then search the World Wide Web automatically for similar material. This moves beyond the constraints of 'keyword' searches.

Case history

Forecasting and planning in practice

How Boeing forecasts aircraft demand

Boeing's planning horizons are long-term. The NPD process can take 20 years from idea generation to commercialization. Boeing must attempt to forecast the future demand for air travel to ensure they are manufacturing the right types of aircraft. There are a number of critical issues to consider when building long-range forecasts:

- o 'Inventory' issues, i.e. annual replacements of aircraft.
- o The markets which drive demand for aircraft. A long-range forecast is developed annually at Boeing to forecast demand for world air travel and cargo growth. This includes forecasts for each main size category of airplane.

It consists of the following:

- o Air travel market forecasts (by econometric model) based on

    1. changes in the cost of air travel
    2. changes in the income of the travelling population.

- o Airplane retirement assumptions
- o Forecasts for commercial jet planes:

    1. airplane deliveries in dollars
    2. airplane deliveries in units
    3. categorization by range and size.

These forecasts are then used within the Boeing business planning process to develop:

- o Financial and production plans
- o Competitor analyses
- o Workforce and inventory requirements
- o Resource allocations
- o New-product evaluations.

These forecasts, combined with forecasts involving risk and opportunities, drive internal planning. Boeing does not include any consideration of unpredictable and random events such as energy crises or wars in their forecasts. The forecast is then broken down into three sections:

1. The world market demand involving growth in air travel and cargo with assumptions about the replacement of retired airplanes
2. The airplane supply requirement
3. The manufacturer's position in the industry.

Source: Adapted from Cravens (2000)

Activity 5.3

Forecasting

Investigate the forecasting approaches employed in your organization. You should consider the:

    c.   part of the organization undertaking the forecast (e.g. department, business unit)
    d.   length of the forecast time horizon and the particular variables that are forecasted
    e.   the forecasting method(s) employed
    f.   data, general information and people involved in the forecast.

Market sensing

Market sensing focuses on the need for managers to understand the market in which they are operating. Piercy (2000) provides the following comments that help to explain the concept of market sensing:

- How those of us inside the company understand and react to the marketplace and the way it is changing (p. 388)
- Our focus is on market understanding and not on marketing research techniques and marketing information systems (p. 426)
- The real challenge is not making market research more sophisticated, it is trying to ensure that the things that managers 'know' and 'understand' are the right things (p. 396).

Information is a key requirement of the decision-making process. However, the type and amount of information available will vary considerably depending on the level at which it is being used in an organization. It is possible to produce copious amounts of market information but this is unlikely to be particularly helpful at a strategic level. Strategic decisions are concerned with the future and much market information is based on the past. It is dangerous to assume that what happened in the past will be of relevance to the future, particularly for firms operating in a dynamic environment. Figure 5.5 illustrates the relationship between the availability and predictability of information in relation to the level of decision-making. At anoperational level there is likely to be much available information that is largely predictable. This may take the form of market research, internal records and marketing intelligence. However, at a strategic level it is likely there will be a shortage of reliable information.

Figure 5.5 Decision-making pyramid
Adapted from Piercy, 2000

A key difference between marketing research and market sensing is that market sensing focuses on a manager's understanding of the marketplace. Marketing research frequently provides information on 'what is', i.e. the current attitudes of consumers, current product preferences and levels of demand. Market sensing is about interpreting these relationships to understand how they impact on the marketplace and consequently on marketing planning.

Question 5.2

Market sensing versus marketing research

Answer Question 5 from the December 1999 Planning and Control paper on market sensing. Go to www.cimeduhub.com to access specimen answers for this question.

Extended knowledge

For further information on techniques for developing a view of the future, refer to:

Drummond and Ensor (2001), Chapter 6.

Mercer (1998), Chapters 2 and 5–8.

For further reading on market information and market sensing, refer to:

Piercy (2000), Chapter 10.

Marketing information systems (MIS) and use of strategic intelligence

Marketing information is a key requirement for any successful marketing plan and therefore the development of effective management and marketing information systems is an important task for marketers. The Planning and Control syllabus does not explicitly include MkIS. However, it is expected that you will be familiar with this subject from studying at Certificate and Advanced Certificate levels, in particular within the Management Information for Marketing Decisions module. Therefore, this coursebook will highlight the areas that you should be familiar with and refer you to further reading, rather than covering the topic in detail.

Senior Marketing Managers should not become too heavily involved in the details of the MIS and marketing research but should be concentrating on how to utilize the information in helping to understand the market and develop successful marketing programmes.

Marketing information systems (MIS)

You should already be fully conversant with the concept of MIS from previous CIM modules. This section will provide a brief overview of the key issues and refer you to further reading. It is essential that organizations develop integrated systems for managing their, often huge, amounts of data. It is a waste of time collecting data if they are then inaccessible and unavailable to decision-makers at the right time and in the right format. Effective and flexible MIS can provide organizations with a competitive advantage if developed appropriately. Figure 5.6 illustrates a typical MIS.

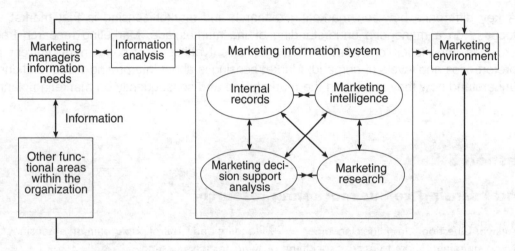

Figure 5.6 The marketing information system
Adapted from Piercy, 2000

It is clear that an MIS has four main components:

1. Internal records – there is a wealth of information available within the organization and it is essential that it is organized in such a way as to facilitate its usage. This may include sales data, customer orders, prices, stock levels, customer complaints, etc.
2. Marketing research – this is concerned with the systematic collection of information that is specific to a particular problem. For example, a piece of marketing research may be commissioned to investigate attitudes to a new advertising campaign.
3. Marketing intelligence – this may include any information that is collected on an *ad hoc* basis, such as competitor intelligence gleaned from the press, customer trends, registered patents, etc.
4. Marketing decision support systems – the processes that convert the data into usable information. For example, statistical tools or modelling techniques.

Extended knowledge

For further discussion of marketing information systems and marketing research, refer to:

Jobber (2001), Chapter 6.

Question 5.3

Market information

Answer Question 4 from the December 1998 Planning and Control paper on market information. Go to www.cimeduhub.com to access specimen answers for this question.

Summary

o The Planning and Control syllabus assumes an understanding of the profit and loss account and of the balance sheet. However, of greater interest in the Planning and Control module is the use of these accounts in the analysis of businesses. This tends to be undertaken using ratio analysis.

o There are five main types of ratios: profitability ratios, capital structure ratios, liquidity ratios, asset utilization ratios and investment performance ratios.

o Productivity analysis concerns the relationship between outputs and inputs. These are expressed as a ratio to measure the efficiency of the relationship, e.g. the increase in sales revenue over the increase in advertising expenditure.

o Segmental analysis forces the marketer to consider the market that is the focus of the analysis and how to segment the market. Consideration of how to segment the market will depend on market attributes, product attributes, company size and objectives.

o A variety of techniques are available to predict the future and to allow the organization to develop a future orientation. The event/situation (including issues concerning breadth and detail) which are to be forecast, and the forecast time horizon, influence the selection of forecasting technique.

o Market sensing is much more than marketing research and marketing research techniques. Its focus is on understanding the market and its future direction, rather than developing an ever-greater understanding of the market in the past. Past analysis has traditionally been the focus of attention, in an attempt to predict the future, based on a detailed understanding of the past. However, the future may be so different that the past may contribute little to future understanding; on the contrary it may hinder it.

o Senior marketing managers should be concerned with how to use the information generated from the MkIS rather than with the details of the system.

Further study and examination preparation

Extended knowledge

Bibliography and links

Cox D and Fardon M (1997). *Management of Finance: A Guide to Business Finance for the Non-Specialist*, Osborne Books.

Craven SD (2000). Current Market Outlook Boeing Commercial Airplane Group, February 1992, p. 11, cited in Craven SD, (1999). *Strategic Marketing* 6th Ed., McGraw-Hill.

Drummond G and Ensor J (2001). *Strategic Marketing Planning and Control*, 2nd Ed., Butterworth-Heinemann.

Financial Times Mastering Marketing Series (1998). Part 1, 21 September.

Jobber D (2001). *Principles and Practice of Marketing*, 3rd Ed., McGraw-Hill.

Mercer D (1998). *Marketing Strategy: The Challenge of the External Environment*, The Open University, Sage Publications.

Piercy N (2000). *Market-led Strategic Change*, 2nd Ed., Butterworth-Heinemann.

www.hps-inc.com.

www.marketing.wharton.upenn.edu/forecast

unit 6 strategic intent

Learning objectives

By the end of this unit you will:

o   Be able to define the terms 'strategic intent'/'vision' and 'mission statement'

o   Know the components of 'good' mission statements

o   Be able to identify the factors that influence the selection of vision and mission statements, and the setting of goals and objectives

o   Be able to discuss the development of appropriate objectives

o   Be able to describe and critically evaluate the balanced scorecard.

Key definitions

Strategic intent/vision – The desired future state or aspiration of the organization (Johnson and Scholes, 1999, p. 243).

Mission statement – A generalized statement of the overriding purpose of the organization (Johnson and Scholes, 1999, p. 241).

Goal – General statement of aim or purpose (Johnson and Scholes, 1999, p. 14).

Objective – Quantification (if possible) or more precise statement of the goal (Johnson and Scholes, 1999, p. 14).

Balanced scorecards – Combine both qualitative and quantitative measures, acknowledge the expectations of different stakeholders and relate an assessment of performance to choice of strategy (Johnson and Scholes, 1999, p. 468).

Stakeholders – Those individuals or groups who depend on the organization to fulfil their own goals and on whom, in turn, the organization depends (Johnson and Scholes, 1999, p. 213).

Study Guide

- This unit will take you about 3 hours to work through
- We suggest that you take a further 3 hours to do the various activities and questions in this unit.

Introduction

The next three units are all concerned with strategy formulation and selection. This unit will discuss the strategic intent of an organization and the factors that influence their overall strategic direction. Unit 7 – Creating strategic advantage – will then concentrate on how companies can develop a strategic advantage with reference to the generic models that companies can use. Unit 8 – Developing a specific competitive position – is concerned with how companies can translate this generic advantage into a specific competitive advantage with particular reference to the role of segmentation, targeting and positioning. Before an organization can make decisions about their strategy and how they are going to compete in terms of their competitive advantage, it is necessary to first establish the general areas in which they wish to operate. Organizations need to have a clear vision of where they want to go in the future in order to decide how they are going to get there.

Strategic intent/vision and mission

Strategic intent refers to the aspirations of an organization rather than just its current activity. Writers often use the terms 'strategic intent' and 'vision' interchangeably because they are essentially referring to the same concept. According to Aaker (1998, p. 158), strategic intent provides:

> *A long-term drive for advantage that can be essential to success. It provides a model that helps break the mould, moving a firm away from simply doing the same things a bit better and working a bit harder than the year before. It has the capability to elevate and extend an organization, helping it reach levels it would not otherwise attain.*

It is apparent that many organizations that have an appropriate and well-constructed vision are focused on the future and ways of continually attaining sustainable competitive advantages. A vision can help guide strategy, identify and maintain core competencies, and provide inspiration and motivation to its managers and its employees by providing them with a sense of purpose.

Hamel and Pralahad (1989) suggested that strategic intent combines:

- 'a dream that energizes the company' (i.e. acts as a motivator)
- implied 'stretch' (looks for new opportunities rather than relying on existing business)
- a sense of direction
- a sense of discovery
- coherence to plans.

 Definition

Strategic intent/vision – The desired future state or aspiration of the organization (Johnson and Scholes, 1999, p. 243).

Case history

Microsoft's vision

'Microsoft's vision is to empower people through great software – any time, any place and on any devices. As the worldwide leader in software for personal and business computing, Microsoft strives to produce innovative products and services that meet our customers' evolving needs. At the same time, we understand that long-term success is about more than just making good products.'

There are two key aspects to Microsoft's past and future success: its vision of technology and the values by which we live, every day, as a company. The values you see below are a set of principles which have evolved since our founding, and which capture the spirit, philosophy and day-to-day business practices of our company. They are not new values, but rather a reinforcement of long-held company principles that underscore our relationships with customers, partners and employees.

Customers: Helping customers achieve their goals is the key to Microsoft's long-term success. We must listen to what they tell us, respond rapidly by delivering new and constantly improving products, and build relationships based on trust, respect and mutual understanding. We will always back up our products with unparalleled service and support.

Innovation: In an industry that moves at lightning speed, innovation is critical to our competitiveness. Microsoft's long-term approach to research and development, combined with our constant efforts to anticipate customer needs, improve quality and reduce costs will enable us to deliver the best products and technologies.

Partners: Helping our partners succeed and grow their businesses with the best platforms, tools and support is central to our mission.

Integrity: Our managers and employees must always act with the utmost integrity, and be guided by what is ethical and right for our customers. We compete vigorously and fairly.

People: Our goal is for everyone at Microsoft to develop a challenging career with opportunities for growth, competitive rewards and a balance between work and home life. In a fast-paced, competitive environment, this is a shared responsibility between Microsoft and its employees.

Entrepreneurial culture: We want our employees to wake up every day with the passionate belief that their work is contributing to the evolution of technology, and making a real difference to the lives of millions of people. We will always preserve the lean, competitive and entrepreneurial culture that has enabled us to grow. We encourage our people to speak out, take risks and challenge conventional wisdom.

Diversity: We are committed to encouraging diversity in the workplace, not only at Microsoft but within our industry. We will practise equal opportunity in all hiring and promotions, and will help to expand access to technology and employment opportunities throughout our industry.

Community: Microsoft and its employees recognize that we have the responsibility, and opportunity, to contribute to the communities in which we live, in ways that make a meaningful difference to people's lives.

Source: Microsoft.com/mscorp

Mission statements

A mission statement (in contrast to a vision) is more concerned with providing daily guidance rather than a vision of the future. According to Piercy (2000, pp. 180–181), mission statements that are to contribute anything must:

- Reflect an organization's core competencies and how it intends to apply and sustain them
- Be closely tied to the critical success factors in the marketplace
- Tell employees, managers, suppliers and partners what contribution is required from them to deliver the promise of value to the customer.

Definition

Mission statement – A generalized statement of the overriding purpose of the organization (Johnson and Scholes, 1999, p. 241).

Case history

Mission statement

The following provides you with examples of mission statements.

Cranfield University

Cranfield's particular mission is to transform world-class science, technology and management expertise into viable, practical, environmentally desirable solutions that enhance economic development. Cranfield will transfer its solutions through its students, and its research, development and consultancy.

Source: www.cranfield.ac.uk

IBM

At IBM, we strive to lead in the creation, development and manufacture of the industry's most advanced information technologies, including computer systems, software, networking systems, storage devices and microelectronics. And our world network of IBM solutions and services professionals translates these advanced technologies into business value for our customers.

BP Group

The world's need for energy is growing steadily day-by-day. Energy and materials, used safely and efficiently, are essential to the prosperity and growth of every country and every region in the world. Sustaining and enhancing our quality of life depends on them. Our goal is to play a leading role in meeting these needs from oil, gas, solar power and petrochemicals without damaging the environment.

Ours is a positive and progressive involvement. Innovation will be the hallmark of the way we work with people, technology, assets and relationships. We will always be constructive, using our know-how to produce constructive and creative solutions to every challenge.

Our success depends on our making, and being seen to make, a distinctive contribution to every activity in which we are involved.

Source: www.bp.com

Greenpeace

Greenpeace is an independent non-profit global campaigning organization that uses non-violent, creative confrontation to expose global environmental problems and their causes. We research the solutions and alternatives to help provide a path for a green and peaceful future.

Greenpeace's goal is to ensure the ability of the earth to nurture life in all its diversity.

Source: www.greenpeace.org.uk

Mission statements are influenced by a number of factors, such as the history of the organization, resource availability, the external environment, the core competencies of the organization and the current preferences of the current chief executive and senior management. The extent to which the mission statement serves its purpose is influenced not only by the quality and relevance of the mission but also by how it is communicated to staff and other stakeholders. A successful mission statement is one that is wholly embraced and 'believed' by staff. Just having a mission statement is insufficient, the staff must also 'buy into' the idea. One organization that failed to understand this, did not involve staff in the process of developing the mission, and then out of the blue all employees were sent a letter and a laminated card informing staff of the organization's new vision and mission. How successful and motivating do you think this mission will be?

Drummond and Ensor (2001) suggest that successful mission statements should demonstrate the following characteristics:

- o Credibility – it must be realistic and believable
- o Uniqueness – not bland and generic
- o Specific capabilities – embrace core capabilities
- o Aspirational – needs to motivate individuals.

The relationship between the vision and mission within the strategic marketing planning framework is illustrated in Figure 6.1.

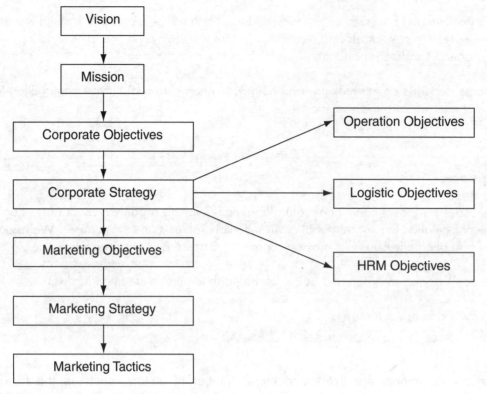

Figure 6.1 Corporate and marketing hierarchy

Activity 6.1

Evaluating mission statements

Piercy (2000), in his book *Market-led Strategic Change* (p. 193), proposes a method for testing mission statements. Refer to this list of criteria and then complete the following:

o Select two different organizations and seek out their mission statements (include your own organization if possible)
o 'Test' these two mission statements against the criteria suggested by Piercy to produce an overall score
o Make conclusions regarding the usefulness of these two mission statements.

Many mission statements were widely adopted by organizations in the 1980s and 1990s but were criticized for being bland and lacking uniqueness, and therefore for not fulfilling the role they were set out for. Many organizations have been accused of paying 'lip service' to mission statements, because they believe that it is necessary to have a 'mission', but do not invest time or energy in producing a relevant and motivating statement. However, advocates of mission statements believe that if written well they can have a powerful influence over strategy and act as a great motivator for staff. Some organizations combine their vision and mission statements whilst others recognize a difference between the two and therefore develop separate statements.

Extended knowledge

Vision and mission

For greater coverage of vision and mission, refer to the following sources:

Drummond and Ensor (2001), pp. 127–134.

Piercy N (2000), Chapter 5.

Johnson G and Scholes K (1999), pp. 13–16 and 241–244.

Influences on organizational strategic direction

The vision, mission and overall strategic direction of an organization will be influenced by a number of factors. Johnson and Scholes (1999) suggest that there are four major types of influence (illustrated in Figure 6.2):

- o   Corporate governance – to whom should the organization be accountable?
- o   Stakeholders – employees, customers, shareholders, suppliers, wider social community, etc.
- o   Business ethics – social responsibility
- o   Cultural context – at a broad national level and within organizational culture.

The strategic direction of an organization is subject to such influences and it can often be difficult to accommodate all these, often conflicting, influences. For example, shareholders may make demands on the organization to improve their return on the investment. However, this may be contrary to the organization's commitment to improve their social responsibility, e.g. by reducing the amount of pollution it creates.

Figure 6.2 Influences on an organization's mission and objectives
Adapted from Johnson and Scholes, 1999

Activity 6.2

Influences on strategic direction

Using Figure 6.2, identify the various influences on your organization's vision/mission. Which factors appear to be the most influential?

What conclusions can you make about your organization's priorities?

Case Study

Strategic direction – tobacco companies

Large cigarette companies have, in the past, been active in diversifying out of this single market. Legal action; with the potential for sizeable financial damages, has been a major driver in this strategy. In addition, consumer debate, in advanced industrial economies, continues on the ethics of producing and marketing this product. However, the resolution of major financial actions, principally in the USA, have encouraged some companies to refocus their strategy away from diversification (to reduce risk exposure) towards a single-minded focus on the cigarette market. BAT, Gallagher and Imperial Tobacco have all reinvested profits into takeovers of rivals in the global market. Imperial Tobacco, for example, has acquired seven tobacco-related businesses since becoming a public company in 1996, while mergers are also common in this global industry. For example, BAT and Rothmans merged in 1999, as have Japan tobacco and RJR International. Brands have been on the shopping list of these aspiring global leaders. Gallagher, for example, bought the rights to Benson and Hedges and Silk Cut brands throughout much of Europe. The Austrian Ducat brand cost the company £1.4 billion. This single-industry focus continues with much financial success, with shareholders very willing to fund requests for funds for expansion. Strategists have so far discounted the growing attention of legislators in developing economies such as India, where the right to smoke in public spaces is beginning to be restricted. They have longer time horizons than stock market investors who downgrade tobacco stock on news of any legal restriction.

Goals and objectives

The vision and mission provide guidance on the overall direction of an organization. Objectives, whether corporate or marketing, are the expected outcomes of the strategy. Goals are often regarded as less specific than objectives and more difficult to measure. However, it is normally accepted that objectives should be SMART:

- Specific
- Measurable – expressed in quantifiable terms
- Acceptable – to stakeholders
- Realistic – attainable
- Time bound – achievable within a certain time frame.

Some writers argue that it is not possible to quantify all types of objectives. For example, it can be difficult to quantify objectives such as innovation leadership.

Case history

BP believe that to be effective, their targets, and objectives should be:

- challenging but achievable
- enduring but responsive to change
- clear and unambiguous to all, both within and outside the company
- agreed and accepted by all whose performance is measured against them
- capable of measurement, yet encompassing aspects which may not have a clear financial or operational benefit and
- capable of delivering the company's long-term strategic and performance goals.

Source: www.bp.com

Definition

Goals and objectives – Goal – general statement of aim or purpose.
Objective – Quantification (if possible) or more precise statement of the goal (Johnson and Scholes, 1999, p. 14).

There are many different types of objectives with which an organization should be concerned. Drucker (1954) identified the following:

1. Market standing – e.g. market share objectives
2. Innovation – e.g. number of new products launched
3. Productivity – e.g. inputs compared with outputs such as increase sales whilst maintaining the same number of sales staff
4. Physical and financial resources – relating to the use of resources
5. Profitability – e.g. return on investment
6. Manager performance and development – performance criteria
7. Employee performance and attitude – loyalty
8. Public responsibility – e.g. reduce dependency on fossil fuels.

It is likely that many organizations will place greater weighting on some areas than others. For example, the Co-operative bank places great emphasis on their responsibility to the public in the form of their ethical banking policy. There may be the danger that some organizations are preoccupied with productivity objectives and trying to improve efficiency of existing activities without actually questioning whether they are doing the right things.

Levels of objectives

Objectives exist at a number of levels within an organization (such as corporate and marketing levels). At whatever level, their purpose is the same: to set out what is to be achieved. There is often confusion as to what constitutes a corporate objective and how this differs from a marketing objective. Corporate objectives are influenced by the vision and mission, relate to the companies' overall direction and are often expressed in financial terms such as return on investment and profitability. From this the corporate strategy will be developed that will hope to meet these objectives. These objectives then need to be translated into functional objectives such as marketing, human resources and operations. For example, marketing objectives will be concerned with markets, products and customers. Appropriate marketing objectives may include market share or sales volume. These objectives will then be cascaded down and be translated into operational plans. In the case of marketing these will relate to the elements of the marketing mix, e.g. promotional, distribution and pricing objectives. This can be further broken down, e.g. promotional objectives could be separated into advertising, public relations and sales promotion objectives. The relationship between these various levels of objectives is illustrated in Figure 6.3.

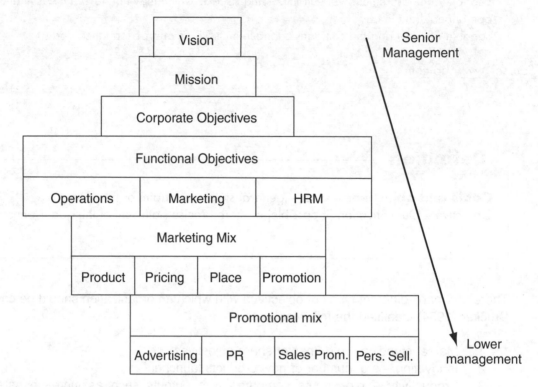

Figure 6.3 Levels of objectives

Activity 6.3

Writing objectives

Drummond and Ensor (2001, p. 138) provide a good example of different types of objectives that may exist in a hotel. Refer to Figure 6.3 in their text and produce a similar table for either your own organization or an organization of your choice.

Strategic direction – trade-offs

It is inevitable that organizations will have to make trade-offs between different types of objectives when developing their strategic direction. For example, they may wish to pursue environmental objectives but this could be at the expense of profitability. Weinberg (1969) suggests that the following trade-offs may have to be made:

- ○ Short-term versus long-term
- ○ Profit margin versus competitive position
- ○ Marketing penetration versus market development
- ○ Related versus non-related growth
- ○ Profit versus non-profit objectives (social, ethical, environmental, etc.)
- ○ Growth versus stability
- ○ Risk avoidance versus risk taking.

Many organizations struggle to achieve a balance between these trade-offs. The balanced scorecard framework can be used to help organizations take a balanced approach to their objectives.

Question 6.1

Strategic objectives and trade-offs

Answer Question 2 from the December 2002 Planning and Control paper. Go to www.cimedu-hub.com to access specimen answers for this question. Question 5 June 2001 and Question 4 December 1999 were both questions on strategic direction.

Balanced scorecard

Objectives cannot be set in isolation from the various organizational stakeholders (see below for a discussion of stakeholders). The balanced scorecard approach was developed by Kaplan and Norton (1992) as a means of acknowledging the various perspectives of different stakeholder groups, whilst at the same time linking objectives with performance measures. In the planning and control cycle, a key part of the process is monitoring and control. Kaplan and Norton suggest that a set of consistent objectives must be established, but that at the same time these should be linked to performance measures. The balanced scorecard approach, illustrated in Figure 6.4, suggests that an organization should view itself from four different perspectives:

- ○ **Customer perspective** – how customers view a company is of obvious importance. They will be concerned with issues such as quality and customer service.
- ○ **Financial perspective** – this is often the area with which many organizations become preoccupied. This represents the view of the shareholders and relates to the financial performance of the company.
- ○ **Internal perspective** – this identifies the internal processes that lead to external customer satisfaction. For example, employees' attitudes and performance.
- ○ **Innovation and learning** – relates to an organization's ability to continually innovate and learn.

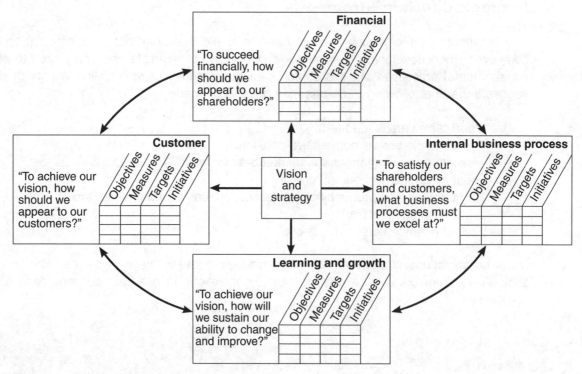

Figure 6.4 The balanced scorecard framework
Kaplan and Norton, 1996

Definition

Balanced scorecard – Combine both qualitative and quantitative measures, acknowledge the expectations of different stakeholders and relate an assessment of performance to choice of strategy (Johnson and Scholes, 1999, p. 468).

This model helps organizations to develop a balanced range of objectives and also relate them to relevant performance measures. Examples of these are illustrated in Figure 6.5.

	Strategic objectives	Strategic measures
Financial	F.1 Return on capital F.2 Cash flow F.3 Profitability F.4 Profitability growth F.5 Reliability of performance	⇨ ROCE ⇨ Cash flow ⇨ Net margin ⇨ Volume growth rate vs. industry ⇨ Profit forecast reliability ⇨ Sales backlog
Customer	C.1 Value for money C.2 Competitive price C.3 Customer satisfaction	⇨ Customer ranking survey ⇨ Pricing index ⇨ Customer satisfaction index ⇨ Mystery shopping index
Internal	I.1 Marketing ■ Product and service development ■ Shape customer requirement I.2 Manufacturing ■ Lower manufacturing cost ■ Improve project management I.3 Logistics ■ Reduce delivery costs ■ Inventory management I.4 Quality	⇨ Pioneer percentage of product portfolio ⇨ Hours with customer on new work ⇨ Total expenses per unit vs. competition ⇨ Safety incident index ⇨ Delivered cost per unit ⇨ Inventory level compared to plan and output rate ⇨ Rework
Innovation and learning	I.L.1 Innovate products and services I.L.2 Time to market I.L.3 Empowered workforce I.L.4 Access to strategic information I.L.5 Continuous improvement	⇨ Percentage revenue from pioneer products ⇨ Cycle time vs. industry norm ⇨ Staff attitude survey ⇨ Strategic information availability ⇨ Number of employee suggestions

Figure 6.5 The balanced scorecard
Kaplan and Norton, 1992, 1993

As illustrated in Figure 6.6, there are causal relationships between the four different perspectives. The knowledge, skills and systems that employees need and the culture that is engendered (innovation and learning) go towards building the right strategic capabilities such as marketing and logistics (internal processes) and in turn this delivers value to the market (customer), which will eventually lead to greater shareholder value (financial).

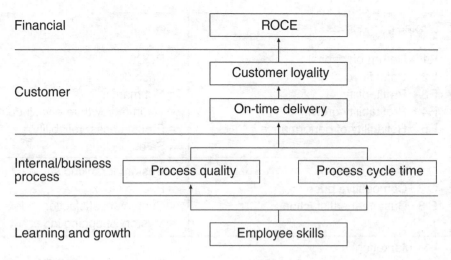

Figure 6.6 Causal relationships within the balanced scorecard
Kaplan and Norton, 1992, 1993

Following Kaplan and Norton's extensive research they suggest the main uses of the balanced scorecard are:

- ○ Clarifying and updating strategy
- ○ Communicating strategy throughout the company
- ○ Aligning unit and individual goals with the strategy
- ○ Linking strategic objectives to long-term targets and annual budgets
- ○ Identifying and aligning strategic initiatives
- ○ Conducting periodic performance reviews to learn about and improve strategy, (Kaplan and Norton, 1992, 1996).

Kaplan and Norton (2000) have developed the balanced scorecard further by suggesting that the framework can be used to help map out organizations' strategies using the cause and effect chain that connects desired outcomes with the drivers of those results.

Extended knowledge

Visit Kaplan and Norton's Web site for further information on the balanced scorecard and examples of companies that have utilized the model. www.bscol.com

Case history

Philips Electronics

Philips Electronics is an example of a company that has adopted the balanced scorecard (BSC) to enable them to 'align company vision, communicate the business strategy (quantitatively), focus employees on how they fit into the big picture and educate them on what drives the business'. The BSC is a key tool in promoting organizational learning and continuous improvement among its 250,000 employees in 150 countries.

The impetus to introduce the BSC came from the top-down as a means of streamlining the complex process of running an international company with diverse product lines and divisions. The BSC has enabled Philips to focus on the factors critical for success and align hundreds of performance indicators that measure their market, operations and laboratories. The critical success factors (CSF) on the Philips Electronics BSC were identified as:

- Competence (knowledge, technology, leadership and teamwork)
- Processes (drivers for performance)
- Customers (value proposition)
- Financial (value, growth and productivity).

The BSC is cascaded down through the organization in order to focus employees on the key business goals. It has three levels: the highest is the strategy review card, next is the operations review card and the third is the business unit card. There is a plan to introduce a fourth level – the individual employee card. This cascading ensures that strategic objectives are translated into everyday tasks and that employees can see how their everyday activities contribute towards the company's long-term goals.

At the business unit level, CSFs were developed for each perspective of the BSC (along with examples):

- Financial – profit, income from operations, working capital
- Customers – rank in customer surveys, market share, repeat order rates, complaints, brand index
- Processes – percentage reduction in process cycle time, order response time, capacity utilization
- Competence – leadership competence, training days per employee, percentage of patent-protected turnover.

As a result of cascading the BSC down from the organizational level to the business unit level, six key indicators were identified:

- Profitable revenue growth (drives the financial perspective)
- Customer delight (drives the customer perspective)
- Employee satisfaction (drives the customer perspective)
- Drive to operational excellence (drives the process perspective)
- Organizational development (drives the competence perspective)
- IT support (drives the competence perspective).

These BSC metrics are used each quarter to review the performance of each business unit. In order to share the results, Philips Electronics employs a traffic-light reporting system to indicate how actual performance compares with targets (green – meeting target, yellow – in line performance, red – below target). This highly visible system is easily interpreted by staff.

The implementation of the BSC has enabled Philips Electronics to identify their CSF and translate these into operational plans, where employees can see how their everyday activities contribute towards company goals.

Source: Adapted from Gumbus, 2002

Extended knowledge

For a more detailed discussion on the balanced scorecard, refer to Drummond and Ensor (2001), pp. 139–141.

The balanced scorecard was introduced in the Marketing Customer Interface module at Advanced Certificate.

If you would like more information on Kaplan and Norton's approach to mapping out strategy then read:

Kaplan and Norton (2000), pp. 167–176.

Activity 6.4

Balanced scorecard

Using the balanced scorecard framework classify your own organization's objectives into the four perspectives as illustrated in Figure 6.5.

Does your organization have a balanced range of objectives? If not what conclusions can you draw about your organization's priorities?

To download a demonstration version of balanced scorecard software visit www.dialog-software.com.

Question 6.2

Balanced scorecard

Answer Question 6 from the June 2002 Planning and Control paper on the balanced scorecard. Go to www.cimeduhub.com to access specimen answers for this question. Question 4 on the June 2000 paper was also on the balanced scorecard.

Stakeholders

A key consideration when developing strategic direction relates to an organization's various stakeholder groups. Stakeholders refer to all the different groups of individuals that are influenced by the activities of an organization. Stakeholders have different expectations and can exert varying levels of influence over the organization. It is important that organizations have a good understanding of the varying needs of their various stakeholder groups. There are three main groups of stakeholders:

- ○ Internal stakeholders (employees, management)
- ○ Connected stakeholders (suppliers, distributors, shareholders, customers)
- ○ External stakeholders (community, government, pressure groups).

Definition

Stakeholders – Those individuals or groups who depend on the organization to fulfil their own goals and on whom, in turn, the organization depends (Johnson and Scholes, 1999, p. 213).

Figure 6.7 illustrates an outline stakeholder map.

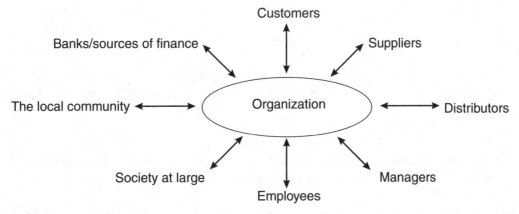

Figure 6.7 A stakeholder map
Kaplan and Norton, 1992, 1993

Activity 6.5

Stakeholder map

Draw a stakeholder map for your own organization and consider the varying needs of each group and the implications on an organization's strategic direction. How does your organization manage the differing expectations of each group?

Question 6.3

Issues to be considered when developing mission, goals and objectives – strategic intent

Refer to December 2000 Planning and Control mini-case study – Freeplay Energy located at www.cimeduhub.com. Answer question 1a only and then compare your answer with the CIM specimen answer and Senior Examiner's reports also located at www.cimeduhub.com and www.marketingonline.com.

Summary

o Strategic intent relates to the aspirations of an organization and is sometimes referred to as the organization's vision. An appropriate and well-constructed vision can help guide strategy, identify and maintain core competencies and can act as a motivator for staff by providing them with a sense of purpose.

o Mission statements are more concerned with providing daily guidance rather than a vision of the future. They should reflect an organization's core competencies, relate to the critical success factors in the market and also inform employees and other stakeholders what contribution is required from them to deliver value to the customer.

o There are a number of influences on strategic direction – corporate governance, stakeholders, business ethics and cultural context. It can be difficult to accommodate these, often conflicting, influences.

o Objectives are a statement of what an organization wants to achieve and, wherever possible, they should be SMART. Objectives exist at a number of levels within an organization. Whatever the level of the objective the purpose is the same, to set out what is to be achieved.

o Organizations will have to make trade-offs between different types of objectives when developing their strategic direction, e.g. short-term versus long-term, profit versus non-profit goals, growth versus stability.

o The balanced scorecard, developed by Kaplan and Norton, is a framework that acknowledges the various perspectives of the various stakeholder groups, whilst at the same time linking objective setting with performance measures. The four different perspectives are the customer perspective, the financial perspective, the internal perspective, and innovation and learning.

o Stakeholders are a key consideration when developing strategic direction. Stakeholders consist of all those individuals that are influenced by the activities of an organization and include internal stakeholders (employees and management), connected stakeholders (suppliers, distributors, shareholders and customers) and external stakeholders (community, government and pressure groups).

Further study and examination preparation

Extended knowledge

Bibliography

Aaker D (1998). *Strategic Market Management*, 5th Ed., John Wiley & Sons.

Drucker P (1954). *The Practice of Management*, Harper & Row, pp. 65–83.

Drummond G and Ensor J (2000). *Strategic Marketing Planning and Control*, 2nd Ed., Butterworth-Heinemann, Chapter 7.

Gumbus A and Lyons B (2002). The balanced scorecard at Philips Electronic, *Strategic Finance*, 84 (5), 45–49.

Hamel G and Pralahad CK (1989). *Harvard Business Review*, 67(3), 63–76.

Johnson G and Scholes K (1999). *Exploring Corporate Strategy*, 5th Ed., Prentice-Hall, pp. 13–16 and 241–244.

Kaplan RS and Norton DP (1992). The balanced scorecard: measures that drive performance, *Harvard Business Review*, 70(1), 71–79.

Kaplan RS and Norton DP (1993). Putting the balanced scorecard to work, *Harvard Business Review*, 71 (5), 134–147.

Kaplan RS and Norton DP (2000). Having trouble with your strategy? Then map it, *Harvard Business Review*, Sept-Oct, pp. 167–176.

Piercy N (2000). *Market-led Strategic Change*, 2nd Ed., Butterworth-Heinemann.

Weinberg R (1969). Developing Marketing Strategies for Short-term Profits and Long-term Growth, Paper Presented at Advanced Management Research, Inc. Seminar, New York.

www.cranfield.ac.uk

www.greenpeace.org.uk

www.microsoft.com/mscorp/articles/mission_values.asp

unit 7
creating strategic advantage

Learning objectives

By the end of this unit you will:

o   Understand the term 'strategic advantage'

o   Be able to describe, discuss and apply the following approaches to develop strategic advantage:

1.   Porter's generic strategies

2.   Sustainable advantage (Davidson's approach)

3.   Competitive positions and strategy

4.   Ansoff's matrix.

o   Be able to discuss and apply offensive and defensive strategies

o   Understand the various types of alliances and networks, be able to discuss the motivations for, and the factors that should be considered when, establishing such relationships

o   Be able to discuss the alternative strategies for declining and hostile markets

o   Understand the concept of and the reasons for, strategic wear-out.

Key definitions

Competitive advantage – The process of identifying a unique and enduring basis from which to compete (sometimes referred to as strategic advantage).

Strategic alliance – business associations in which knowledge and resources are shared to the benefit of the partners.

Strategic wear-out – Occurs when an organization no longer meets customer needs and the pursued strategy is surpassed by competitors (Drummond and Ensor, 2001).

Study Guide

- ○ This unit will take you about 4 hours to work through
- ○ We suggest that you take a further 4 hours to do the various activities and questions in this unit.

Introduction

Once an organization has undertaken its business analysis as outlined in Units 2 and 3 and developed a view of the future (see Unit 5 – Financial analysis and techniques for developing a view of the future) they need to translate their findings into a winning strategy. The previous unit discussed strategic intent and how this influences the overall strategic direction of an organization. This unit is concerned with analysing the various ways in which organizations can create strategic advantage in an attempt to develop a winning strategy. A number of approaches will be outlined that organizations can use to help them develop strategic advantage. Alliances and partnerships are increasingly being seen as a means of gaining strategic advantage. The growth in, and issues relating to, these relationships will be explored. Successful strategies will not endure indefinitely and this unit will conclude with a discussion of the dangers of, and reasons for, 'strategic wear-out'.

Strategic advantage

One of the greatest challenges for any organization is developing a coherent and appropriate strategy that builds on their internal resources and capabilities, capitalizes on external opportunities and will provide a distinct competitive advantage. Competitive advantage is the process of identifying a unique and enduring basis from which to compete, some authors refer to it as strategic advantage. Aaker (1998) provides a useful framework for considering sustainable competitive advantage (SCA) (see Figure 7.1). According to Aaker there are numerous ways in which organizations can compete – through their distribution strategies, their pricing strategies, global strategies and their positioning strategies. However, Aaker believes that how you compete is only part of the equation. The basis of competition, the markets in which you compete and to whom you compete against are all key elements of SCA.

Basis of competition

Aaker (1998) suggests that organizations must also consider the basis of competition (i.e. in terms of available assets and competencies). Without the support of assets and competencies it will be unlikely that the SCA can be sustained. Aaker gives the example that anyone can distribute cereal or detergent through supermarkets but few actually have the assets and competencies needed to do it effectively.

Where you compete

This relates to the market in which you decide to compete. An organization may have an excellent distribution strategy and the assets and competencies to deliver this strategy but may fail because the market does not value them. Aaker provides the example of Pringles crisps, which had great assets – long shelf life and a crushproof container. However, it failed in the market because customers did not value these characteristics, being primarily concerned with taste, which this product failed to deliver. It was not until the taste was improved that the product succeeded.

Whom you compete against

For an asset or competency to lead to an SCA it may need the right set of competitors. For example, many financial services were traditionally regarded as poor at customer service. Companies such as Virgin saw this as an opportunity to enter this market due to their ability to deliver high levels of customer service.

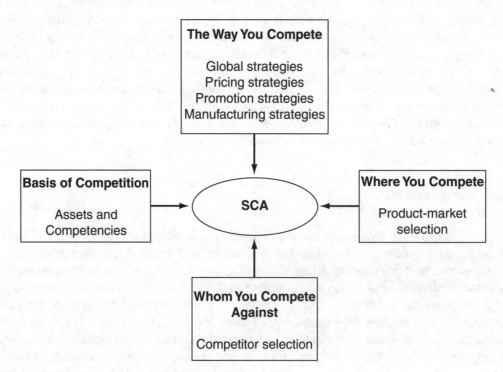

Figure 7.1 The sustainable competitive advantage
Adapted from Aaker, 1998, p. 142

Extended knowledge

SCA

For a more detailed discussion of SCA, refer to Aaker (1998), Chapter 8, pp. 141–144.

Approaches to developing strategic advantage

The next section will outline a number of approaches to develop strategic advantage. They are not mutually exclusive and many organizations use a combination of approaches to develop their own distinctive competitive advantage.

Porter's generic strategies

Porter (1980), a major contributor to the discussion of competitive strategy, suggests that there are three generic types of strategy that can provide organizations with a competitive advantage:

- o Cost leadership
- o Differentiation
- o Focus.

Figure 7.2 illustrates the alternative sources of competitive advantage and highlights the options open to companies in terms of defining their source of advantage and their competitive scope (i.e. targeting a broad or narrow range of customers).

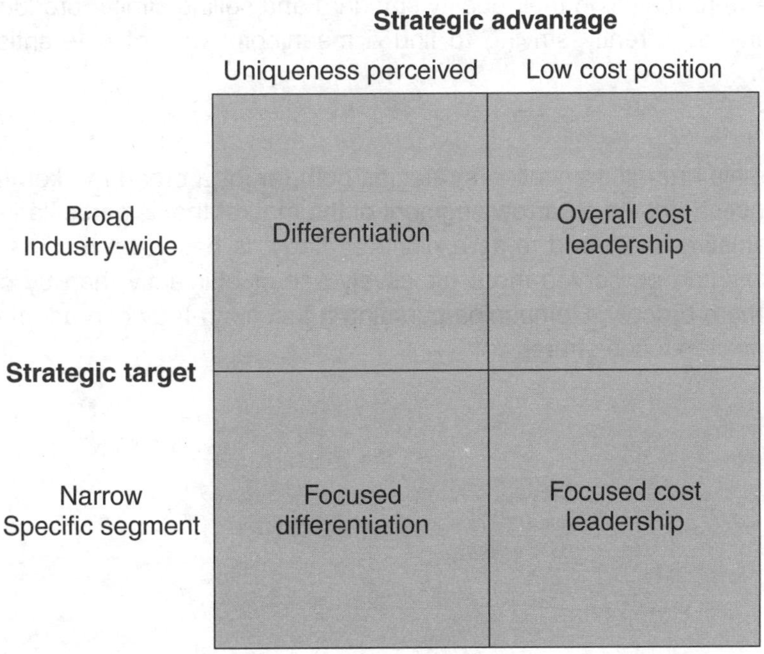

Strategic advantage

	Uniqueness perceived	Low cost position
Broad Industry-wide	Differentiation	Overall cost leadership
Narrow Specific segment	Focused differentiation	Focused cost leadership

Strategic target

Figure 7.2 Competitive advantage
Adapted from Porter, 1980

159

Cost leadership

One possible source of competitive advantage lies in the ability of a firm to be the lowest cost producer in the industry. Firms pursuing a cost leadership strategy would typically concentrate on continually striving to reduce their cost base and improving efficiencies. This could be achieved through activities such as achieving economies of scale, cutting costs, global sourcing and using technology to develop more efficient means of production. Low-cost producers do not necessarily need to offer the lowest price. Instead, they could use the additional revenue to invest back into research and development so that new ways can be identified to reduce costs. Cost leadership relies on large-scale production and the presence of the experience curve. Retailers specializing in a narrow product range that seek out-of-town locations (such as PC World) are able to achieve economies of scale and therefore pursue a cost leader strategy.

Cost leadership can be a difficult strategy to sustain in the long-term due to the threat of competitors that may have even lower cost structures. For example, the UK-based discount retailer Kwik Save was threatened by the entry of German-based Netto and Aldi into the low-cost retail market.

Differentiation

Companies pursuing a differentiation strategy strive to offer products or services that are regarded as superior to those offered by competitors. The uniqueness of the product enables companies to charge a premium price. For this strategy to be successful customers must perceive that the higher price is justified in terms of the additional features and benefits they accrue. For example, Gap sell children's clothing at a significantly higher price than other high-street retailers. Many parents are prepared to pay this price premium because of the imagery and brand values associated with Gap clothing. A differentiation strategy is sustainable as long as customers perceive a firm's offering to be of greater value than those of its competitors. For example, Marks & Spencer's differentiation strategy based on quality failed because the competitors were matching their quality standard and selling similar products at a lower price. The company is currently striving to find a meaningful way of differentiating itself from its competition.

Focus

Cost leadership and differentiation strategies both target a broad market. In contrast, a focus strategy concentrates on a narrow segment of the market that is particularly attractive. A focus strategy, sometimes referred to as a niche strategy, is based on the assumption that these niche markets can be served more effectively and/or efficiently than by companies that are competing more broadly. Companies pursuing a focus strategy can adopt either a cost focus or a differentiation focus strategy.

Cost focus

Companies pursuing a cost focus strategy are concentrating on a niche market but are also concentrating on reducing costs. It can be argued that easyJet has adopted a cost focus strategy. It has concentrated on a narrow segment of the population and has driven costs down by direct bookings and removing all the peripheral services associated with air travel, such as on-board meals. It could be argued that easyJet is now moving from a narrow focus to more broad market appeal.

Differentiation focus

This is concerned with producing superior products for narrow market segments, such as Rolex watches and Ferrari.

Case history

Small is beautiful – Palmair

Palmair Express, based at Bournemouth airport, has just one aircraft and its 73-year-old Chairman waves off every flight. The airline was founded in 1957 by Peter Bath, the current Chairman, employs 22 cabin crew and operates 14 flights a week, mainly to European destinations. The Chairman is keen that the airline should maintain the personal service for which it has become famous, and to help ensure the personal touch, he greets every passenger on their departure. In March 2001, Palmair was voted third best airline in the world in a survey of 31,000 passengers conducted by *Holiday Which?* Although narrowly beaten by Air New Zealand and Singapore Airlines, Palmair left other British carriers, including Virgin and British Airways, on the runway. Palmair goes to show that you do not have to be big to be successful.

Source: De Bruxelles (2001), www.Lexis-Nexis.com

Question 7.1

Focus strategy

Read the mini-case study 'MG Rover and China Brilliance Holdings (CBH)' in the December 2002 exam paper and answer question 1a only. Go to www.cimeduhub.com to access specimen answers. Question 5 from the December 2000 paper was also on focus strategy.

Give yourself 10 minutes to read the mini-case study and no more than 20 minutes to write your answer. Compare your answer with the CIM specimen answer and Senior Examiner's report.

Figure 7.3 compares the benefits and possible limitations of each of Porter's three generic strategies.

Type of strategy	Ways to achieve the strategy	Benefits	Possible problems
Cost leadership	• Size and economies of scale • Globalization of operations • Relocating to low cost parts of the world • Modification/simplification of designs • Greater labour effectiveness • Greater operating effectiveness • Strategic alliances • New sources of supply	The ability to: • Out-perform rivals • Erect barriers to entry • Resist the five forces	• Vulnerability to even lower cost operators • Possible price wars • The difficulty of sustaining it in the long term
Focus	• Concentration upon one or a small number of segments • The creation of a strong specialist reputation	• A more detailed understanding of particular segments • The creation of barriers to entry • A reputation for specialization • The ability to concentrate efforts	• Limited opportunities for sector growth • The possibility of out-growing the market • The decline of the sector • A reputation for specialization which ultimately inhibits growth and development into other sectors
Differentiation	• The creation of strong brand identities • The consistent pursuit of those factors which customers perceive to be important • High performance in one or more of a spectrum of activities	• A distancing from others in the market • The creation of a major competitive advantage • Flexibility	• The difficulties of sustaining the bases for differentiation • Possibly higher costs • The difficulty of achieving true and meaningful differentiation

Figure 7.3 Porter's three generic strategies

Inconsistent strategy

Porter (1980) argues that if companies fail to consistently pursue one of these generic strategies they will become 'stuck in the middle' with no discernible competitive advantage, as illustrated in Figure 7.4.

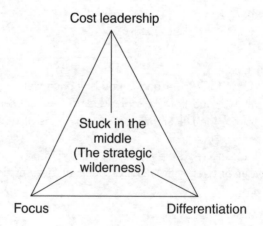

Figure 7.4 Stuck in the middle

Extended knowledge

This coursebook has provided you with a brief overview of Porter's generic strategies. For a more detailed discussion, refer to Drummond and Ensor (2001), Chapter 8, pp. 144–150.

Activity 7.1

Porter's generic strategies

Select an industry of your choice and identify an example of a company that pursues each of the generic strategies. In your opinion is there a company that is 'stuck in the middle'? To what extent does this model help companies to identify their competitive advantage?

Question 7.2

Competitive advantage

Read the mini-case study 'Howden Joinery' in the June 2002 exam paper and answer question 1a only. Go to www.cimeduhub.com to access specimen answers.

Give yourself 10 minutes to read the mini-case study and no more than 20 minutes to write your answer. Compare your answer with the CIM specimen answer and Senior Examiner's report.

The June 2001 case Marks & Spencer examined strategic position and evaluation of alternative strategies.

Sustainable advantage – Davidson's approach

Davidson (1997) has identified 10 ways of attaining a sustainable competitive advantage. Each of these is outlined below.

Superior product or service
This strategy is based on having a product or service that is in reality better than competitors, e.g. Mercedes-Benz cars.

Perceived advantage
Rather than the product *actually* being superior to competing products it is *perceived* as different. For example, when George Michael paid £1.45 million for John Lennon's Imagine Piano, he was not just buying a piano, he was buying a piece of history. The competitive advantage lies in the branding and perceived benefits the product delivers.

Global skills
This competitive advantage lies in the ability of companies to operate on a global basis. Coca-Cola and McDonald's have both achieved competitive advantage through their global strategies.

Low-cost producer
This equates to Porter's cost leadership strategy.

Superior competencies

Competencies, as discussed in Unit 2 – External analysis – often take a long time to develop and can therefore be a very important source of competitive advantage. For example, Sony has superior competencies in the area of product development and innovation.

Superior assets

Assets may take the form of cash, brands or property. For example, it is now being acknowledged that brands can make a great contribution to the value of a company.

Scale advantages

In Unit 4 – Auditing tools – you were introduced to the PIMS research, which indicated that market share was a key determinant of profitability. Therefore achieving economies of scale can be a source of competitive advantage.

Attitude advantages

The attitudes of managers and staff can be a source of competitive advantage if, for example, they have vision and commitment.

Legal advantages

A competitive advantage can be gained if a company can protect its position, e.g. through patents. James Dyson created a competitive advantage when he patented the cyclone technology in his bagless vacuum cleaner.

Superior relationships

Superior relationships may exist between suppliers, distributors, partners, customers, government and other opinion leaders. For example, Disney and McDonald's have a long-term promotional agreement. Boots the Chemist is developing a strategic partnership with Granada Media to launch a combined TV, Internet and broad-based health and beauty company.

Davidson suggests that some of the following sources of competitive advantage are going to increase in importance:

- Low-cost operations
- Superior competencies
- Superior relationships.

Davidson also suggests that competitive advantage based on actual product superiority and legal advantages will decline in importance.

Extended knowledge

For a more detailed discussion of Davidson's approach to developing competitive advantage, see Davidson H (1997), pp. 261–269.

Activity 7.2

Davidson's approach

Give an example for each of Davidson's 10 types of competitive advantage.

Competitive positions and strategy

The position that a firm holds in the marketplace is going to influence the basis of their competitive advantage. Kotler and Singh (1981) developed a framework that classified companies according to their position in the industry and identifies four distinct categories: market leaders, market challengers, market followers and market nichers. This framework can be compared with military strategies where competitors are regarded as the enemy, and where the fighting takes place in the marketplace rather than on the battlefield.

Market leaders

Market leaders are usually dominant in terms of market share. They are often the target of aggressive competitors that strive to take market share away from them. There are a number of options available to market leaders:

- **Expand the total market** – by identifying new uses or users for the product or by increasing usage. This will expand the total market and as a result the leader will have a share of a larger market
- **Expand current market share** – through offensive strategies they attempt to take share away from competitors. This may include developing new products, expanding distribution channels, mergers, acquisitions or strategic alliances and expanding into new geographical markets
- **Defend market share** – through strong market positioning, development and refinement of an effective competitive advantage, a proactive approach, continuous innovation, strong distribution channels, good customer relationships and substantial advertising. There are a number of defence strategies a company can adopt:

  - position defence
  - flank defence
  - pre-emptive defence
  - counter-defence
  - mobile defence
  - contraction defence.

These defensive strategies are illustrated in Figure 7.5.

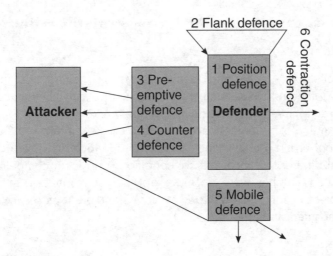

Figure 7.5 Defensive strategies
Kotler et al., 1999

Position defence

Position defence is concerned with blocking out competition and trying to improve current position. Market leaders have to continually look at ways to improve their business in an attempt to fend off the threat of challengers. For instance, to maintain their market leadership Microsoft is continually investing in their business to stay ahead of competition.

Flank defence

This strategy involves defending the business's non-core activities. For example, Abbey National recognized their weakness in remote access banking when they launched Cahoot.

Pre-emptive defence

This involves attacking competitors before they attack you. This strategy may employ any of the attacking strategies detailed below. For example, electricity-generating companies entered the gas market as a pre-emptive strike following de-regulation.

Counter-defence

These are largely reactive strategies where a market leader responds to an attack by a competitor. WH Smith launched an on-line bookshop in response to the threat of Internet sales operators such as Amazon.com.

Mobile defence

This is concerned with continually looking for new opportunities and moving into new areas of business in order to remain flexible. For example, easyJet has moved into car rental, financial services and Internet cafes in an attempt to stay ahead of the competition.

Contraction defence

Market leaders may find they are spreading themselves too thinly across many sectors and markets and may decide to concentrate on their core business and withdraw from other markets. Marks & Spencer is currently adopting this strategy by concentrating on UK business and withdrawing from Europe and the USA.

Case Study

Boots the Chemist contraction defence – strategic withdrawal from Asia

Boots the Chemist attempted to expand their business by moving into international markets. However, like many other retailers, such as Marks & Spencer, they encountered unforeseen difficulties when operating in markets outside their home markets. In order to succeed they need to have a deep understanding of customer needs in various markets. There is a danger that companies try to develop a 'global brand' but in doing so present 'one face to the world' without taking into consideration cultural differences, local market conditions and local competition. In the spring of 2001, Boots announced that they were closing 19 of their stores in Asia in an attempt to reduce their losses of the previous year. Boots decided to close stand-alone stores in Taiwan and Thailand as part of their retrenchment strategy.

Source: Mazur (2002)

Market challengers

The characteristic of market challengers is that they are number 2 in the market and often aggressively attack market leaders in an attempt to take market share from them. Market leadership is seen as an attractive position due to the assumed associated benefits of economies of scale, power and status. There are number of attacking/offensive strategies open to market challengers. These are illustrated in Figure 7.6:

- ○ Frontal (head-on) attack
- ○ Flank attack
- ○ Encirclement attack
- ○ Bypass attack
- ○ Guerrilla attack.

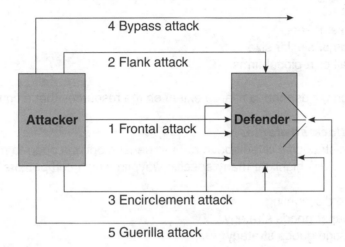

Figure 7.6 Attacking strategies
Kotler et al., 1999

For successful frontal attacks three key conditions should be present:

- ○ The market challenger must have a sustainable competitive advantage
- ○ The challenger has to be able to negate the leader's advantage, generally by being able to deliver the leader's key attributes at almost the same level
- ○ There has to be an obstacle hindering the leader from retaliation.

Frontal attack

Competitors are attacked head on. For market challengers to be able to sustain this type of attack, which can be very costly, they must have sufficient resources to sustain any short-term damage they may incur. For example, Virgin has taken on BA head to head in Business Class on transatlantic flights.

Flank attack

This strategy relies on the identification of a competitor's weak spots and attacking them. Ford acquired Land Rover to help attack their competitors' weaknesses in the areas of off-road vehicles.

Encirclement attack

This strategy is based on the idea of 'surrounding the enemy' and attacking on all sides. This can prove a costly option due to the additional resources necessary to serve multiple segments. The Volkswagen group offers a diverse product range that serves a wide range of segments – Skoda, Seat, Audi and Volkswagen.

Bypass attack

This strategy relies on the ability of a company to identify new opportunities in new areas. This can be achieved by identifying new market segments, new geographical markets and also technological leapfrogging. For example, Royal and Sun Alliance has moved into new markets such as China.

Guerilla attack

The military similarities are apparent here because this type of attack relies on random and sporadic attacks on competitors. Tactical marketing programmes such as price promotions are used to achieve short-term gains, which it is hoped will erode market share in the longer term. Supermarket retailers often employ this attack strategy.

Market challengers have to decide not only how to attack but also whom to attack:

- o Market leader
- o Firms of similar size
- o Small or regional firms.

This decision will depend to a large extent on the resources that a company has at its disposal.

Specific attack strategies

All attacking strategies listed above refer to generic options open to market challengers. Kotler and Singh (1981) highlight many specific ways in which competitors can be attacked:

- o Price discounting
- o Cheaper goods strategy
- o Prestige goods strategy
- o Product-proliferation strategy
- o Product innovation strategy
- o Improved services strategy
- o Distribution innovation strategy
- o Manufacturing cost reduction strategy
- o Intensive advertising promotion.

Market followers

These types of competitors are likely to be positioned third, fourth or fifth in the market and often duplicate the strategies of the market leader. There are obvious cost advantages in being a follower – for instance, R&D costs are lower. The extent to which a follower replicates the leader's strategy may range from counterfeiting, cloning, imitating through to adaptation. Sony is renowned for their innovative approach to consumer electronics and rival Japanese companies often follow them.

Market nichers

Market nichers do not attempt to compete against the market leaders: they identify a specialist segment and concentrate their efforts on serving the needs of this niche market. There are many current examples of niche strategies such as Ben and Jerry's ice cream, Rolex watches and Morgan cars. Market nichers can specialize by end use, vertical level specialization, specific customer specialization, quality/price specialist or channel specialist (Kotler and Singh, 1981).

Exam hint

Offensive and defensive strategies

Some authors refer to market leader strategies as defensive strategies. In contrast, market challenger strategies are often referred to as attacking or offensive strategies. In the exam, you may be asked to discuss these types of strategy. It is important that you are familiar with this terminology.

Extended knowledge

Market position and influence on strategy

For a detailed discussion of the influence of market position on strategy, refer to Chapter 14 of Hooley et al. (1998).

Activity 7.3

Leaders and challengers

Identify two different industries where there is evidence of a clear market leader and market challenger. Identify the strategies pursued by:

1. Market leader to defend its position
2. Market challenger to attack the leader.

How effective have their strategies been?

Question 7.3

Market leader and challenger strategies – mini-case

Read the mini-case study 'X-Box' in the December 2001 exam paper and answer questions 1a and 1b. Go to www.cimeduhub.com to access specimen answers.

Give yourself 10 minutes to read the mini-case study and no more than 1 hour to write your answers. Compare your answers with the CIM specimen answer and Senior Examiner's report.

The June 1999 Planning and Control mini-case study – The Wet Shave Market was also concerned with market leader and challenger strategies.

Ansoff's matrix – product/market strategy

You should already be familiar with the Ansoff matrix from previous studies at Advanced Certificate, particularly Marketing Operations. This will provide you with a brief overview of the model in order to refresh your memory. Ansoff (1957) developed the matrix, illustrated in Figure 7.7, which provides a useful framework for identifying alternative strategies based on products and markets. It does not focus specifically on the way in which competitive advantage is gained but it does help firms to consider the different options available to them in terms of growth strategies. The matrix is based around 'new and existing markets' and 'new and existing products'. The further a firm moves away from existing customers and existing products, the higher the level of risk involved. Therefore, diversification is regarded as the most risky and market penetration the least risky strategy.

		Products	
		Existing	New
Markets	Existing	Market penetration	Product development
	New	Market development	Diversification

Figure 7.7 Ansoff's matrix

Market penetration

Pursuing a market penetration strategy involves selling more of the same product to the same customers. This strategy could involve:

o   Increase usage – encourage customers to use a product more frequently (e.g. increase visits to a store by offering loyalty bonuses)
o   Convert non-users into users – by offering incentives such as 'recommend a friend'
o   Attract competitors' customers – some on-line banks have enticed customers away from competition by offering incentives such as reducing their credit card balance.

This is a viable strategy if the market is not already saturated.

Product development

This involves developing new products for existing customers. For example, Boots the Chemist has developed new services such as dentistry, aromatherapy and homeopathy for their existing customer segments.

Market development

This is concerned with developing new markets for existing products and can be achieved by either targeting new segments or entering new geographical markets. With globalization, the opportunities for market development strategies are likely to increase significantly for many companies. For example, Royal and Sun Alliance adopted a market development strategy when they formed a joint venture with an Indian financial services group in an attempt to enter this potentially attractive market.

Diversification

This is probably the most risky strategy because it involves entering areas with which a firm has little or no experience. The level of risk is affected by the extent to which the new strategy is related or unrelated to existing business. Diversification into unrelated areas can be particularly risky. This strategy is often pursued via strategic partnerships or acquisition to reduce the risk.

For example, the Danish toy manufacturer Lego is entering the car market by seeking a partner with a view to launch the 'ultimate family vehicle'. The car will be designed to build on Lego's goal of becoming a leading family brand.

Extended knowledge

For a further discussion of Ansoff's matrix, refer to Chapter 8, pp. 260–262, Jobber (2001).

The *FT Mastering Strategy* series included an interesting article on growth strategies. Five Ways to Grow the Market and Create Value (*FT Mastering Strategy*, 1999).

Activity 7.4

Applying Ansoff

For your own organization or an organization with which you are familiar use the Ansoff matrix to identify the various growth strategies that could be pursued. To what extent is this model helpful in identifying competitive advantage?

Alliances and networks

Increasingly, businesses are recognizing that to gain a sustainable competitive advantage they may have to enter into alliances with other firms. Strategic alliance is not a new phenomenon, as illustrated by the array of alliances in the car industry in the early 1990s. However, the number and types of companies entering into these alliances and partnerships has proliferated in recent years and it is expected that this trend will continue. The case of IBM illustrates the growing importance of alliances to firms. In 1993 only 5% of IBM's sales outside personal computers were derived from alliances. Now IBM juggles almost 100,000 alliances, which contribute over one-third of its turnover. The company has been quoted as saying it expects these partnerships to boost sales by an extra $10 billion by 2003 (Mazur, 2001a).

Much has been written on strategic alliances and partnership. This coursebook will highlight the key issues relating to alliances and networks, provide contemporary examples and provide signposts for further reading on the subject.

Definition

Strategic alliance – Business associations in which knowledge and resources are shared to the benefit of the partners.

There are many environmental changes that are forcing firms to develop collaborative relationships. These include:

o Increasing pace of change in the environment (e.g. technological change)
o Limited resources
o Increase in competition from both existing and new firms

- o Increased customer expectations
- o Globalization
- o Unstable and unpredictable markets
- o Increased power of certain types of companies (e.g. retailers).

Motivations for companies to enter into strategic partnerships include:

- o Desire to exploit economies of scale
- o Desire to create new knowledge and increase level of innovation
- o Reduce risk
- o Share costs
- o Enter new geographical markets
- o Exploit others assets and competencies, e.g. easyJet entered into a strategic partnership with Mercedes to provide cars for their car rental venture
- o Acquiring learning and innovation.

Types of alliances

There are many different types of alliances ranging from an informal buying co-operative to a joint venture where a legally separate company is formed. Table 7.1 illustrates the major types of alliances.

Table 7.1 Main categories of alliances

Type of alliance	Characteristics	Examples
Acquisitions and mergers	Includes both co-operative and hostile takeovers. Often motivated by desire to increase efficiencies and to create synergy	Glaxo Wellcome merged with SmithKline Beecham in 2000 to form GlaxoSmithKline, the largest pharmaceutical company in Europe
Consortia and joint ventures	Involves independent organizations setting up specific projects or ventures with other firms	Eurofighter, a European collaboration consisting of four partner companies – BAE Systems (UK), Alenia (Italy), CASA (Spain) and DASA (Germany). The rationale was to reduce risk by sharing the significant development costs
Contract or licensing	Contractual agreements where the right to a product is legally signed over to another party. This may take the form of franchising or sub-contracting	Franchising is utilized by a wide variety of companies such as McDonald's, Ford dealerships, Hertz car rental, and the Body Shop
Networks	Informal agreements based on co-operation rather than contractual agreements	Many airlines have informal code sharing agreements that allow passengers to use several different airlines on the same ticket

Adapted from Johnson and Scholes, 1999

Case Study

Whitbread expands through partnerships

The leisure group Whitbread has expanded its network of David Lloyd fitness clubs through partnerships with schools. The first partnership was established with a secondary school in Surrey. The clubs are opened on school property. In return Whitbread fund the building of a music department, recording studio and all weather hockey pitch. Pupils will be able to use the facilities of the David Lloyd centre at certain times. Whitbread hopes to replicate this type of agreement with other schools and colleges. This public–private agreement will enable Whitbread to expand their network of David Lloyd centres whilst at the same time enabling schools to secure the quality of sports facilities they require.

Factors to consider when establishing an alliance

There are many factors to consider when seeking a partner and the process of selection can be a time-consuming process. The following identifies the key factors that organizations should consider.

Strategy
Strategy should be at the core of any alliance. The strategy should dictate why each partner and structure is better than any other option, company expectations, risk management and how the new alliance will be co-ordinated. According to Gomes-Casseres (2000), a coherent alliance strategy has four elements:

o A *business strategy* to shape the logic and design of alliances
o A *dynamic view* to guide the management of each alliance
o A *portfolio approach* to enable co-ordination among alliances
o An *internal infrastructure* to maximize the value of collaboration.

Core competencies and strategic fit
It is important that the core competencies of each partner are complementary and that there is strategic fit. Strategic fit refers to the level of compatibility between the two organizations.

Resources
Sufficient resource allocation is a key factor on the success of a relationship.

Risk
There is a high degree of risk involved in setting up alliances. It is important that all parties are aware of these risks and have developed strategies to deal with them.

Cultural fit
It is imperative that each partner has similar goals and aspirations. Culture should play a key role in identification of suitable partners.

Flexibility
All parties must be willing to be flexible so that the alliance can respond to changes in the external environment.

Long-term focus

Partners should not only be focusing on the short-term gains of the alliance but also on the long-term opportunities that the relationship may deliver.

There are many examples of successful strategic alliances. However, many partnerships do not deliver the predicted benefits. According to a report from KPMG and The Conference Board (cited in Mazur, 2001b), 70% of today's mergers and acquisitions fail to deliver expected business benefits, and 70% of those failures occur during post-merger integration. IMD (cited in Mazur, 2001) gives the following as reasons why alliances fail:

- ○ Differences in vision
- ○ Incompatible cultures/brand fit
- ○ Attrition of talent and capabilities
- ○ Loss of intangible assets
- ○ High co-ordination costs
- ○ Synergy gridlock
- ○ Back-office IT disintegration.

A recurring problem for many partnerships lies in the lack of cultural fit and even what has been described as a 'culture clash'. Alliances and partnerships are one means of building a sustainable competitive advantage. However, the energy, commitment and resources needed to make them successful should not be underestimated.

In order to overcome some of the problems the following actions could be taken:

- ○ Focus on core competencies
- ○ Gain commitment from staff, i.e. role of internal marketing
- ○ Gain trust
- ○ Be aware of the balance of power
- ○ Agree strategic priorities and develop long-term strategic plans
- ○ Develop joint project groups

Extended knowledge

Refer to Chapter 8 of Hooley et al. (1998) for a comprehensive discussion of alliances and strategic partnerships.

Activity 7.5

Alliance examples

Scan the quality press, such as the *Financial Times,* and journals such as *Marketing* and *Marketing Week* and identify examples of strategic alliances and partnerships. Classify these according to Table 7.1 and identify the motivations for each of these partnerships. To what extent do you think they will help to gain a competitive advantage?

Case history

MG Rover and China Brilliance holdings

In the spring of 2002 MG Rover announced they were entering into a partnership with China Brilliance. China Brilliance is a Shanghai- based manufacturer of cars and components and is the largest producer of minibuses in China. MG Rover is now focusing their business on attracting a new younger market with their MG sports cars.

The rationale for entering into the strategic alliance was that MG Rover and China Brilliance did not have products that competed directly. They both believed they could both benefit from the alliance, without their plans conflicting. The alliance would enable both companies to share development programmes, manufacture cars together and spread costs over bigger volumes. It was anticipated that the partnership would also enable both firms to grow in the expanding Chinese market.

This strategic alliance was the focus of the December 2002 Planning and Control mini-case.

Question 7.4

Strategic alliance

There have been several questions on strategic alliances on recent Planning and Control Papers.

Read the mini-case study 'MG Rover and China Brilliance Holdings (CBH)' in the December 2002 exam paper and answer Question 1b only. Go to www.cimeduhub.com to access specimen answers.

Give yourself 10 minutes to read the mini-case study and no more than 25 minutes to write your answer. Compare your answer with the CIM specimen answer and Senior Examiner's report.

Question 7 from the December 2000 paper and Question 6 from the June 2000 paper relate to strategic alliance. Answer either or both of these. Go to www.cimeduhub.com to access specimen answers.

Declining and hostile markets

Much discussion about strategy development and gaining a competitive advantage is concerned with the search for growing and attractive markets. However, many firms are faced not with healthy markets but ones that are mature or even declining. Many organizations assume that the most suitable strategy in this situation is one of strategic withdrawal. This is not necessarily the only strategy available to them and these markets can often be a source of opportunity if the right strategy is selected.

Declining markets

A declining market may be as a result of a variety of factors, often caused by changes in the external environment, for example:

o   Development of new technology such as the Internet may replace traditional buying habits
o   Changes in Government policy such as regulations relating to financial services
o   Changing customer needs such as the increase in concern about smoking and the subsequent drop in demand for cigarettes
o   Growing interest in shopping on-line may prompt a decline for traditional retailers.

Aaker (1998, p. 239) proposes four alternative strategies for firms facing a declining market:

1.   Revitalize market
2.   Encourage other competitors and stay to be the profitable survivor
3.   Milk or harvest
4.   Divest or liquidate.

Revitalization

Depending on the specific market it may be possible to rejuvenate the market to extend the life of the sector. Rejuvenation can be achieved in a variety of ways, as illustrated in Table 7.2.

Table 7.2 Rejuvenating a declining market

Method of rejuvenation	Explanation	Example
Seek new markets	This can be achieved by targeting new segments or new geographical areas	The development of mobile phones to attract teenagers
Develop new product	New products can make existing products obsolete and speed up the replacement cycle and create growth	Digital cameras have created a growth in this market
Find new uses	Seek new uses for existing products to extend its usage	Kelloggs cornflakes were promoted as suitable for meals other than breakfast
Rejuvenate product	Changing the mix (i.e. using new methods of distribution, rebranding, promotion or new packaging) can revitalize an existing product	Blue Nun wine (see below), Lucozade, Polo, Walkers' salt and shake crisps, Pepperami
Government policy	Government can stimulate growth by changing policy	The launch of ISAs (Individual Savings Accounts) stimulated growth in savings products
Target growing sub-segments	Despite the market declining overall it may be possible to identify sub-segments that are growing	The brewing industry is a mature market and yet 'alco-pops' and strong ales are growing segments

Adapted from Aaker, 1998, p. 241

Case history

Blue Nun wine

Blue Nun is an instantly recognizable brand of wine. However, its popularity has declined rapidly since its peak in popularity in 1985. According to Fellowes (2001): 'Until recently, the mere suggestion of buying a bottle of Blue Nun was likely to induce guffaws and embarrassment'. Langguth Wine and Spirits bought the ailing brand in 1995 with the aim of relaunching and repositioning the brand and increasing global sales. Consumer research revealed that, despite the brand's outdated image, it still held very positive memories for many consumers, particularly those that bought it in the 1970s and associated it with their youth. In order to reposition the brand Langguth has made a number of changes.

- Modern consumer preferences for wine have changed. The original sweet Liebfraumilch no longer appeals and therefore the wine itself has been changed to a Qualitatswein to accommodate consumer preferences for drier wines.
- A whole new range of Blue Nun wines is being launched, including reds and sparkling wines.
- The brand is being targeted at the mainstream consumer who wants an affordable, reliable bottle of wine, not the wine connoisseur. It is positioned on the brand values of fun memories.
- Blue Nun is sold in over 80 countries including most of Europe, the USA, Australia, China, Japan, Taiwan and Singapore. To ensure consistency across countries, a 'brand book' containing strict guidelines on the brand message and brand values has been developed.

The rejuvenated brand is apparently being successful. Sales in the USA have doubled in the last 2 years and are continuing to grow. Over 500,000 cases were sold in the UK last year, where it has been the market leader for the last 2 years. In the Asian markets in 2000 there was an 18% growth in sales.

Source: Adapted from Fellowes (2001)

Profitable survivor

It may be possible to stay in the market and strengthen one's position as other competitors leave the market. This would mean that despite a shrinking market, a firm would be increasing its market share and therefore this may be a very attractive strategy.

Milk or harvest

This strategy would involve reducing investment in the market. It is likely that this will reduce sales and market share. However, the ability to invest in other more lucrative sectors outweighs this decline. The rate at which a firm milks the market will vary depending on the specific situation. Alternatively a firm may decide to adopt a 'hold' strategy that involves maintaining an adequate level of investment.

Divest or liquidate

When markets are experiencing rapid decline, margins are extremely low, other competitors have achieved a dominant position or where exit barriers can be broken down then the most likely strategy is one of withdrawal, as illustrated in Figure 7.8.

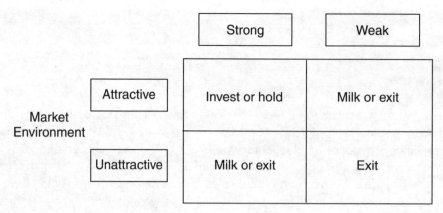

Figure 7.8 Strategies for declining markets
Adapted from Aaker, 1998, p. 245

There are many factors that will influence the choice of strategy for managing a declining market, such as:

- Predicted growth of market
- Level and intensity of competition
- Level of exit barriers
- Business position within the market (strong or weak)
- Relationship with other areas of business – synergy?

Activity 7.6

Declining markets

Identify one example of a declining market and within this market two major competitors. Compare and contrast the marketing strategies that each company has adopted in response to a declining market.

Hostile markets

Hostile markets are those with low margins, intense competition and over-capacity. Hostile markets may result from (a) declining demand and/or (b) increase in competition. Therefore, they may even be growing markets.

The Windermere study cited in Aaker (1998, pp. 250–251) identified six stages of hostility as illustrated in Table 7.3.

Table 7.3 Six stages of hostility

Stages of hostility	Explanation
1. Margin pressure	This is often due to over-capacity and therefore many competitors seek profitable segments
2. Share shifts	This may result from acquisitions or loss of share by overpriced competitors
3. Product proliferation	Competitors try to compete for market share by improving customer value through product proliferation
4. Self-defeating cost reduction	Due to declining margins firms may concentrate on cost reduction, which in turn may lead to decline in product or service quality
5. Consolidation and shake-out	This may consist of downsizing, followed by mergers and acquisitions and finally the formation of international players
6. Rescue	Many markets can emerge from hostility, often through consolidation with fewer competitors present in the market

Adapted from Aaker, 1998, p. 250

Hostile markets may not pass through all these stages in the same sequence. However, this model can help companies to identify and manage hostile markets.

The Windermere study (cited by Aaker, 1998, p. 252) suggests that there are five possible strategies for firms operating in hostile markets:

o Focus on large customers
o Differentiate on reliability
o Cover broad spectrum of price
o Turn price into a commodity
o Have an effective cost structure.

Extended knowledge

Chapter 13 of Aaker (1998) provides a comprehensive discussion of strategies in declining and hostile markets.

Question 7.5

Strategic options in response to price war – mini-case

Read the mini-case study 'Weetabix' in the June 2000 Planning and Control exam paper and answer Question 1a only. Go to www.cimeduhub.com to access specimen answers.

Give yourself 10 minutes to read the mini-case study and no more than 25 minutes to write your answer. Compare your answer with the CIM specimen answer and Senior Examiner's report.

Strategic wear-out

There are many examples of companies that once had a successful strategy but have failed to adapt to the changing environment and have therefore suffered from 'strategic wear-out'. Strategic wear-out or strategic drift refers to the lack of fit between an organization's strategy and the needs of the market place (Figure 7.9). Marks & Spencer is a prime example of a company that is currently trying to overcome the problems of strategic wear-out. Their successful strategy of the 1980s and early 1990s is no longer effective. They have lost market share to a new species of retailers that have a much better understanding of customer needs.

According to Davidson (1997, p. 285), there are a number of reasons for strategic wear-out:

o Market changes:

  o changing customer needs (e.g. increased interest in environmental issues)
  o developments in distribution such as the Internet

o Competition – from either existing or new competitors
o Internal factors:

  o insufficient investment
  o lack of management control of company costs
  o misguided changes to winning strategy.

 Definition

Strategic wear-out – Occurs when an organization no longer meets customer needs and the pursued strategy is surpassed by competitors (Drummond and Ensor, 2001).

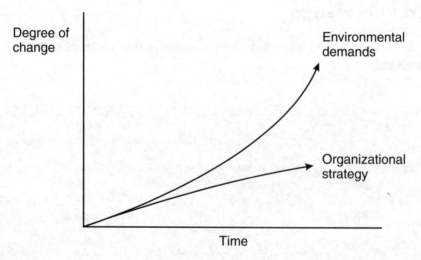

Figure 7.9 Strategic wear-out

In order to avoid strategic wear-out companies should:

o Undertake regular and detailed reviews of each element that makes up the external environment
o Identify the ways in which these elements are changing

    ○ Evaluate the impact of these changes on the organization
    ○ Undertake an internal audit to establish the appropriateness of actions both currently and for the future to ensure that customer needs continue to be met.

Extended knowledge

Strategic wear-out is discussed in greater detail by Davidson (1997), Chapter 7, pp. 285–286.

Activity 7.7

Strategic wear-out

Identify two examples of firms whose strategies are suffering strategic wear-out. What factors have led to this strategic drift? To what extent do you think this could be avoided? What, if any, actions are the companies taking to try to rectify their position?

Question 7.6

Strategic wear-out

Answer Question 4 from the December 2001 Planning and Control paper.
Go to www.cimeduhub.com to access specimen answers for this question. Question 7 from the December 1999 paper was also on strategic wear-out.

Summary

○ One of the greatest challenges for any organization is to develop a coherent and appropriate strategy that builds on their internal resources, exploits external opportunities and provides a distinct competitive advantage.

○ Sustainable competitive advantage is not just related to how firms compete but also the basis of competition, where they compete and whom they compete against.

○ Porter suggests that there are three generic forms of strategy than can provide a competitive advantage: cost leadership, differentiation or focus. Those companies that fail to consistently pursue one of these generic strategies will become 'stuck in the middle'.

○ Davidson has identified 10 alternative ways of attaining a sustainable competitive advantage: superior product/service, perceived advantage, global skills, low-cost producer, superior competencies, superior assets, scale advantages, attitude advantages, legal advantages and superior relationships.

o Companies can be classified according to their position in the market: market leaders, market challengers, market followers and niche marketers. There are a number of offensive and defensive strategies that firms can pursue either to attack or defend their position.

o The Ansoff matrix is a useful framework for identifying the various growth strategies open to a company: market penetration, market development, product development or diversification.

o Strategic alliances are increasingly being regarded as a means of gaining a sustainable competitive advantage.

o Much writing about strategy development is focused on the search for growing and attractive markets. However, many firms are faced not with healthy markets but with ones that are mature or even declining. Firms must develop coherent strategies to deal with these declining or even hostile markets.

o Companies that once had a successful strategy but have failed to adapt to the changing environment are in danger of suffering from strategic wear-out. This refers to a lack of strategic fit between an organization's strategy and the market's needs.

Further study and examination preparation

Extending knowledge

Bibliography

Aaker D (1998). *Strategic Market Management*, 5th Ed., John Wiley & Sons.

Ansoff H (1957). Strategies for diversification, *Harvard Business Review*, 25 (5), 113–125.

Davidson H (1997). *More Offensive Marketing*, Penguin.

De Bruxelles S (2001). One-plane outfit puts top airlines to flight, *The Times*, 3 March.

Drummond G and Ensor J (2001). *Strategic Marketing Planning and Control*, Butterworth-Heinemann.

Fellowes J (2001). Message in a bottle, *Marketing Business*, May, pp. 16–19.

Financial Times Mastering Strategy (1999). Five ways to grow the market and create value, *Financial Times*, 18 October, p. 8.

Gomes-Casseres, B (2000). Strategy must lie at the heart of alliances, *Financial Times, Mastering Management* Series Part 3, 16 October.

Hooley GJ, Saunders JA and Piercy NF (1998). *Marketing Strategy and Competitive Positioning*, 2nd Ed., Prentice-Hall.

Jobber D (2001). *Principles and Practice of Marketing*, 3rd Ed., McGraw-Hill.

Johnson G and Scholes K (1999). *Exploring Corporate Strategy*, 5th Ed., Prentice-Hall, pp. 13–16 and 241–244.

Kotler P and Singh (1981). cited in Kotler P (2000). *Marketing Management, The Millenium Edition*, Prentice-Hall.

Kotler P, Armstrong G, Saunders J and Wong V (1999). *Principles of Marketing*, 2nd European Edition, Prentice-Hall.

Mazur L (2001a). The Only Way to Compete Now is with an Alliance, *Marketing*, 15 February, p. 20.

Mazur L (2001b). Acquisition Activity is on a High, But in Most Cases the Deals Fail to Deliver, *Marketing*, 8 February, p. 26

Mazur L (2002). Global retailing can trip up even the best brands, *Marketing*, 21 February, p. 18.

Porter M (1980). *Competitive Strategy: Techniques for Analysing Industries and Competitors*, Free Press.

www.Lexis-Nexis.com

unit 8
developing a specific competitive position

By the end of this unit you will:

o   Understand and be able to describe the strategic alignment process

o   Understand the importance of segmentation in creating competitive advantage

o   Be able to discuss the process of segmentation and the various methods of segmenting both consumer and organizational markets

o   Be able to discuss the various criteria that will influence segment choice and targeting strategy

o   Appreciate the importance of positioning as a means of achieving competitive advantage

o   Understand the role the marketing mix plays in achieving a specific positioning strategy

o   Be able to discuss the various types of branding strategies

o   Be able to discuss the relative advantages and disadvantages of brand extensions and brand stretching

o   Understand the role of innovation in achieving a competitive advantage and the methods of encouraging an innovative culture

o   Understand the importance of building customer relationships

o   Be able to discuss ways in which relationships can be built

o   Understand the criteria by which strategies can be evaluated.

Key definitions

Segmentation – The identification of groups of individuals or organizations with characteristics in common that have significant implications for the development of marketing strategy (Jobber, 2001).

Brand equity – A set of assets and liabilities linked to a brand's name and symbol that add to or subtract from the value provided by a product or service to a firm and/or that firm's customers (Aaker, 1998, p. 173).

Brand extensions – Brand extensions occur when companies launch new products, under the same brand name into the same broad market.

Innovation – The commercialization of something new, which may be: a new technology, a new application in the form of a new product, service or process, a new market or market segment, a new organizational form or a new management approach or a combination of two or more of these elements (Janszen, 2000).

Relationship marketing – The purpose of relationship marketing is to establish, maintain and enhance long-term relationships with customers and other parties so that the objectives of both parties are met (Gronroos, 1991).

Study Guide

- ○ This unit will take you about 5 hours to work through
- ○ We suggest that you take a further 5 hours to do the various activities and questions in this unit.

Introduction

The previous unit identified a number of generic frameworks that could be used to identify various ways of achieving competitive advantage. This unit is concerned with how organizations can convert this generic advantage into a unique and sustainable advantage. A key aspect of developing a successful strategy lies in the ability of an organization to match their internal capabilities with the external market needs. This approach will be discussed and the importance of segmentation, targeting and positioning in helping to achieve a sustainable competitive advantage will be outlined. The marketing mix plays a central role in helping to achieve the desired positioning strategy. The marketing mix has been covered in detail in previous CIM modules at Certificate and Advanced Certificate in Marketing Fundamentals and Marketing Operations. It is assumed you are familiar with all aspects of the mix and therefore this coursebook will only highlight the areas with which you should be familiar and concentrate on the specific issues of branding, innovation and new product development and relationship marketing. The unit will then conclude with discussion of the criteria by which organizations can select the most appropriate strategy.

Strategic alignment process

Strategy can be regarded as the matching of an organization's resources and capabilities to the environment in which it operates. This process is sometimes referred to as 'strategic fit'. It is a key step in the strategy development process and ensures that by matching markets, channels and customers with internal assets and competencies a sustainable competitive advantage is developed. It is not enough to just identify unmet customer needs. The company must have the necessary skills and resources to meet these needs. This process is referred to as the strategic alignment process and is illustrated in Table 8.1.

Table 8.1 The strategic alignment process

Stage	Process	Explanation
1	Identify utilizable assets	Assets could include brands, property, patents, finance, relationships and scale advantages
2	Identify utilizable competencies	Competencies relate to skills and may include marketing (e.g. ability to develop new and innovative products), selling (e.g. customer relationship management) and operations (e.g. inventory control)
3	Select and rank business opportunities in terms of attractiveness	This involves identifying market opportunities and then developing criteria to measure the attractiveness of each option. Portfolio analysis can be used to identify the most attractive strategies (This will be discussed later in greater detail in relation to segmentation.)
4	Match internal assets (stage 1) and competencies (stage 2) with market opportunities (stage 3)	This process will identify the areas in which it will be most effective for a company to compete
5	Identify any assets or competencies that need to be strengthened	During the strategic alignment process it may be that market opportunities are identified but the firm lacks the ideal assets and competencies to capitalize on this opportunity. A firm may decide to develop or acquire the necessary competencies to exploit this market (e.g. entering into a strategic alliance, employing new staff, acquiring brands)

Adapted from Davidson, 1997, p. 82

For a detailed discussion of assets and competencies refer to Unit 3 – Internal analysis. This process of alignment can also be used to identify suitable market segments and will be discussed further in the next section.

Segmentation, targeting and positioning

The process of segmentation, targeting and positioning (STP) plays a critical role in the development of any marketing strategy. Markets consist of individuals, all with different needs and wants, rather than a homogeneous mass of customers. Segmentation acknowledges these differences and suggests that a marketer's role is to identify groups of individuals who have similar needs and to develop products/services to meet these needs. In some markets, such as luxury yachts or individually commissioned jewellery, it is possible to adopt the practice of one-to-one marketing where the firm can produce a customized individual product for each and every customer if they so wish. However, for the majority of companies it is not feasible to adopt this practice and therefore they seek out groups of customers who have similar needs and develop products to match their requirements. The practice of segmentation is becoming increasingly important because people today are continuously seeking individualism and looking for products/services that reinforce their own identity. This is in stark contrast to the 1960s where customers were actively seeking out mass produced products. This trend, away from mass marketing has been fuelled by three major factors as illustrated in Figure 8.1. Some companies are responding to customer's needs for individuality by adopting a mass customization strategy. For example, Levi jeans offers customers the opportunity to have a customized pair of jeans made to measure. The customer selects the style and fabric, provides measurements, and the Levi tailor makes the jeans. The challenge for firms today is to strike the right balance between mass marketing (the most cost efficient means of serving the market) and producing tailor-made products (meeting individual customer needs). This is the role of segmentation.

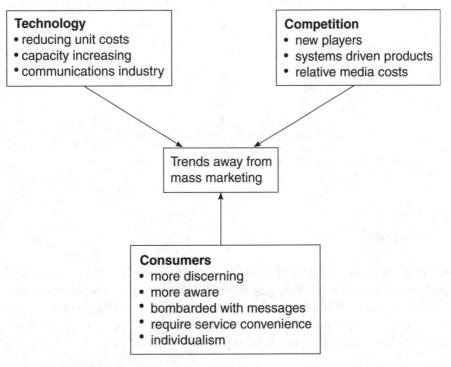

Figure 8.1 Trends away from mass marketing
Adapted from Kotler et al., 1999

You should already be familiar with the concept of segmentation, the ways in which markets can be segmented, targeting strategies and positioning from previous CIM modules such as Marketing Operations and the Marketing Customer Interface. Therefore, this section does not attempt to provide an in-depth discussion of all the issues relating to STP. Instead, it will identify the issues with which you should already be familiar, direct you to appropriate reading to refresh your memory, highlight key topics and provide examples. There are six major steps in STP, as illustrated in Figure 8.2. Many organizations will probably not approach segmentation in such a formal and systematic manner. However, these six steps provide a structure that can help discussion of the key issues in relation to the process of segmentation.

Segmentation

1. Identify methods of segmentation (bases)

↓

2. Develop profiles for these segments

↓

Market Targeting

3. Evaluate market segment attractiveness

↓

4. Select target segments

↓

Market Positioning

5. Identify positioning for each segment

↓

6. Develop marketing mix to achieve the desired positioning

Figure 8.2 Stages of market segmentation, targeting and positioning
Adapted from Kotler et al., 1999

Exam hint

Segmentation plays an important role in understanding customer needs and identifying opportunities. It is central to any marketing strategy and has therefore featured on many of the Planning and Control exam papers in the past. Segmentation is also a key aspect of the Analysis and Decision exam and provides you with the opportunity to put the theory into practice in the context of a particular organization or industry.

Segmentation

The process of segmentation involves identifying groups of customers who have similar needs and developing products to meet these needs. Doyle (1998, p. 179), identifies a number of benefits of segmentation:

- ○ Better matching of customer needs
- ○ Enhanced profits
- ○ Enhanced opportunities for growth
- ○ Retention of customers
- ○ Targeted communications
- ○ Stimulation of innovation
- ○ Market segment share.

The first stage in the STP process is identifying the most effective means of segmenting the market. It would be possible to segment any market with any type of base. However, the base selected must relate to differences in purchase behaviour. For example, you could segment purchasers of coffee according to the colour of their eyes, although eye colour is not relevant to the purchase of coffee. Choice of segmentation base will also be influenced by company resources and competitor activity. It is important to remember that markets segment themselves. Those companies that segment markets for administrative ease are in danger of failing to understand what drives customers to purchase. There are many different bases that can be used to segment both consumer and organizational markets, and these are outlined below.

Definition

Segmentation – The identification of groups of individuals or organizations with common characteristics that have significant implications for the development of marketing strategy (Jobber, 2001).

Segmentation bases

Consumer markets

The methods by which consumer markets can be segmented are closely associated with buyer behaviour (covered in Unit 2 – External analysis). There are numerous ways of segmenting consumer markets and companies are continuously developing new methods in an attempt to segment their markets more finely. However, there is a general agreement that consumer markets can be segmented by customer characteristics and behavioural characteristics.

Customer characteristics:

- o Demographic – age, gender, income, occupation, education, religion, family life-cycle
- o Geographic – country, region, county, city size, town
- o Geodemographic – this combines information on household location with demographic socioeconomic information, e.g. ACORN, FiNPiN
- o Psychographic – social class, personality and lifestyle. VALS and Taylor Nelson's Monitor Framework are both examples of lifestyle segmentation.

Behavioural characteristics:

- o Benefits sought
- o Usage frequency (e.g. occasional or regular)
- o Usage status (e.g. non-user, lapsed user, user)
- o Purchase occasion
- o Attitude towards the product
- o Buyer readiness stage.

It is important that you are familiar with each of these bases and are able to critique and provide examples of each. In the Analysis and Decision major case you will be expected to apply this knowledge in a practical situation. This unit will provide some examples of segmentation bases; however, for a detailed discussion refer to extending knowledge for relevant sources.

Extended knowledge

For further discussion of segmenting consumer markets refer to: Drummond and Ensor (2001) Chapter 4, pp. 52–69 and or Jobber (2001) Chapter 7, pp. 186–196.

Demographic – FLC (family life cycle)

Classifying consumers according to their family circumstances can be a useful method for segmenting many different types of markets. This framework can be helpful for products such as financial services. Earning potential, levels of expenditure and the need for different types of financial services will change as a person moves through this cycle. A modern family life-cycle model is illustrated in Figure 8.3.

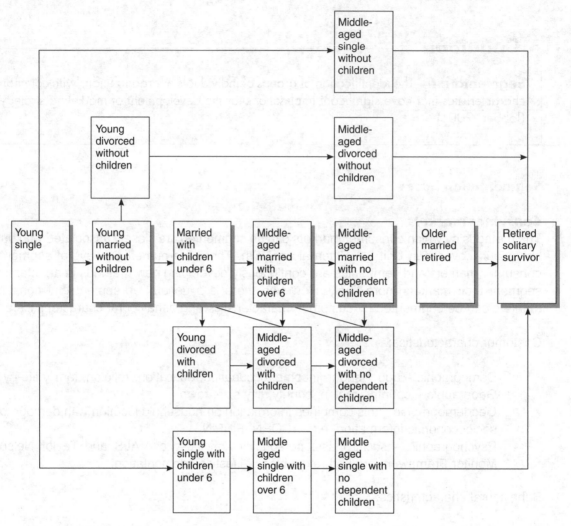

Figure 8.3 A contemporary family life-cycle
Adapted from Murphy and Staple, 1979

Geodemographics – ACORN (a classification of residential neighbourhoods)

Figure 8.4 illustrates the various categories into which consumers are divided according to the type of housing in which they live.

ACORN Types	% of households in GB	ACORN Groups
ACORN category A: THRIVING		
1.1 Wealthy Suburbs, Large Detached Houses	2.2%	1 Wealthy Achievers, Suburban Areas
1.2 Villages with Wealthy Commuters	2.8%	
1.3 Mature Affluent Home Owning Areas	2.7%	
1.4 Affluent Suburbs, Older Families	3.4%	
1.5 Mature, Well-Off Suburbs	2.9%	
2.6 Agricultural Villages, Home Based Workers	1.5%	2 Affluent Greys, Rural Communities
2.7 Holiday Retreats, Older People, Home Based Workers	0.7%	
3.8 Home Owning Areas, Well-Off Older Residents	1.5%	3 Prosperous Pensioners, Retirement Areas
3.9 Private Flats, Elderly People	1.3%	
ACORN Category B: EXPANDING		
4.10 Affluent Working Families with Mortgages	1.8%	4 Affluent Executives, Family Areas
4.11 Affluent Working Couples with Mortgages, New Homes	1.3%	
4.12 Transient Workforces, Living at their Place of Work	0.3%	
5.13 Home Owning Family Areas	2.5%	5 Well-Off Workers, Family Areas
5.14 Home Owning Family Areas, Older Children	2.6%	
5.15 Families with Mortgages, Younger Children	1.9%	
ACORN Category C: RISING		
6.16 Well-Off Town & City Areas	1.1%	6 Affluent Urbanites & City Areas
6.17 Flats & Mortgages, Singles & Young Working Couples	0.9%	
6.18 Furnished Flats & Bedsits, Younger Single People	0.5%	
7.19 Apartments, Young Professional Singles & Couples	1.4%	7 Prosperous Professionals, Metropolitan Areas
7.20 Gentrified Multi-Ethnic Areas	1.1%	
8.21 Prosperous Enclaves, Highly Qualified Executives	0.9%	8 Better-Off Executives, Inner City Areas
8.22 Academic Centres, Students & Young Professionals	0.6%	
8.23 Affluent City Centre Areas, Tenements & Flats	0.7%	
8.24 Partially Gentrifed Multi-Ethnic Areas	0.8%	
8.25 Converted Flats & Bedsits, Single People	1.0%	
ACORN Category D: SETTLING		
9.26 Mature Established Home Owning Areas	3.4%	9 Comfortable Middle Agers, Mature Owning Areas
9.27 Rural Areas, Mixed Occupations	3.4%	
9.28 Established Home Owning Areas	3.9%	
9.29 Home Owning Areas, Council Tenants, Retired People	3.0%	
10.30 Established Home Owning Areas, Skilled Workers	4.3%	10 Skilled Workers, Home Owning Areas
10.31 Home Owners in Older Properties, Younger Workers	3.2%	
10.32 Home Owning Areas with Skilled Workers	3.3%	
ACORN Category E: ASPIRING		
11.33 Council Areas, Some New Home Owners	3.7%	11 New Home Owners, Mature Communities
11.34 Mature Home Owning Areas, Skilled Workers	3.3%	
11.35 Low Rise Estates, Older Workers, New Home Owners	2.9%	
12.36 Home Owning Multi-Ethnic Areas, Young Families	1.0%	12 White Collar Workers, Better-Off Multi-Ethnic Areas
12.37 Multi-Occupied Town Centres, Mixed Occupations	2.0%	
12.38 Multi-Ethnic Areas, White Collar Workers	1.0%	
ACORN Category F: STRIVING		
13.39 Home Owners, Small Council Flats, Single Pensioners	2.3%	13 Older people, Less Prosperous Areas
13.40 Council Areas, Older People, Health Problems	2.1%	
14.41 Better-Off Council Areas, New Home Owners	2.0%	
14.42 Council Areas, Young Families, Some New Home Owners	2.7%	14 Council Estate Residents, Better-Off Homes
14.43 Council Areas, Young Families, Many Lone Parents	1.6%	
14.44 Multi-Occupied Terraces, Multi-Ethnic Areas	0.7%	
14.45 Low Rise Council Housing, Less Well-Off Families	1.8%	
14.46 Council Areas, Residents with Health Problems	2.1%	
15.47 Estates with High Unemployment	1.3%	15 Council Estate Residents, High Unemployment
15.48 Council Flats, Elderly People, Health Problems	1.1%	
15.49 Council Flats, Very High Unemployment, Singles	1.2%	
16.50 Council Areas, High Unemployment, Lone Parents	1.5%	16 Council Estate Residents, Greatest Hardship
16.51 Council Flats, Greatest Hardship, Many Lone Parents	0.9%	
17.52 Multi-Ethnic, Large Families, Overcrowding	0.5%	17 People in Multi-Ethnic, Low-Income Areas
17.53 Multi-Ethnic, Severe Unemployment, Lone Parent	1.0%	
17.54 Multi-Ethnic, High Unemployment, Overcrowding	0.3%	

Figure 8.4 The ACORN consumer targeting classification

Question 8.1

Geodemographic segmentation

Answer Question 3 from the December 1999 Planning and Control paper on geodemographic segmentation. Go to www.cimeduhub.com to access specimen answers for this question.

Case history

FRuitS

The financial division of NOP, the market research group, and Berry Consulting, a database and modelling company, has developed a method of segmenting financial service markets according to lifestyle. They have segmented people according to a) life stage, b) financial strength and c) their pattern of purchasing of financial products, and have produced a typology based on a fruit bowl.

The FRuitS model has been developed from research that examines the financial behaviour of consumers through 60,000 interviews each year. The following segments have been identified.

Plums (10% of UK population)

Typically male. Aged 44–65, living in the south, married, university educated, high income (over £35,000), homeowner with 2+ cars. Has a strong financial portfolio, 3.5 times more likely to own shares and twice as likely to have a credit card.

Pears (9% of UK population)

Slightly older than plums, more likely to be retired. Income of £7,500 to £17,500. More cautious, but twice as likely to own stocks and shares. Interested in savings, but not in the market for mortgages or bank loans.

Cherries (14% of UK population)

Around 35–54 with family, usually own their own home and 2 cars and have an income over £17,500. Prime candidates for mortgages, bank loans and credit cards.

Apples (12% of UK population)

Similar age to cherries, but income under £17,500. Likely to live in the north, Midlands or Wales, to be married, have one car, be self-employed or possibly working part-time. Moderate savings and good prospects for mortgages, loans and personal pensions, since they are less likely to be in a company pension scheme.

Dates (15% of UK population)

More likely to be female, 55+, not educated beyond age 14. Widowed or retired, they live alone as owner/occupiers or in council housing. Income up to £7,500, no car, and are more likely to have life insurance and a building society account.

Oranges (16% of UK population)

Aged 16–34. Single, most likely to be in private rented accommodation, are either unemployed or studying, with income up to £7,500. Oranges are interesting for their potential.

Grapes (13% of UK population)

Coming in bunches, they are more likely to live in households with five members or more. Aged 15–55 they're usually working but with relatively low incomes immediately consumed. Candidates for loans.

Lemons (11% of UK population)

Like dates, they are typically older, single or widowed, living on their own, with income below £7,500. But they are worse off, being half as likely to have household insurance, and unlikely to have loans, cards or personal pensions.

Adapted from Anon (1996), www.Lexis-Nexis.com

Case history

Behavioural segmentation – Internet shopping

Shopping on-line is still a relatively new phenomenon. As consumers get into the swing of clicking, rather than queuing for their goods, they develop new shopping habits – habits that retailers are keen to cash in on.

Last year, a survey by market analysts Datamonitor found that web consumers have habits quite different from those shopping on the high street. On-line customers fall into certain categories, exhibiting characteristics which identify them as a particular 'breed' of e-shopper.

Despite the wealth of dot.com publicity and advertisements many people are still very wary of making a purchase on-line. Although 80% of respondents had browsed the net for anything from CDs to cars, less than a third had actually taken the plunge and ordered on-line, and even fewer – just 15% – had paid over the Internet.

But, according to the report, all this is about to change. Falling prices mean that computer ownership will continue to increase, the proliferation of interactive TV, games consoles and WAP phones will all fuel the growth in on-line shopping. More than 70% of Europeans already own at least one interactive device and it is thought that, by 2004, more than three-quarters of all households with PCs will be connected to the Internet, increasing the potential on-line shopping population.

Overall, the proportion of Internet users who buy on-line is expected to rise from 25% to 70% over the next four years.

Once consumers progress from starter to expert they will inevitably spend more time, and money, on the Internet. Datamonitor spoke to a total of 12,000 people, aged from 18 upwards, in the UK, Sweden, Germany, France and Spain. According to their findings, we are all shopping animals. Which one are you?

The rhino

Not always, but mostly, elderly, with 61% of the group being over 65. Rhinos tend to belong to a relatively low income household, often due to retirement. This consumer wants to see, feel – and if possible sniff – their groceries before they hand over the ready cash. In fact, cash is the preferred method of payment and the thought of putting credit card details on to a computer and clicking on a 'mouse' which sends them to someone they've never met or spoken to is enough to send even the toughest, most thick-skinned rhino charging into the bushes for cover. Only a third of all rhinos have gone on-line at least once.

The puma

At the opposite end of the shopping jungle lies the puma. Usually young, often single, with a high income and fearless disposition, these predators want their shopping delivered yesterday and aren't afraid to try out new technology. If you can get it on-line, they'll buy it, anything from the latest Nike (or possibly Puma?) trainers to a new car. They'll even hunt for food on-line – provided it can be delivered within the hour – and can usually be relied on to try anything once. However, this big cat should remember what curiosity did, and be a little more cautious when handing over their financial details if they don't want to get their claws burned.

The gazelle

Generally 30-somethings, and usually computer literate, these are the lowest spending group in the younger categories. Youthful and energetic, yes, but the gazelle has a more timid approach to shopping on the Internet than the puma. Moving in herds, often with a young family in tow, they prefer to hang back, saving their hard-earned cash for the things they really need. They're not averse to the Web, and will occasionally dip their toe in the water, but they'd rather wait to see if it's safe before wading in. Their average on-line spend in the past six months was £170.

The gorilla

Still preferring to spend most of their substantial income on the high street, this group is not as conservative as the rhinos and is open to new suggestions. They will eventually get into the swing of shopping on the Net, but only after carefully weighing up the pros and cons. Classic gorilla behaviour involves starting slowly with low-risk, familiar items – something from Amazon perhaps – and then moving on to bigger transactions as confidence builds. Despite being financially better off than rhinos only 18% of this group, had logged on to the Internet.

The jackal

This pack animal has got the Internet sussed and spends most of their day persuading other, less adventurous types, to try out the latest technology. If they're not surfing for a new coat or digging up a bargain CD, they're ordering groceries at home and breathing a contented sigh at not having to fight their way through the crowds in the high street. Around 10 years younger than gorillas or rhinos, jackals spend approximately 10 times more money on Internet shopping – an impressive average of £440 over six months.

Source: Adapted from Eames L (2000) www.Lexis-Nexis.com

Activity 8.1

VALS

The VALS framework (values, attitudes and lifestyles) classifies consumers according to their nine lifestyle groups, as shown in Figure 8.5.

Visit the VALS Web site at the following address, click on VALS survey, complete the mini-questionnaire and obtain the results. If possible, discuss your results with fellow students.

http://Future.sri.com/VALS/VALSindex.shtml

- o   To what extent do you think this framework is helpful in segmenting markets?
- o   In which markets do you think this type of segmentation may be helpful?
- o   What are the limitations of this type of framework?

Developmental stage	Grouping (% of US population)
Need-driven	**Survivors**. This is a disadvantaged group who are likely to be withdrawn, despairing and depressed (4%). **Sustainers** are another disadvantaged group, but they are working hard to escape poverty (7%).
Outer-directed	**Belongers** are characterized as being conventional, nostalgic, reluctant to try new ideas and generally conservative (33%). **Emulators** are upwardly mobile, ambitious and status conscious (10%). **Achievers**. This group enjoys life and makes things happen (23%).
Inner-directed	**'I-am-me'** tend to be young, self engrossed and act on whims (5%). **Experientials** wish to enjoy as wide a range of life experiences as possible (7%). **Societally conscious** have a clear sense of social responsibility and wish to improve society (9%).
Nirvana	**Integrateds** are completely mature psychologically and combine the positive elements of outer and inner directedness (2%)

Figure 8.5 The VALs framework (Developed by Arnold Mitchell at the Stanford Research Institute)

Question 8.2

Lifestyle segmentation

Answer Question 5 from the December 2002 Planning and Control paper on lifestyle segmentation. Go to www.cimeduhub.com to access specimen answers for this question. Question 5 from the December 1998 paper also featured lifestyle segmentation.

Question 8.3

Geodemographic or pyschographic segmentation

Answer Question 6 from the June 2001 Planning and Control paper on geodemographic or psychographic segmentation. Go to www.cimeduhub.com to access specimen answers for this question.

Organizational markets

The methods used to segment consumer markets are not appropriate for organizational markets due to the complexity of purchase decisions and the decision-making group. Organizational buying behaviour was discussed in Unit 2 – External analysis. Organizational markets can be segmented according to macrofactors and microfactors. Figure 8.6 illustrates the major variables for segmenting organizational markets and examples of each. You must be able to discuss each of these variables. Refer to extended knowledge for relevant sources.

Variables	Examples
Macro segmentation	
■ Size of organization	Large, medium or small
■ Geographic location	Local, national, European Union, Worldwide
■ Industrial sector	Retail, engineering, financial services
■ End market served	Defined by product or service
Micro segmentation	
■ Choice criteria	Quality, delivery, value in use, supplier reputation price
■ Structure of decision-making unit	Complexity, hierarchical, effectiveness
■ Decision-making process	Long, short, low or high conflict
■ Buy class	New task, straight or modified re-buy
■ Importance of purchasing	High or low importance
■ Type of purchasing organization	Matrix, centralized, decentralized
■ Innovation level of organization	Innovative, follower, laggard
■ Purchasing strategy	Optimizer, satisfier
■ Personal attributes	Age, educational background, risk taker/adverse, confidence level

Figure 8.6 Organizational macro and microsegmentation
Reproduced from Drummond and Ensor, 2001, p. 80

The nested approach illustrated in Figure 8.7 provides a logical approach to organizational market segmentation. This approach starts with the broad organizational factors (macrofactors) and then moves through layers of segmentation variables to the often more complex factors such as situational and personal characteristics (microfactors).

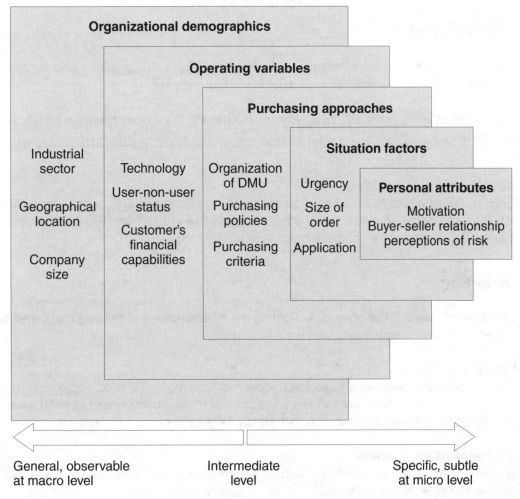

Figure 8.7 The major factors for segmenting organizational markets (a nested approach)
Adapted from Bonoma and Shapiro, 1983

Question 8.4

Organizational buyer behaviour and segmentation

Answer Question 5 from the December 2001 Planning and Control paper on organizational buyer behaviour and segmentation. Go to www.cimeduhub.com to access specimen answers for this question.

Extended knowledge

For further discussion of the bases used to segment organizational markets refer to:

Drummond and Ensor (2001), Chapter 4, pp. 78–81; Jobber (2001) Chapter 7, pp. 197–201.

Activity 8.2

Consider your own organization or one that you are familiar with. Consider how you currently segment the market. How effective is this method?

What alternative, more effective, ways of segmenting the market could be adopted?

Development of profiles

Once the most effective bases have been identified, the next step is to develop profiles of the resulting segments. In many cases companies will use not just one base for segmenting the market. They may use a combination of factors.

Targeting

Targeting consists of two stages: evaluating the attractiveness of the segments and selecting a market coverage strategy.

Which segments to target?

Once appropriate segments have been identified, the next step is to decide which of these segments to serve. There are two issues to consider: the attractiveness of each segment and the extent to which an organization can match the needs of the segment.

Segment attractiveness

According to Hooley et al. (1998) segment/market attractiveness can be assessed by the criteria illustrated in Table 8.2.

Table 8.2 Factors to consider when evaluating market segments

Market factors

- o Segment size
- o Segment growth rate
- o Stage of industry evolution
- o Predictability
- o Price elasticity and sensitivity
- o Bargaining power of customers
- o Seasonality and cyclical pattern of demand

Economic and technological factors

- o Barriers to entry
- o Barriers to exit
- o Bargaining power of suppliers
- o Level of technology utilization
- o Investment required
- o Margins available

Competitive factors

- o Competitive intensity
- o Quality of competition
- o Threat of substitution
- o Degree of differentiation

Environmental factors

- o Exposure to economic fluctuations
- o Exposure to political and legal factors
- o Degree of regulation
- o Social acceptability and physical environment impact

Adapted from Hooley et al., 1998, pp. 301–307

Extended knowledge

For a detailed discussion of these factors refer to:

Hooley et al. (1998), Chapter 12, pp. 302–309 or Drummond and Ensor (2001), Chapter 9, pp. 172–177 or Jobber D (2001), Chapter 7, pp. 201–203.

Determining organizational strengths
A market segment may be regarded as attractive, but if the company does not have the necessary resources and skills to serve this segment then it is not going to be suitable. Organizational strengths can be broken down into three areas, as illustrated in Table 8.3.

Table 8.3 Criteria for assessing company strengths

Current market position	
	o Relative market share
	o Rate of change of market share
	o Exploitable market assets
	o Unique and valued products and services
Economic and technological position	
	o Relative cost position
	o Capacity utilization
	o Technological position
Capability profile	
	o Management strength and depth
	o Marketing strength
	o Forward or backward integration

Adapted from Hooley et al., 1998, pp. 309–312

Extended knowledge

For further discussion of these factors refer to: Hooley et al. (1998), Chapter 12, pp. 309–312.

Aligning market opportunities with company strengths

Once the attractive segments and internal company strengths have been identified, it is necessary to match them in order to identify the most appropriate segments to pursue. This is the same process as strategic alignment (discussed at the beginning of this unit). Portfolio analysis can play an important role in this process. Portfolio analysis, discussed in Unit 4 – Auditing tools, has traditionally been used to summarize current business activity and, to a lesser degree, the alternative business investment opportunities open to a multi-product company. However, they can equally well be used to help identify target markets. The process is similar to that explained in Unit 4 – Auditing tools, when discussing the plotting of strategic business units on the General Electric model:

1. Identify the appropriate criteria for measuring (a) segment attractiveness and (b) company strength/fit with company assets and competencies
2. Weight each factor according to its importance
3. Evaluate each criterion (for both segment attractiveness and company strength) using a scale of, say, 1–5, where '5' is excellent and '1' is poor
4. Calculate an overall score for (a) segment attractiveness and (b) company strength for each segment under investigation
5. Plot these scores on a multi-factor portfolio matrix as illustrated in Figure 8.8

(Refer to Unit 4 – Auditing tools for full details of this process.)

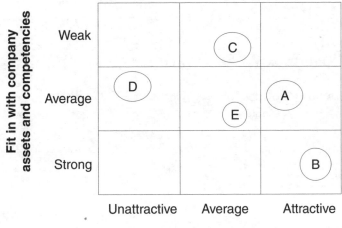

Figure 8.8 Adapted Shell directional policy matrix applied to target market selection
Shell, 1975

Extended knowledge

The following provide further discussion on the use of portfolio analysis in target market selection:

Hooley et al. (1998), Chapter 12, pp. 312–314 and

Drummond and Ensor, (2001), Chapter 9, pp. 177–181

Question 8.5

Segment selection

Evaluating segment attractiveness is an important aspect of marketing strategy and questions have appeared on this topic in recent papers.

Answer Question 3 from the June 2000 and Question 6 from the June 1999 Planning and Control papers. Go to www.cimeduhub.com to access specimen answers for this question.

In reality, many organizations select target markets using a more informal process than the one outlined above. In many cases there are subjective factors that must also be taken into consideration, such as:

○ Does it create a sustainable market position?
○ Is it compatible with the mission statement?
○ Is it consistent with organizational culture and values?
○ Can the current organizational structure serve the proposed market?
○ Does it facilitate an innovative approach to market entry?
○ Does it provide a focal point for action and future development?
○ Is it compatible with current internal information flows and reporting lines?

(Adapted from Drummond and Ensor, (2001), p. 181).

Question 8.6

Attractiveness of Overseas Markets – Mini-case

Read the mini-case study 'Howden Joinery' in the June 2002 Planning and Control exam paper and answer Question 1b only. Go to www.cimeduhub.com to access specimen answers.

Give yourself 10 minutes to read the mini-case study and no more than 25 minutes to write your answer. Compare your answer with the CIM specimen answer and Senior Examiner's report.

Market coverage strategies

Once the attractive segments have been identified it is necessary to decide which targeting strategy to pursue. Kotler et al. (1999) suggest that there are three broad approaches that can be adopted:

o **Undifferentiated marketing**: This is sometimes referred to as mass marketing and involves producing one product that is designed to appeal to all segments. In today's highly fragmented markets, it is rare that this strategy is appropriate

o **Differentiated marketing**: This involves developing a different product for each different segment. For example, Ford has identified a number of different segments with different requirements for cars and therefore produces different cars to meet the needs of each segment

o **Focused marketing**: Companies adopting a focused strategy select one or a few segments on which to concentrate. For example, Morgan cars adopt a focus strategy concentrating on sports car enthusiasts.

Jobber (2001) suggests a fourth approach:

o Customized marketing: Individual customer needs are unique and it is financially viable to offer them customized products/services tailored to individual customer requirements.

Extended knowledge

For further discussion of market coverage strategies refer to Jobber D (2001), Chapter 7, pp. 203–205.

Positioning

Once the target markets have been identified, it is necessary to clearly position the product or service in the marketplace. The aim of a company is to identify on what basis they are to compete, and then to position their product or service clearly and uniquely in the minds of their customers. For example, Stella Artois has successfully positioned itself as 'reassuringly expensive' in the UK, despite being a relatively inexpensive lager in France. According to Kotler et al. (1999) a brand can be positioned using the following associations:

o product attributes
o usage occasions
o users

  o   activities
  o   personality
  o   origin
  o   competitors
  o   product class
  o   symbol.

Extended knowledge

For further discussion of these positioning associations and examples refer to Drummond and Ensor (2001), Chapter 9, pp. 182–184.

According to Jobber (2001) there are four factors that are critical to successful positioning:

  o   **Clarity**: the positioning strategy must be clear and simple – for example 'Have a break, Have a Kit Kat'
  o   **Credibility**: the differential advantage must be credible in the minds of the target market
  o   **Consistency**: it is important that the target market receives consistent messages about a product. Rover has been criticized for failing to identify a clear position because there has been a lack of consistency over the last few years
  o   **Competitiveness**: the basis on which a product is to be positioned must exceed what the competitors provide.

Perceptual maps can prove to be very valuable when researching customer perceptions of products and services. Perceptual maps, which are based on two axes that represent key attributes, enable a company to assess where their product sits relative to the competition. They can also identify any possible gaps in the market. Figure 8.9 illustrates a perceptual map for breakfast products and indicates that there was a gap in the market for a product that appealed to children but could be 'eaten on the hoof'. Kelloggs filled this gap when they launched their Frosties and Coco-pops cereal bars.

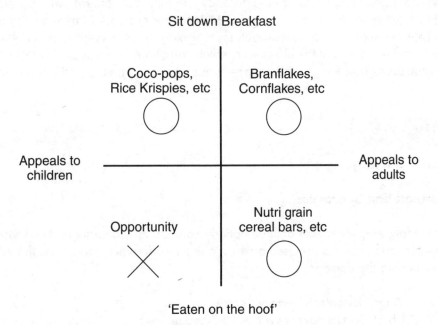

Figure 8.9 A perceptual map of breakfast products

A number of brands have failed to establish clear positions in the minds of the customer. These positioning mistakes may be as a result of any of the following:

- o **Confused positioning**: the brand fails to establish a clear position in the customer's mind relative to the competitors
- o **Underpositioning**: customers cannot see any significant advantages of this product
- o **Overpositioned**: positioning of a product is so focused that customers fail to appreciate that the brand covers a wider product range.

Extended knowledge

For further coverage of positioning and perceptual maps refer to: Drummond and Ensor (2001), Chapter 9, pp. 182–188.

For an interesting overview of segmentation refer to: Doyle (1998), Chapter 3.

Question 8.7

Segmentation, targeting and positioning – mini-case

Read the mini-case study 'Freeplay Energy' in the December 2000 Planning and Control exam paper and answer Question 1b only. Go to www.cimeduhub.com to access specimen answers.

Give yourself 10 minutes to read the mini-case study and no more than 25 minutes to write your answer. Compare your answer with the CIM specimen answer and Senior Examiner's report.

The marketing mix

The final stage of the STP process relates to the development of the marketing mix to achieve the desired positioning. You should already be fully conversant with all elements of the extended marketing mix from previous CIM Modules such as Marketing Fundamentals and Marketing Operations. This coursebook is not going to discuss in detail each element of the mix. Instead it will highlight the areas with which you should already be familiar and concentrate on those aspects that are of particular relevance to the Planning and Control module.

 Activity 8.3

Activity briefing

Segmentation in practice

Visit the following Web sites of three holiday companies. Compare and contrast the various segmentation bases that are used by each company. To what extent does the Web site help in positioning the company?

- o Voyages Jules Verne www.vjv.co.uk
- o Club 18-30 Holidays www.club18-30.co.uk
- o The Discerning Traveller www.chycor.co.uk/holidays/discerningtraveller

Extended knowledge

If you wish to revisit the marketing mix refer to the following texts, which all contain separate chapters on each element of the mix.

Jobber (2001).

Davidson (1997).

Doyle (1998).

Branding

Branding has traditionally been dealt with as an aspect of 'product' within the marketing mix. However, it is increasingly being recognized that brands can be very powerful and can in fact be the driving force of a successful marketing strategy. For example, the Virgin brand has enabled Richard Branson to enter many and varied markets due to its brand equity. Richard Branson's greatest asset is probably the Virgin brand.

 ### Definition

Brand equity – A set of assets and liabilities linked to a brand's name and symbol that add to or subtract from the value provided by a product or service to a firm and/or that firm's customers (Aaker, 1998, p. 173).

Brand equity is the sum of:

- o brand awareness
- o brand associations/identity
- o perceived quality
- o brand loyalty.

(Aaker, 1998, p. 173).

Benefits of branding

The benefits of branding are well documented in a wide range of sources. Doyle (1998) suggests four ways in which strong brands generate value for companies:

- o Strong brands usually obtain price premiums from consumers or resellers
- o Strong brands obtain higher market shares
- o Because of customer loyalty, successful brands generate more stable and less risky earning streams
- o Successful brands offer avenues for further growth.

Brand valuation

Many companies are beginning to realize the value of their brands and are looking for ways to quantify this value. According to Doyle (1998) there are five main methods of valuing brands:

- ○ Price premium valuation – the price premium over unbranded products is used as the basis for brand valuation
- ○ Incremental sales valuation – if brands achieve higher sales than unbranded products these incremental sales can be used to value the brand
- ○ Replacement cost value – the estimated cost of developing a similar brand
- ○ Stock market valuation – the residual value estimated once physical assets, industry factors and other intangible assets have been removed
- ○ Future earnings valuation – probably the most appropriate method. This is where the discounted present value of future earnings attributable to the brand is estimated.

No doubt the debate as to how best to value brands will continue. Drummond and Ensor (2001, p. 189) suggest a list of factors that act as indicators of a brand's value:

- ○ Market type
- ○ Market share
- ○ Global presence
- ○ Durability
- ○ Extendability
- ○ Protection
- ○ Superior products and services
- ○ Country of origin
- ○ Market domination.

Extended knowledge

For further information on the factors influencing brand value refer to:

Drummond and Ensor (2001) Chapter 9, pp. 189–192.

For further discussion on valuing brands refer to:

Doyle (1998), Chapter 6, pp. 193–194 and Hooley et al. (1998) Chapter 12, pp. 120–123.

Branding strategies

There are a number of alternative branding strategies that can be adopted. The four main strategies are illustrated in Table 8.4.

Table 8.4 Alternative branding strategies

Strategy	Explanation	Examples
Company brand	Firms retain the company name for their brand across their portfolio. This allows for economies of scale, strong image and provides reassurance to customers moving into a new market. Problems may occur if a poor product detracts from brand image and organic growth can be more difficult by moving into new market segments (i.e. how far can the brand be stretched?)	Virgin, Cadbury's
Individual brand names (multi-brands)	Each product has a unique brand name. This allows companies to cope with increasingly segmented markets, facilitates innovation and creative marketing. Companies can provide products of differing standards and quality without damaging their brand image. This strategy can be very costly and risky	Procter and Gamble with Ariel, Daz and Bold Unilever with Cif, Cha's Teashops, Persil, Domestos
Company and individual brand (endorsed approach)	This uses both the company name and an individual brand name. This strategy benefits from association with the company but enables firms to cope with increasingly segmented markets. It is difficult to enter niche segments with this strategy and the failure of one brand may impact on the overall brand image	Vauxhall Astra, Vectra and Corsa Kelloggs Rice Krispies, Cornflakes and Coco-pops
Range branding	Products are grouped and each group has a separate brand name. This provides firms with the increased opportunity to enter new market segments with a new range brand. They can then capitalize on this brand by launching under this brand name	RHM – Sharwoods and Bisto, Heinz Weight Watchers

Adapted from Doyle, 1998, p. 167

In addition to these four main branding strategies companies can also opt for private brands or generic brands. In reality companies can use a combination of branding strategies. There are a number of factors that will influence choice of branding such as the number of products and product lines and their differential advantage, competitor strategies, target market characteristics and of course the level of available resources.

Extended knowledge

For a more detailed discussion of the advantages and disadvantages of each of the branding strategies refer to: Drummond and Ensor (2001) pp. 195–197.

Case history

Banking on a new identity

Banks have spent decades convincing us that our money is safe. Why is it that many of them have created completely new identities for their Internet offerings? The Co-operative bank with Smile, Abbey National with Cahoot and Halifax with IF (intelligent finance) have all invested a great deal of time and money in building new brands from scratch. There are two main reasons as to why these banks have opted for a multi-brand strategy:

Attracting a different customer

By adopting a different brand name it was hoped that non-users would be attracted to the brand. Abbey National has used Cahoot to target a different, and indeed a more affluent, customer base, and the crossover between Cahoot and Abbey National customers is only 1%. Therefore they are not cannibalizing their existing sales.

Creating a different identity

Many banks have suffered from poor reputations and did not want to tarnish the image of their new operations with this reputation. For example, when the Prudential launched Egg they were left with no choice but to give it a different identity, given the problems in the financial service industry, (for example the pensions mis-selling scandal).

However, there are some limitations to this strategy:

Focus on security

The key for financial service organizations is that individuals feel they are dealing with a company that provides them with security. All the banks launching on-line banks have found the need to reassure potential customers of the link to the parent brand.

From on-line to high street

Recent reports have suggested that Egg is to establish a 'real world' presence, possibly through a concession in branches of Boots. Maybe they are recognizing that the Internet is not a market (it is a channel), and that customers want to use a variety of channels that are integrated rather than a purely Internet-based offering.

Source: Adapted from Murphy (2001), www.Lexis-Nexis.com

Brand extensions

One of the benefits of branding lies in the ability to launch new products on the back of existing ones. Brand extensions occur when companies launch new products, under the same brand name, into the same broad market. For example, Mars extended their brand from countlines to boxed chocolates when they launched Celebrations. It is believed that brand extensions can be a less risky strategy than launching completely new products because customers will trust the brand. In fact it is reported that five out of every ten brand extensions fail. This is not as high as the failure rate of new products (as high as nine out of ten) but obviously cause for concern (Lury, 2000).

Case history

Flora Pro-Activ – extending the brand

Flora Pro-Activ is a spread that is designed to lower cholesterol levels. It was launched in Europe in 2000 and since then sales have continued to grow (last year sales grew by 15.3%). Unilever Bestfoods has decided to leverage the Pro-Activ's premium health positioning by extending the brand into milk and yoghurts. These brand extensions are to target those people who have raised cholesterol levels and yet do not eat spreads. These brands will challenge the market leader Benecol in a range of different food markets.

Source: Kleinman (2002)

Brand stretching

Traditionally, brands tended to confine themselves to certain product areas. However, there are many examples of companies that are stretching their brands into unrelated areas, for example Nike is moving to consumer electronics, Virgin is selling cars and Coca-Cola has launched a new range of urban clothing. The success of these ventures will be influenced by the 'stretchability' of the brand. For example, the Virgin brand's core values appear to be transferable into a number of unrelated markets. However, if you think of Coca-Cola you think of a brown fizzy drink and it is difficult to see how these core values can be transferred into the clothing market (Tomkins, 2000). The same principle could be applied to Guinness, where the brand is also the product, and the brand is therefore less elastic. The factors to consider when thinking about brand stretching are:

- o Does the brand fit the new product class?
- o Does the brand add value to the offering in the new product class?
- o Will the extension enhance the brand name and image?
- o What effect will the new brand have on the image of the existing brand?
- o Are the same or different segments being targeted?
- o Is the brand positioned on the same or different differential advantage as the existing brand?
- o Does the brand offer the customer something better, different or cheaper than is already available?

According to Lury (2000) brands can be stretched using a number of approaches:

- o Core personality – the brand's personality is used to stretch into often unrelated markets. For example, Virgin has used its positioning as a customer champion to stretch into many unrelated markets (see activity 8.3 below).
- o Functional approach – the brand is developed by offering products in similar formats. For example, confectionery brands moving into ice creams and chilled desserts.
- o Core ingredient – in America Arm and Hammer's products are all based on bicarbonate of soda and are available as toothpaste, deodorant, a detergent and cat litter.
- o Core competencies – brands develop according to their core competencies. For example, Bic's expansion is based on their expertise in cheap, disposable plastic engineering, e.g. razors and biros.

There are many examples of co-branding where two brands are brought together to create a new brand extension. For example, Milky Way and McVities have joined forces to create cake bars.

Activity 8.4

Stretchability of the Virgin brand

Visit the Virgin Web site at www.virgin.com. Consider the wide range of markets that the Virgin brand has entered and answer the following questions:

- Why do you think Virgin has been able to successfully enter unrelated markets?
- To what extent do you think the problems associated with Virgin Trains have had an impact on the Virgin brand?

Case history

Unilever

Unilever is attempting to exploit some of its leading brands by stretching them into new markets. Unilever has set up a home-cleaning and laundry business in West London, called Myhome, whose services are branded with the Persil and Cif names. It has also launched men's barbershops in Oxford Street and Kingston that carry the name of its Lynx brand.

'Unilever's trial domestic cleansing service is a good example of the radical thinking necessary to enter new markets. It means a more intelligent understanding of what a brand's core meaning is – rather than just a literal knowledge of what it does – on the part of the marketer. Unilever seems to have come to realize that its offer is not 'household cleaning products', but 'clean houses'. It's like the old marketing saying that Black & Decker defines its business not as selling drills, but selling holes.'

Myhome chief executive David Ball says Unilever has recognized that services will be an important part of the future for the group. The intention is to expand Myhome, which already has 150 employees, into other parts of the UK and abroad. Unilever already has a Surf Laundry Cleaning operation in India and has a company called Riverstone in the USA that provides similar services.

'People have more disposable income and as such are looking at spending it in a trade-off to create time,' says Ball. He argues that Myhome will build the standing of the Persil and Cif brands while at the same time not encroach on retail sales of the products.

The initial concept for Myhome came out of a Unilever working group on brand extensions. Given that Unilever is moving into service businesses on a number of fronts, it has what it refers to internally as a Quality Time team, drawn from the new service businesses, which shares learning and best practice.

Source: Adapted from Gray (2001), www.Lexis-Nexis.com

Case history

A Stretch too Far?

When Jack Daniels (Bourbon brand) decided to enter a co-branding agreement with Heinz to produce a premium range of barbecue grilling sauces, many people thought that this would not be a successful strategy. The Jack Daniels' brand stands for U.S Southern heritage, original, high quality craftsman and flavour. It was hard to see how these brand values could be successfully translated into a non-alcoholic and non-beverage category. However, the partnership has been successful with Heinz reporting a 12% share of the premium barbecue sauce segment.

The success of this brand extension has been attributed to the fact that the Jack Daniels' brand is synonymous with the American Deep South, and grilling and barbecuing also has long-standing roots with the region. It builds on the synergy between the two brands as well as the core competencies of both Heinz and Jack Daniels.

In contrast, Samsonite, a brand of virtually indestructible luggage, failed to capitalise on new market opportunities when it attempted to extend its brand into the clothing market. Samsonite's functional brand values are associated with quality, durability and efficiency of design. In contrast, its emotional values are innovative and smart. It was the latter values that Samsonite hoped to capitalize on when it launched a range of 'Hauteutilitarian' clothes that was positioned as both functional and glamorous. Unfortunately, it seemed that the fashion conscious consumer did not want to buy clothes from a luggage maker. The clothing range was to some extent seen as high-style and well-made, however it failed to capitalise on the travel element of the brand.

The confusion surrounding the brand and its values has been further exacerbated by previous attempts by Samsonite to stretch its brand. For example, it licensed its brand to produce cast and extruded aluminium furniture in addition to launching a Samsonite grill. These two strategies were far too removed from the travel category and therefore failed to be relevant to the brand's core values.

Brand stretching can seem like an ideal and low risk strategy for entering new markets. However, companies should consider long and hard whether the new market is synergistic with the brand's current core values.

Source: Marchese (2002)

Question 8.8

Branding issues

Answer Question 2 from the December 2001 Planning and Control paper on branding issues. Go to www.cimeduhub.com to access specimen answers for this question.

Brand revitalization

It is likely that over time brands will become less relevant to their target markets and therefore companies will have to take action to improve the performance of the brand. Drummond and Ensor (2001, p. 199) suggest that brand revitalization involves gaining sales volume by expanding the market and this can be achieved by four methods:

- Enter new markets – new geographical areas
- Exploit new market segments
- Increase frequency of use
- Increase quantity used.

Brand repositioning

As markets change and new opportunities arise, it may be necessary to reposition a brand to align it with the new opportunities. Brands may also require repositioning because they have been either underpositioned or overpositioned or suffer from a confused positioning. Lucozade was one of the first brands that successfully repositioned its brand from a drink for unhealthy old people to an energy drink for healthy active young people. According to Doyle (1998, p. 188), there are a number of ways in which brands can be repositioned:

- **Real positioning** – the actual brand is changed, for example Skoda cars
- **Psychological positioning** – the company seeks to change customer's beliefs about a brand, for example Pepperami
- **Competitive depositioning** – firms can try to alter beliefs about competitors' products and suggest they are inferior. Many on-line banks are using this strategy
- **Reweighting values** – buyers may be persuaded to attach a greater importance to certain values in which the brand is market leader. For example, the benefits of drinking bottled water with added calcium have been publicized
- **Neglected values** – sometimes new choice criteria can be introduced to buyers. The Co-operative Bank is positioned on ethical issues, which in the past were irrelevant to most customers
- **Changing preferences** – it may be possible to switch buying preferences
- **Augmenting the product** – a brand may be enhanced by offering additional services such as warranties and after-sales service.

Extended knowledge

For further discussion on brand revitalization and repositioning refer to: Drummond and Ensor (2001) Chapter 9, pp. 199–204.

Activity 8.5

Select two brands:

- One that has been successfully revitalized or repositioned and
- One that in your opinion has failed to be revitalized or repositioned.

Compare and contrast the strategies used by the two companies. Why in your opinion did one fail and one succeed?

Case history

Apple

Apple is a good example of a brand that has successfully repositioned itself. The brand's early success was built on innovation, design and product capability. However, they became complacent and allowed Microsoft and IBM to steal their customers and market share. It deserted its core mass consumer market and lost sight of what it stood for and its customers' needs. By 1998, Apple's situation was so bad that it lost £690 million in a single quarter.

In an attempt to turn the business around, the Apple founder, Steve Jobs returned to the company and set out to undertake a fundamental review of the business and to refocus on Apple's core values. The result was the iMac, launched in 1998. 'The Internet was opening up and, as well as looking attractive and different, the iMac was a great tool to address a sector we had lost our way in' says European Marketing Communications Manager Alan Hely.

Revenue in 2001 is expected to be in the region of £4.15 billion. Market share in the UK rose from 1.5% in 1999 to 2.7% in November 2000. Apple is continuing to innovate and have realized that rarely does one product save a company.

Source: www.Lexis-Nexis.com

Question 8.9

Brand repositioning strategy

Answer Question 2 from the December 2000 Planning and Control paper on brand repositioning strategy. Go to www.cimeduhub.com to access specimen answers for this question.

Global brands

Firms are increasingly adopting global branding strategies in an attempt to benefit from economies of scale and consistent messages and images throughout the world. For a detailed discussion of global brands, refer to the CIM International Marketing module.

Case history

Jif to Cif

Unilever renamed cleaning cream Jif as 'Cif' in an attempt to align the brand across the globe. The move formed part of Unilever's strategy of paring its brand range from 1,600 down to 400 products. The company put £1 billion behind marketing its core brands. Its core brands including Cif, Lipton, Dove and BirdsEye Wall's account for 90% of the company's turnover.

Jif was known as Cif in more than 80% of markets where the Lever Bros product is sold. The Jif brand until recently was available in the UK, Northern Ireland and Holland, among other markets. Jif was replaced in stores in the UK and other markets. The UK launch of Cif was supported by a £2 million TV campaign created by Lowe Lintas, as well as by direct mail and in-store activity. The product logo and range will be unchanged.

A spokeswoman for Unilever says: 'Cif is the most widely used brand name for Jif around the world. The name change brings Cif closer to becoming a global brand behind which resources can be marshalled, so enabling us to innovate better and faster to meet consumers' needs.'

Unilever has benefited from the economies of scale in terms of manufacturing, marketing and advertising that comes from a concentration of these core global brands. However, they have maintained a number of profitable 'local jewels', brands such as Marmite in the UK, that are only strong in one country.

Source: Marketing Week (2000), www.Lexis-Nexis.com

Question 8.10

Pan-European branding

Answer Question 2 from the June 1999 Planning and Control paper on Pan-European branding. Go to www.cimeduhub.com to access specimen answers for this question.

Extended knowledge

For further discussion of branding refer to:

Aaker (1998), Chapter 9.

Doyle (1998), Chapter 6.

Question 8.11

easyJet branding strategy – mini-case

A compulsory question on branding was asked as part of the mini-case on the December 1999 Planning and Control Exam paper. Answer Question 1b only. Go to www.cimeduhub.com to access specimen answers for this mini-case.

Innovation and new product development

Innovation has been referred to as the 'lifeblood' of an organization. A company must continuously seek real product and marketing improvements in order to continuously satisfy customers and fend off competitors. Innovation is most often associated with new product development. However, this is only part of the equation and innovation also relates to changes in products, processes and practices. Janszen (2000) defines innovation as: 'The commercialization of something new, which may be:

- ○ A new technology
- ○ A new application in the form of a new product, service or process
- ○ A new market or market segment
- ○ A new organizational form or a new management approach

Or a combination of two or more of these elements.

Many organizations are striving to develop organizational cultures that encourage innovation. For example, in 1999 Procter and Gamble announced a major internal restructuring, sacking 13% of the workforce to streamline management and speed up decision-making. Innovation teams were set up within the company and the management of new ideas was passed to new business managers rather than existing businesses. These changes resulted in the successful launch of Swiffer, Febreze and Dryel.

Innovation is not the same as invention. There are very few 'inventors' that have successfully invented a commercial business opportunity, notable exceptions being James Dyson, Bill Hewlett and Dave Packard. 'Inventors' rarely develop innovations that change markets, make fortunes and change the way the world operates. Innovation is led by commercial application, whilst invention is led by the scientific process.

New product development (NPD)

It is apparent that new product development is a key aspect of the innovation process. The reality of new product launches is that the majority are not unique or novel. Many of the NPD launches are variations of existing products. Booz et al. (1982) identified four types of new products:

- ○ New to the world
- ○ New product lines or line additions
- ○ Product revision
- ○ Reposition.

There is much risk attached to new product development. Research in the USA found that less than 1% of products launched in 1998 achieved $100 million of sales in their first year. More than two-thirds failed in their first year.

Failure of new products

There are a number of reasons that may account for the high failure rate of new products. Drummond and Ensor (2001) suggest the following:

○ Under-investment
○ Failure to deliver customer benefits
○ Forecasting errors
○ Internal politics
○ Industry response.

To this list could also be added:

○ Lack of management enthusiasm
○ The NPD process too slow and beaten by market competitors.

Extended knowledge

Amazon.com is taking orders for the world's first dynamically stabilized, self-balancing human transporter – the Segway at a cost of $4,950.00. Is this the new C5 or a truly innovative new product? Visit www.amazon.com, click on Segway and see what you think. Make sure you watch the videoclip.

Process

Traditionally, companies adopted a linear process to NPD, as illustrated in Figure 8.10. However, it is still a useful framework for ensuring that all the major factors have been reviewed and considered. Firms are facing the dilemma of ensuring that new product ideas are assessed rigorously but at the same time getting new ideas to market first. The challenge facing organizations is to develop NPD processes that are still rigorous and yet enable firms to get to market quickly. Drummond and Ensor (2001) suggest the following strategies for optimizing the NPD process.

○ Multi-functional teams – to ensure a balanced viewpoint
○ Completeness and evaluation – complete all stages of the NPD process
○ Customer involvement – used to evaluate possible ideas and products
○ Parallel processing – undertaking activities concurrently
○ Strategic direction – links must be made between corporate strategy and NPD
○ Knowledge management – the transfer of knowledge is essential to help develop a 'learning organization'.

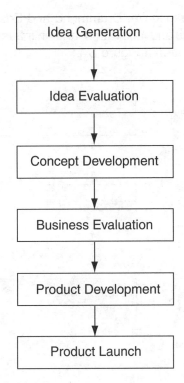

Figure 8.10 Linear new product development process
Adapted from Drummond and Ensor, 2001

Case history

Idea generation

Many companies are continually looking for new ways of generating ideas. Norse Dairy Systems (NDS) based in Columbus, Ohio is a supplier of baked ingredients and novelty packaging. They provide their customers with product development support. In order to generate new frozen novelty ideas NDS conducts a company wide '100 New Ideas Workshop'. This unconventional multi-step brainstorming session is based on 'lateral thinking' where new ways of looking at things are adopted in order to develop creative thinking. This process has produced many successful new products. Rather than using wooden spoons to scoop ice-cream out of tubs, they developed edible cone chips for scooping. A 'strip cup' was produced that got rid of the need for a spoon. Instead of using a spoon to eat the dessert, the customer tore the cup down in strips along horizontal perforations and ate the dessert directly from the cup. NDS also developed a system for embossing images and logos on ice cream wafers and cones to create a three dimensional effect. This helped processors to build brand equity and differentiate themselves in the marketplace.

Source: Dairy Foods (2003)

Managing innovation

Ambler (1999) suggests that if a company can get the right organizational conditions, then innovation will take care of itself. The challenge to organizations is how to create the right conditions. Generating creative ideas is only one part of the process (and often the easiest). The difficulty lies in how to convert this idea into a marketable business opportunity that adds value from a customer's perspective. Drummond and Ensor (2001) suggest that, to create a culture that embraces change and innovation, and an infrastructure to support this, firms should consider the enablers illustrated in Figure 8.11.

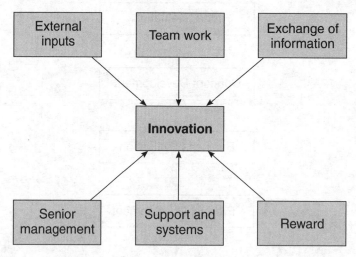

Figure 8.11 Generating innovation
Drummond and Ensor, 2001

Extended knowledge

For a full discussion of the strategies for optimizing the NPD process and managing innovation refer to:

Drummond and Ensor (2001) Chapter 10.

Organizational structures can impede or assist the innovation process. Hooley et al. (1998) suggest a variety of ways in which organizations can change their structure to facilitate innovation:

- º The functional approach
- º A taskforce
- º A project team-functional matrix
- º Venture teams
- º Spin-outs
- º Inside-outside venture.

Extended knowledge

For a full discussion of these six approaches refer to Hooley et al. (1998) p. 386. (Chapter 16 provides a comprehensive discussion of innovation and NPD.)

Case history

3M

3M is regarded as one of the leading companies in the art of innovation. The challenge for many companies is how to get to market quickly whilst at the same time ensuring that they have selected the winning idea. 3M is adopting the following strategies to try and increase the pace of innovation:

- 3M Acceleration to drive growth – this initiative is focused on prioritizing projects and shifting resources to those that have the strongest potential for growth and profitability.
- Acquisition – the company is pursuing a strategy of accessing fast-growing markets by acquiring companies with strong market positions and technologies.
- Special Thanks and Recognition (STAR) scheme – a reward system that has been set up in the UK to encourage individuals and teams to increase the pace of innovation.
- Seeking and implementing new methods to drive innovation faster – IT for example is helping to speed up the process. The use of extranets has helped to build relationships with distributors and channel partners and this can lead to new ideas.
- Dedicated Teams – specialist teams are selected to focus on innovation. For example, in the UK, the Enterprise Growth Team has been established to develop new applications/new markets for existing 3M technologies. So far it has been a successful venture and became self-financing in 6 months. Its success has been attributed to several factors:

  - The team is sponsored at the highest level
  - It is a multi-disciplinary team with representatives from technical, marketing, manufacturing and sales
  - It has no restraints or boundaries
  - The team is physically located together
  - The team is driven by stretch goals and lives and dies by its results.

The team identified new uses for 3M's multi-layer technology that traditionally had been used for high-tech applications such as enhancing electronic LCD displays. The bright radiant colour-changing film is now being used in decorative applications on luxury goods such as packaging and point of sale material for brands such as Christian Dior perfume and Storm watches.

Source: Adapted from www.wnim.com/issue13/pages/innovationprint.htm

Activity 8.6

Consider your own organization. To what extent is your organizational climate conducive to developing innovative ideas? Consider the six factors highlighted in Figure 8.11.

Question 8.12

Innovation

Innovation is a key theme on the Planning and Control syllabus and several questions have been asked on this topic.

Answer Question 3 from the June 2001 paper. Go to www.cimeduhub.com to access specimen answers for this question. Question 6 from the December 1999 paper was also on innovation.

Relationship marketing

Relationship marketing recognizes the importance of the lifetime value of a customer. The key to successful long-term business success relies not just on getting new customers but, more importantly, on encouraging customer loyalty.

Research has shown that it takes significantly more investment to acquire a new customer that it does to retain an existing one. In fact, studies have shown that it costs 5–10 times more to acquire a new customer than to retain an existing one (Murphy, 1996). Analysts at Bain and Company Management Consultants have found that a 5% increase in customer retention can significantly increase profitability, for example by 25% in a bank (Murphy, 1996).

Therefore, companies are increasingly recognizing the need to develop strategies that build customer loyalty and develop profitable relationships. The concept of relationship marketing is not limited to building relationships with customers but can equally be applied to the other markets with which a firm is associated. Building effective relationships with the various markets as illustrated in Figure 8.12 will, in the longer term, enable firms to more effectively meet their customers' needs and develop stronger relationships with their customers. The importance of developing relationships in terms of strategic alliances and partnerships was discussed in the previous unit.

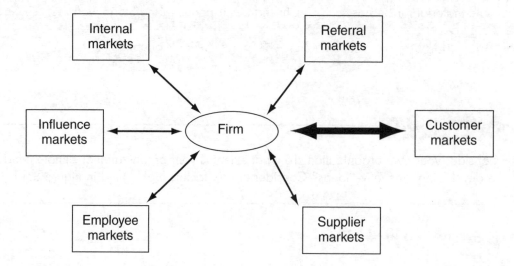

Figure 8.12 The six market model
Adapted from Christopher et al., 1994

Definition

Relationship marketing – The purpose of relationship marketing is to establish, maintain and enhance long-term relationships with customers and other parties so that the objectives of both parties are met (Gronroos, 1991).

Characteristics of relationship marketing

Traditional marketing techniques, often referred to as transactional marketing, view marketing and selling as one-off transactions, as opposed to relationship marketing which is concerned with the management of long-term relationships. Figure 8.13 contrasts these two approaches.

Transaction marketing	*Relationship marketing*
Focus on single sales	Focus on customer retention and building customers' loyalty
Emphasis upon product features	Emphasis upon product benefits that are meaningful to the customer
Short timescales	Long timescales recognizing that short-term costs may be higher, but so will long-term profits
Little emphasis on customer retention	Emphasis upon higher levels of service that are possibly tailored to the individual customer
Limited customer commitment	High customer commitment
Moderate customer contact	High customer contact with each contact being used to gain information and build the relationship
Quality is esentially the concern of production and no one else	Quality is the concern of all and it is the failure to recognize this that creates minor mistakes that lead to major problems

Figure 8.13 Transaction vs relationship marketing
Adapted from Christopher et al., 1994

According to De Souza (1999) customer retention has a more powerful and direct effect on profits than market share, scale advantages and other variables commonly associated with competitive advantage. This approach to marketing should not only lead to increased profitability through repeat business but should also provide opportunities for cross-selling, and the generation of positive word of mouth and new business from 'loyal' satisfied customers.

Developing relationships

Figure 8.14 illustrates the relationship marketing ladder developed by Christopher et al. (1993). This framework clearly identifies a number of stages of relationship building. The objective of relationship marketing is to move people up the ladder from prospect through to advocate and to maintain this position.

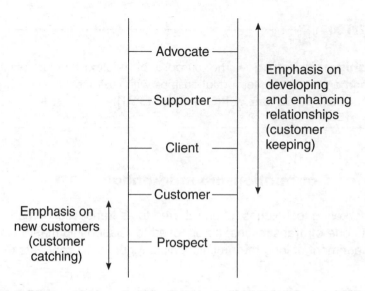

Figure 8.14 The relationship marketing ladder
Christopher et al., 1993

Of course, all customers are not equally profitable and worth the investment to move them up the ladder. In fact, many companies may choose to 'deselect' those that are unprofitable. Identification of various customer groupings is an important part of any relationship marketing strategy. For example, financial service companies may not want to maintain some groups of customers (e.g. those that are unprofitable – such as the 'lemons' in the FRuitS segmentation approach outlined earlier) (Thilo and Leventhal, 1998). Companies may choose to 'deselect' these types of customer groups. In some cases unprofitable customers are a significant group. For example, when considering the retail banking sector, the percentage of profitable customers is 42% with 27% of customers deemed to be non-profitable (*The Banker*, May 1999).

For relationship marketing to be successful it is vital that there are obvious benefits to all parties involved. Figure 8.15 illustrates the 'cornerstones' of relationship marketing as described by Hooley et al. (1998).

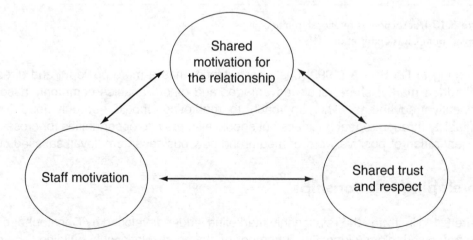

Figure 8.15 Cornerstones of relationship marketing
Adapted from Hooley et al., 1998, p. 355

The benefits for companies in developing relationships with their customers are obvious. The benefits to customers are not always as apparent. For example, customers may prefer to remain anonymous – do customers really want to develop relationships with their super-markets, banks or DIY stores? For many customers, there is a perceived lack of benefits in entering into many relationships. Supermarkets are obviously keen to retain their customers and many of these have instigated 'loyalty cards' that purport to reward loyal customers. However, many customers see very little actual benefit for the privilege of handing over a great deal of personal information that can then be used to bombard them with irrelevant and annoying direct mail. The success of the relationship also depends on the development of mutual trust between the two parties. Without the commitment of employees to deliver the expected levels of service, the relationship will break down as customers defect to other companies in search of better service.

Drummond and Ensor (2001) suggest a number of common principles of relationship marketing:

o   Use appropriately – it is not always the best strategy
o   Establish relationship drivers – identify the key factors for success
o   Build customer value – ensure that there is real benefit to customers to enter the relationship
o   Retain customers – concentrate on increasing customer loyalty.

Implementing relationship marketing

The key to building successful relationship marketing strategies lies in the implementation of these programmes. Kotler et al. (1999) suggest the following stages of implementation:

o   Identify key customers
o   Assign a 'relationship manager' to each of them
o   Develop clear job descriptions
o   Appoint a manager to supervise relationship managers
o   Develop long-term plans for developing relationships.

This list is not exhaustive and may not apply in all situations. However, it does highlight the importance of effective management of the relationship. Many organizations have restructured their sales force based on relationship management.

Day (1998), in an article in the *FT Mastering Marketing* series suggested that, for relationships to be successful they should focus on:

o   Delivering superior value – continually develop ways to add value for your customer
o   Demonstrating trustworthiness – the firm must gain and maintain their customers' trust
o   Tightening the connections – make it more attractive for the customer to remain loyal
o   Co-ordinating capabilities – all activities should be co-ordinated
o   Engage the entire organization – both hearts and minds – the company culture must support this strategy
o   Tighten organizational alignment – identify any weak links and strengthen them
o   Make learning a priority – continually seek ways to improve
o   Refresh and maintain databases and records – this is a time-consuming but essential task.

Extended knowledge

For further coverage of relationship marketing refer to: Hooley et al. (1998), Chapter 15, (in particular pp. 354–355) and Day (1998).

Question 8.13

Relationship marketing programme

Answer Question 7 from the June 1999 Planning and Control paper. Go to www.cimeduhub.com to access specimen answers.

Strategic evaluation

Once an organization has identified the various strategic options available, it is then necessary to evaluate them in order to identify the 'best' strategy that will gain the best source of competitive advantage. In reality, many companies do not adopt formal processes and instead rely on 'gut feel'. However, there are a number of approaches that can be adopted to assess strategies.

Criteria

Johnson and Scholes (1999, p. 355) suggest a list of criteria by which companies can evaluate alternative strategies:

○ **Suitability** – does it:

1. Exploit strengths and competencies?
2. Rectify weaknesses?
3. Deflect threats?
4. Seize opportunities?

○ **Feasibility** – can it be implemented?
1. Sufficient finances?
2. Deliver the goods?
3. Deal with competitor's response?
4. Access to technology, etc.?
5. Time?

○ **Acceptability:**
1. To stakeholders?
2. Legislation and environmental impact?

Aaker (1998, p. 30), provides a slightly different list of criteria to that of Johnson and Scholes and in particular highlights the importance of how the proposed strategy fits with existing strategies.

- o Consider in the context of environmental opportunities and threats
- o Sustainable competitive advantage?

  1. Exploit strengths or competitor's weaknesses?
  2. Neutralize weaknesses or competitor's strengths?

- o Consistent with vision/objectives?

  1. Achieve long-term ROI?
  2. Compatible with vision?

- o Be feasible:

  1. Need only available resources
  2. Be compatible with the internal organization.

- o Relationship with other strategies:

  1. Balanced portfolio?
  2. Consider flexibility?
  3. Exploit synergy?

Use of portfolio analysis in strategy evaluation

The use of portfolio analysis in assessing target markets was discussed earlier in this unit. This technique can be used to assess alternative strategic options. The resulting matrix will identify those strategies that would be the most attractive to pursue and those which a company should avoid.

Summary

- o Successful strategies rely on strategic fit between an organization's resources and capabilities and the environment in which it is operating. This process is referred to as the strategic alignment process. Segmentation, targeting and positioning, all play a critical role in the development of any successful marketing strategy. Segmentation is concerned with identifying groups of customers with similar needs and developing marketing mixes to satisfy these needs.

- o Consumer markets can be segmented by: customer characteristics (demographic, geographic, geodemographic and psychographic) and behavioural characteristics (benefits sought, usage frequency, usage status, purchase occasion, attitude towards the problem and buyer readiness stage).

- o Organizational markets can be segmented by macrofactors (organizational size, geographic location, SIC, end market served) and microfactors (choice criteria, buy class, level of innovation, etc.).

o Once appropriate segmentation bases have been identified and profiles developed for each segment it is necessary to select those segments to target and those to avoid. In order to do this, two issues need to be considered: the attractiveness of the segment and the extent to which an organization can match the needs of the segment.

o Positioning is the final stage of the STP process and is concerned with clearly and uniquely positioning a product or service in the minds of the customers. This can be achieved through the marketing mix.

o It is increasingly being recognized that brands can be very powerful and in fact can be the driving force of a successful marketing strategy. The importance of brands is being reflected by the inclusion of brand values on the balance sheet.

o There are four main branding strategies that can be adopted: company brand, individual brand names, company and individual brand and range branding.

o Companies are increasingly using their brands to stretch into related or new market sectors. The success of this will depend on the 'stretchability' of the brand.

o Many brands are being repositioned in the hope that they will be aligned with new market opportunities or to achieve a clearer positioning in the minds of the customers.

o Many companies are developing global brands in an attempt to benefit from economies of scale and to achieve a consistent brand image.

o Innovation is more than just developing new products. It relates to changes in products, processes and practices. Innovation has been referred to as the lifeblood of an organization and companies are increasingly looking for ways to improve their level of innovativeness.

o The new product development process has traditionally been regarded as a linear process. In order to speed up the development of new products it is increasingly being recognized that companies have to develop techniques such as parallel processing to increase the pace of development.

o Firms need to concentrate on creating the right organizational conditions and culture in order to facilitate effective innovation.

o Relationship marketing is concerned with developing long-term relationships with profitable customers rather than achieving one-off transactions. Research has shown that it is more profitable to retain existing customers than to gain new ones.

o Once an organization has identified various strategic options it must evaluate them in order to identify the 'best' strategy. Some firms may rely on 'gut feel', others develop criteria by which to evaluate the alternative strategies.

Further study and examination preparation

Extended knowledge

Bibliography

Aaker D (1998). *Strategic Market Management*, 5th Ed., John Wiley & Sons.

Ambler, T (1999). Sorting through the innovations to find real gold, *Marketing*, 11 February, p. 7.

Anon (1996). Juicy prospects for finance products, *Financial Times*, 16 May.

Booz, Allen and Hamilton (1982). *New Product management for the 1980's*, Booz, Allen and Hamilton.

Christopher M, Payne A and Ballantyne D (1993). *Relationship Marketing*, Butterworth-Heinemann.

Dairy Foods (2003). Be a trend setter, Dairy Foods, 2003 Frozen Novelties Planning Guide, pp. 6–7.

Davidson H (1997). *More Offensive Marketing*, Penguin.

Day G (1998). Building relationships that last, *Financial Times Mastering Management* series, 28 September.

De Souza (1999). Rules of Attraction, *Financial World*, February, pp. 28–31.

Doyle P (1998). *Marketing Management and Strategy*, 2nd Ed., Prentice-Hall.

Drummond G and Ensor J (2001). *Strategic Marketing Planning and Control*, 2nd Ed., Butterworth-Heinemann.

Eames, L (2000). Consumer Shopping animals: so what kind of Internet consumer are you – a gazelle or a gorilla?, *The Guardian*, 25 May.

Gray, R (2001). Products stretch out into services – brands can build reputations by creating experiences for customers, *Marketing*, 1 March.

Gronroos C (1991). The Marketing Strategy continuum, towards a marketing concept for the 1990's, *Management Decision*, 29:1, pp. 7–13.

Hooley GJ, Saunders JA and Piercy NF (1998). *Marketing Strategy and Competitive Positioning*, 2nd Ed., Prentice-Hall.

Janszen F (2000). *The age of Innovation*, FT Prentice-Hall.

Jobber D (2001). *Principles and Practice of Marketing*, 3rd Ed., McGraw Hill.

Johnson G and Scholes K (1999). *Exploring Corporate Strategy*, 5th Ed., Prentice-Hall.

Kleinman M (2002). Flora Pro-Activ to extend brand into milk and yoghurt, *Marketing*, August 29, pp. 1.

Kotler P, Armstrong G, Saunders J, and Wong V (1999). *Principles of Marketing*, 2nd European Ed., Prentice-Hall.

Lury G (2000). Extension heads: are brands elastic?, *Brand Strategy*, 4 September.

Marchese L (2002). Brand Schizophrenia: Today's epidemic, *Brandweek*, Vol 43 Issue 38, pp. 28.

Mazur L (2000). Good inventions need marketing to come real, *Marketing*, 14 December.

Murphy D (2001). Banking on a new identity – why do banks adopt separate on-line brands?, *Marketing*, p. 33.

Murphy J (1996). Customer Loyalty: happy customers add directly to the bottom line, *Financial Times, Mastering Management* series, 1 November.

Murphy P E and Staples W (1979). A Modernised Family Life Cycle, *Journal of Consumer Research*, June.

Thilo P and Leventhal B (1998). *The Use of Market Segmentation in Customer Management*, MRS Conference Papers.

Tomkins R (2000). Stretching a selling point, *Financial Times*, 26 May.

unit 9
implementation and control

Learning objectives

By the end of this unit you will:

o Be aware of, and be able to discuss, barriers to implementation of marketing plans

o Understand the importance of internal marketing

o Be able to develop an internal marketing plan

o Understand the importance of leadership and project management in the implementation of plans

o Know the dimensions of an effective marketing feedback and control system

o Identify suitable control mechanisms for measuring the success of plans.

Key definitions

Internal marketing – Has the goal of developing a type of marketing programme aimed at the internal market place in the company that parallels and matches the marketing programme aimed at the external market place of customers and competitors (Piercy, 2000, p. 592).

Project management – Project management involves achieving unity of purpose and setting achievable goals within given resources and timescales (Drummond and Ensor, 2001).

Control – Control consists of verifying whether targets have been achieved. Its purpose is to identify any problem or error in order to rectify them and prevent recurrence. It operates on everything: things, people and actions.

Benchmarking – A systematic and ongoing process of measuring and comparing an organization's business processes and achievements against acknowledged process leaders and/or key competitors, to facilitate improved performance (Drummond and Ensor, 2001).

Study Guide

- o   This unit will take you about 3 hours to work through
- o   We suggest that you take a further 3 hours to do the various activities and questions in this unit.

Introduction

The last three units have concentrated on the development of marketing strategies that help to achieve competitive advantage. This unit, in contrast, is concerned not with the development of plans, but with the implementation and control of them. The challenge of marketing lies not only in the ability to produce a winning marketing strategy but also more importantly, in transforming this plan into commercial reality. The implementation of plans is probably one of the most difficult tasks facing marketers. These difficulties arise because marketers have to rely on other people, some of whom may be in a different department, another city or even another country, to implement these plans. There are many barriers within organizations that can hamper implementation. In order to overcome these barriers there is a need for strong leadership and vision, effective management, sufficient resources and effective systems. This unit will highlight the techniques that marketers can use to facilitate effective implementation.

The second part of the unit will concentrate on aspects of control. Control is a vital component of any planning process. It is necessary in order to measure the success of the plan and to also inform future strategies. A range of financial and non-financial control measures are discussed.

Implementation

Marketing implementation is concerned with translating marketing plans into action. The marketing plan is the vehicle for communicating the strategy within the organization and addresses the issues of 'what' should happen and 'why' it should happen. Implementation is concerned with 'how' the strategy should be carried out, 'who' is to be responsible, 'when' things will take place and 'where' things will happen. Too often in organizations the implementation stage is overlooked and as a result a 'good strategy' can fail. It is important that organizations devote as much time and energy to the implementation of plans as they do to creating marketing strategies.

Strategy success

There are two factors that contribute to the success of a strategy:

- o   The strategy itself
- o   The ability to implement the strategy.

Bonoma (1984) suggested that the various combinations of these factors would lead to four alternative business outcomes, as illustrated in Figure 9.1.

Strategy

Appropriate   Inappropriate

<table>
<tr><td></td><td>Success</td><td>Chance</td></tr>
<tr><td></td><td>Problem</td><td>Failure</td></tr>
</table>

Good | Success | Chance
Bad | Problem | Failure

Execution skills

Figure 9.1 Strategy and execution
Adapted from Bonoma, 1984

Success
This is the most desirable situation where an effective strategy is well implemented.

Chance
In this situation the strategy is weak. However, if the strategy is well implemented there could be a chance that it will be successful.

Problem
This occurs often. A strong strategy has been developed but is poorly executed, resulting in problems. It is interesting to note from this model that it is probably better to have an inappropriate strategy that is effectively implemented than a good strategy that is poorly implemented.

Failure
This is the least desirable outcome – a strategy is neither appropriate nor effectively implemented.

Obviously this is a simplified model that will vary depending on the specific situation and the degree to which strategies are inappropriate. However, it does present a graphical representation of the importance of implementation in the planning process. The next section will identify the reasons why strategies are often ineffectively implemented.

Activity 9.1

Success of marketing plans

Refer to Figure 9.1 and consider which quadrant your organization's marketing strategies would normally fall into. Consider the reasons for your selection.

Marketing strategy failure and barriers to implementation

There are a variety of factors that can lead to marketing planning failure. One of the major contributions to failure occurs at the implementation stage. So why do plans fail?

According to Aaker (1998, p. 299), there are a number of pitfalls of the planning process:

- o **Spreadsheet mode** – many plans are based on income statements and balance sheets that are therefore internally driven. Often plans are an extension of last year's plans rather than being driven by external factors
- o **Focus on short-term financial objectives** – the results of this often involve under investment in critical areas to improve short-term financial performance
- o **Annual cycle constraints** – threats and opportunities do not coincide with annual planning cycles. Managers often breathe a sigh of relief once they have submitted their annual plans and forget about them until next year
- o **Plans without souls** – the danger of a formal planning process is that the resultant plan can lack creativity, and often the emotional commitment needed for successful implementation is missing
- o **Rigid plans** – firms are operating in dynamic environments and therefore plans should be flexible
- o **Lack of commitment to the final plan** – this can be a major problem. The strategic plan has little relevance to actual operations or the link between strategy and operations is not clear. There maybe also be a lack of commitment because people have not 'bought into' the plan.

The following could also be added to the list:

- o **Lack of time and other resources** – in some cases plans are developed but little thought is given to how they are to be financed or staffed
- o **Separation of planning from management** – this can result in a lack of commitment to the plan because those responsible for implementing the plan have not been involved in the planning process
- o **Implementation is recognized too late and is bolted on at the end** – implementation converts ideas into reality and requires planning. However, in many situations this is not recognized
- o **Lack of fit with organizational culture** – culture can have a major affect on the success of plans
- o **Does not fit well on the existing organizational structure** – new plans may cross departmental boundaries and therefore there can be conflict about ownership and budgets.

The major problem with implementation of plans lies in the failure of companies to manage change successfully. Inevitably a new strategy is going to result in the need for change. Many people are resistant to change because they are familiar with the status quo and fear the consequences of change. Therefore any new marketing strategy is going to be met with suspicion, unless the company can engender a culture that not only accepts change but also welcomes it. Marketing managers need to be aware of the internal barriers that exist, and then need to develop strategies to overcome these barriers. Organizations need to learn how to effectively manage change.

Activity 9.2

Internal barriers

Critically review the internal barriers to successful implementation that exist in your organization. What barriers exist, why are they present and how might they be overcome?

Managing change

The development of a culture that embraces change is an essential ingredient in the successful implementation of marketing strategy. The transition curve can help in understanding how people adapt to change (see Figure 9.2).

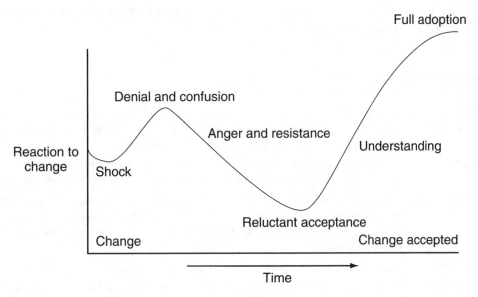

Figure 9.2 Reaction to change
Adapted from Wilson, 1993

This model is useful because it illustrates that eventually people will internalize the new status quo (or will have left the organization). Adapting to change can be a very painful process and the expression of anger and frustration is a natural part of this adaptation. The implications for marketers is that the acceptance of major changes in working practices and responsibilities will take time.

Activity 9.3

Managing change

Select one example of change that has been instigated within your organization. To what extent did the model in Figure 9.2 fit your experiences of this change? How can managers use this model to their advantage?

Implementation process

The development of a market orientation is a key ingredient of successful implementation. Without a customer-centred philosophy it is likely that any new strategy will encounter problems. The development of a market orientation is a key task of the marketing department. However, this is often a difficult process due to the inherent conflicts that exist within organizations. Market orientation is discussed in Unit 1 – Market-led planning and the strategic marketing process. Jobber (2001, p. 649) suggests the following process for ensuring the successful execution of the marketing plan:

1. Gain the support of key decision makers and overcome the opposition of others
2. Gain the required resources such as people, time and budget

3. Gain commitment of individuals and departments in the company who are involved in front-line implementation

4. Gain the co-operation of other departments needed to implement the plan.

Internal marketing, discussed below, can be used to facilitate this process.

Drummond and Ensor (2001) identify a number of factors that will contribute to the successful implementation of plans, illustrated in Table 9.1.

Table 9.1 Factors in successful implementation

Factor	Comment
Leadership	A strong and effective leader that is able to motivate and build teams is an essential ingredient for successful implementation
Culture	Culture refers to the shared values and beliefs. If a plan goes against the dominant culture it is likely the plan will fail, unless support is gained via internal marketing
Structure	Organizational structures not only denote levels of responsibility but also facilitate communication. Communication is a key aspect of implementation and organizations must ensure that the structures do not act as barriers to effective communication
Resources	Appropriate levels of resources should be available – time, money and staff
Control	Effective controls should be established to measure the progress and success of plans
Skills	Skills necessary for successful implementation include: technical/marketing skills, HRM skills and project management skills
Strategy	An appropriate and relevant strategy must be communicated to all participants
Systems	Effective systems should be in place. For example, marketing information systems that generate relevant and timely information

Adapted from Drummond and Ensor, 2001, p. 150

These factors are embodied in the 7-S model developed by McKinsey and Co as illustrated in Figure 9.3. This model consists of two categories of factors:

o Soft or HRM aspects – style, staff, shared values and skills
o Hard or process aspects – strategy, structure and systems.

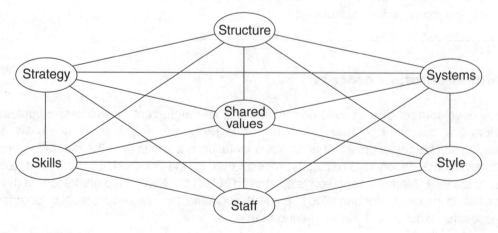

Figure 9.3 McKinsey 7-S framework
Adapted from Drummond and Ensor, 2001

Extended knowledge

For a more detailed discussion of the factors in successful implementation refer to:

Drummond and Ensor (2001) Chapter 13, pp. 251–256.

Jobber (2001) Chapter 19 provides a comprehensive discussion of implementation.

Assessing ease of implementation

The ease with which a strategy will be implemented can depend on strategic fit, i.e. the extent to which the strategy fits into current activities. The better the fit the more likely that implementation will succeed. The importance of the change and the degree of change will influence the extent to which implementation is successful. Figure 9.4 illustrates the relationship between change and importance.

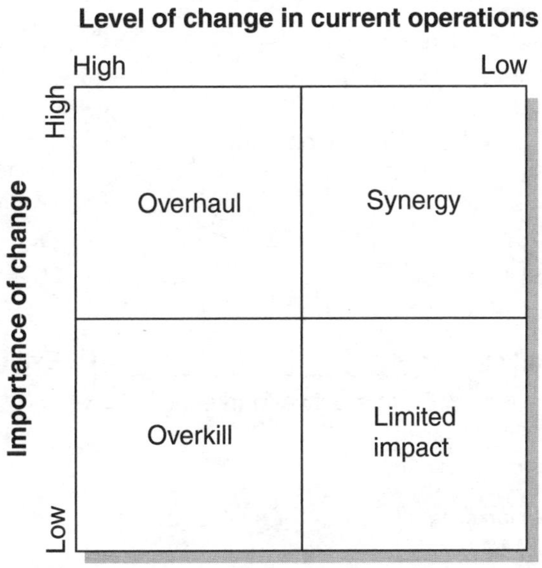

Level of change in current operations

	High	Low
High	Overhaul	Synergy
Low	Overkill	Limited impact

Importance of change

Figure 9.4 Strategic fit

- **Overhaul**: implementation will have a significant impact and is likely to meet much resistance
- **Synergy**: the degree of change is low but it is very important. Resistance should be limited as long as the level of change required is minimal. Problems can occur if ultimately more change is required than first anticipated
- **Limited impact**: the importance of the change and the degree of change are both minimal
- **Overkill**: high degree of change to deal with relatively unimportant changes. This can alienate staff because they do not appreciate why change has to take place.

Internal marketing

According to Berry (1986), 'The most important contribution the marketing department can make is to be exceptionally clever in getting everyone else in the organization to practise marketing'. This is essentially what internal marketing is concerned with.

Definition

> **Internal marketing** – Has the goal of developing a type of marketing programme aimed at the internal market place in the company that parallels and matches the marketing programme aimed at the external market place of customers and competitors (Piercy, 2000, p. 592).

Internal marketing can play a key role in the implementation of plans. It is concerned with adopting the principles and practices of external marketing to the internal market. Figure 9.5 illustrates that in fact there are three types of marketing that occur within an organization. The success of external marketing lies in the ability of the organization to satisfy the needs of the customer. Organizations are dependent on their staff to achieve this, particularly in high customer contact service businesses. Therefore, successful internal marketing is increasingly being seen as a prerequisite for effective external marketing.

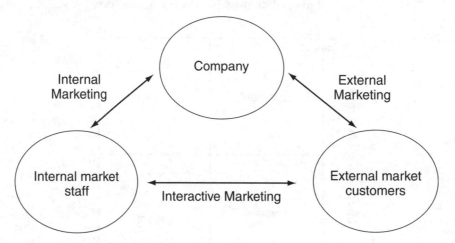

Figure 9.5 Three types of marketing
Adapted from Kotler et al., 1999

Internal marketing suggests that employees should be treated as internal customers and marketing plans need to be 'marketed' internally to gain acceptance and to ensure that employees understand the rationale behind the plans, can see how they can contribute to the success of the plan and importantly, 'buy into' the plan. This is not an easy task. A survey of employees in British companies with 1000 people or more, published by the Marketing & Communications Agency (MCA) and MORI, shows the scope of the challenge. The majority of employees said they feel undervalued, uninvolved and lack confidence in their organizations' leaders and vision (Mazur, 1999). Employees that lack motivation and confidence in their organizations are unlikely to buy into new ideas readily.

Increasingly organizations are recognizing that one of their greatest untapped assets is their own employees and that getting staff to act as brand ambassadors is one of the few things competitors cannot directly copy. Research among marketers at the Marketing Forum found that almost half the delegates now had a dedicated budget for internal marketing (Mazur, 1999).

Internal marketing is therefore not only important to ensure that staff buy into plans. It can also be used to transfer employees themselves into a source of competitive advantage.

Case history

Richer Sounds

Julian Richer, the founder of Richer Sounds, embraces the concept of internal marketing wholeheartedly. He is probably unaware that this is what he is doing but the result is the same. Richer refers to this as the Richer Way: 'make sure your staff are happy in order to give good customer service, increase turnover, reduce complaints, cut theft and absenteeism'. Richer Sounds consists of 27 hi-fi stores located in the cheaper ends of towns and specializes in end of line equipment. In the London Bridge shop the average sales per square foot are £5,500 compared with £630 at PC World and £520 at Currys. The general philosophy of these stores is to 'pile 'em high, sell them cheap but also have great customer service'. Richer Sounds' competitive advantage is its staff. Julian Richer realized that if staff were happy and motivated they were more likely to provide a better service to the customers. His methods of creating a happy workforce are numerous and legendary, including free access for staff to seven holiday homes in the UK and Paris (regardless of sales performance), trips on the Orient Express for staff who come up with the best ideas, a fiver every month to each employee so they can go down to the pub and brainstorm, and use of a Bentley or Jaguar for a month for the best performing shop. The company annual attitude survey shows that 95% of staff love working for the company, which speaks volumes about the success of Julian Richer's techniques.

Other companies, such as Asda and Halifax, are now recognizing the benefits of the 'Richer Way' and have employed Julian Richer as a consultant to advice them on staff motivation schemes and internal communication issues

Source: Beenstock (1998), www.Lexis-Nexis.com

The internal marketing plan

The internal marketing plan should take the same format as an external marketing plan with objectives, strategy, market segmentation, marketing mix programmes and evaluation.

Internal market segmentation

Internal markets could be segmented in a number of different ways such as by job function, role or location. However, these methods may not be the most appropriate. It may be useful to segment according to the extent to which people are likely to accept the proposed change. Jobber (2001) suggests that three different segments can be identified:

o **Supporters** – likely to gain from the change
o **Neutrals** – will neither gain nor lose
o **Opposers** – likely to lose from the change or are traditional opponents.

A separate marketing mix can then be developed for each of these segments. It may also be possible to identify influential individuals that are opinion leaders.

Internal marketing mix
Product
The internal product can be viewed as the marketing plan, the company itself or even the individual's own job or function. Employees need the benefits of the 'product' communicated to them.

Promotion

This is a crucial element of the mix and refers to any medium that can be used to communicate with the target groups. The promotional mix could include newsletters, discussion groups, presentations, workshops, the use of the company Intranet etc. It is also concerned with the message that is being transmitted. A key aspect of internal communication is that it is two way. It is important to include staff in the process from the beginning rather than just telling them what is going to happen.

External communication is also an important feature of an internal communication plan. It is essential that any external communication be in line with the messages being transmitted internally. This will ensure that staff are receiving consistent messages from all sources. In the worse-case scenario external communication can even alienate staff. This is exactly what happened to Boots, when its staff complained about a TV campaign that portrayed Boots' staff as incompetent.

Distribution

This refers to the places where the product and communication will be delivered to internal customers such as seminars, meetings, away days, informal conversations, company Intranet, etc. There is some overlap between distribution and communication mediums.

Price

Price relates to the price the staff have to pay as a result of accepting the plan. Change may result in change of job role, loss of status, office moves etc.

Internal marketing execution

Successful execution of the internal plan is reliant on three key skills (Jobber, 2001, p. 658):

- o **Persuasion** – the ability to develop a persuasive argument and to support words with action
- o **Negotiation** – it is likely that some negotiations will have to take place so that all parties are happy
- o **Politics** – organizations are made up of people, all with their own personal agendas. Therefore it is essential that the sources of power are identified and used to help implement the plan.

Internal marketing evaluation

In order to evaluate the success of internal marketing programmes appropriate measures have to be used, such as:

- o The extent of support of key players
- o Employee satisfaction levels
- o Reduced customer complaints
- o Higher customer satisfaction scores.

Many companies are now conducting regular surveys to monitor levels of staff motivation, acceptance of the marketing concept and perceptions of the organization. In addition, it could be argued that if internal marketing is being effective then it should be having an impact on external marketing. By measuring levels of customer satisfaction and numbers of customer complaints it may give an indication of the success of internal marketing programmes.

Potential problems

There are a number of potential problems associated with internal marketing. For example:

- o Opposers create convincing counter arguments
- o Insufficient time to implement effective internal plans

○ High staff turnover that causes problems in ensuring all staff are involved
○ Low-paid shop (front-line) staff – this may result in a 'why should I bother?' attitude
○ Cost–internal marketing programmes can be costly and many organizations are still slow to recognize their importance.

Activity 9.4

Internal marketing

○ To what extent do you think your organization has embraced the concept of internal marketing?
○ What impact does this have on their external marketing activities?
○ How has your company embraced technology, e.g. an intranet in an attempt to improve their internal marketing/communications? How effective is this strategy?

Extended knowledge

For further reading on internal marketing refer to the following sources:

Jobber (2001), Chapter 19.

Piercy (2000), Chapter 14.

Drummond and Ensor (2001), Chapter 13.

Question 9.1

Internal marketing

Answer Question 2 from the June 2001 Planning and Control paper on internal marketing. Go to www.cimeduhub.com to access specimen answers for this question. Question 2 from the June 1998 paper was also on internal marketing.

Project management

The ability to manage projects effectively is a key aspect of implementing plans. Project management is concerned with the achievement of predetermined goals within a certain timescale and with a limited amount of resources. The skills associated with project management are the same in whatever context they are being used. They are highly applicable to the implementation of marketing projects that are often complex, involve and impact on, a wide variety of people from different areas of the business. It is inevitable that project managers will have to deal with 'opposers' and overcome other barriers to implementation. It is essential that project managers acquire the necessary skills to integrate activities, motivate participants, develop a sense of teamwork and monitor progress. Drummond and Ensor (2001) suggest five common tasks of project management (Table 9.2).

Definition

Project management – Involves achieving unity of purpose and setting achievable goals within given resources and timescales (Drummond and Ensor, 2001).

Table 9.2 Common tasks in project management

Task	Comment
Objective setting	It is important that objectives are SMART (Specific, Measurable, Action, Realistic and Timebound)
Planning	This involves breaking down the project into manageable tasks, co-ordinating activities and monitoring progress
Delegation	The key to successful management is the recognition that you cannot do everything yourself
Team building	An essential skill for a project manager is the ability to build a successful team
Crisis management	There will be times when things do not go to plan and urgent action is required. In order to try to anticipate likely problems, scenario planning can be used

Adapted from Drummond and Ensor, 2001, p. 262

Extended knowledge

For a more detailed discussion of project management see:

Drummond and Ensor (2001) Chapter 13, p. 261–265.

Question 9.2

Overcoming internal barriers

Answer Question 3 from the December 2002 Planning and Control paper on overcoming internal barriers. Go to www.cimeduhub.com to access specimen answers for this question. Question 4 from the June 1999 paper was also on overcoming internal cultural barriers.

Exam hint

Successful implementation of marketing strategies is often an important aspect of the Analysis and Decision exam.

Extended knowledge

For an interesting article on perceptions of marketing within organizations and strategies for improving its internal standing see the following article:

Wicks M (2002), Marketing the Marketing Department, located at the CIM's 'What's New in Marketing Website' www.wnim.com/issue13/pages/marketingdepsprint.htm

Control

The marketing planning process would not be complete without some form of evaluation of performance and assessment as to whether the marketing objectives have been achieved. There are three main components of control:

1. Setting targets/objectives against which performance can be measured
2. Measurement of performance
3. Corrective action.

A key aspect of control is that it should lead to corrective action. Failure to meet targets may be as a result of (a) unrealistic objectives (and therefore targets may have to be reviewed) or (b) poor performance of individuals (and therefore additional training, advice, etc., may have to be offered). If targets are met then individuals should be rewarded and objectives may also have to be reviewed for the future.

Definition

Control – Consists of verifying whether targets have been achieved. Its purpose is to identify any problems or errors in order to rectify them and prevent recurrence. It operates on everything: things, people and actions.

Evaluation of marketing plans can also be used to inform future marketing decisions. Therefore, the planning and control cycle is a continuous feedback loop. The objectives and control measures must be fully integrated to ensure that what is intended to happen is in fact what is evaluated. The balanced scorecard is a useful framework for ensuring that objectives are linked to performance measures. The balanced scorecard also highlights the importance of ensuring that a balanced range of objectives has been developed. The balanced scorecard is discussed in Unit 6 – Strategic intent.

Effective control systems

The most obvious question, yet one that is frequently overlooked is, 'What is it that we seek to control?' Too often marketers focus on what is easy to measure rather than what is important. Therefore, much effort is put into measuring quantifiable processes such as market share, efficiency of sales staff or number of hits on the website rather than important issues such as customer satisfaction. Control measures can broadly be categorized into financial and non-financial measures.

The linkage between control and the planning process is summarized in Figure 9.6

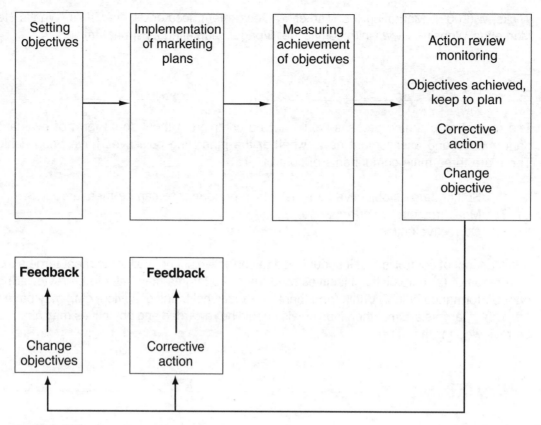

Figure 9.6 The control process

Factors influencing control measures

The marketing control process has been referred to as 'closing the (planning) loop'. Most marketing practitioners have experienced a planning situation where considerable effort has been placed on the planning activity but people have been 'too busy' to review and change the plan, an activity frequently left to the end of the marketing plan year, by which time it is too late. Control issues have moved towards the top of the marketing agenda. The specific control measures selected will depend on:

1. Hierarchy – i.e. the hierarchical level within the organization that is being considered
2. Whether it is an interim or final control
3. Whether control is being used to monitor efficiency or effectiveness.

Hierarchy
The place of the marketer in the organizational hierarchy has a large influence on the type of marketing planning which is undertaken and consequently on the planning and implementation controls. The level of focus and the time horizon are two of the main differences that result from hierarchy. Control measures for long-term time horizons for the whole organization (strategic corporate marketing planning) are very different to those that are required for tactical planning for a product division.

Interim or final control
Final controls are those that are linked to the planning cycle, usually one year. Such controls are usually directly linked to marketing objectives, e.g. increase market share by 6 percentage points. Control in this case is straightforward, whether or not the marketing objective has been

met. Interim controls are more complex. For example, how can we tell that we are on target to achieve a 6 percentage points increase in market share over the year? This is highly unlikely to occur in terms of an increase of 0.5 percentage points each month.

Use to monitor efficiency or effectiveness

This is measured by the ratio of inputs over outputs and was discussed in Unit 5 – Financial analysis and techniques for developing a view of the future. Writers often make the distinction between efficiency (which indicates how well resources are used) and effectiveness (whether particular actions should be taken, i.e. is the business moving in the correct direction?). In the context of control, efficiency tends to be measured, while effectiveness is analysed and considered in formulating marketing objectives and strategy following analysis of the marketing environment. It is essential that control measures focus on both effectiveness and efficiency.

Characteristics of effective control systems

In order to develop effective and meaningful control measures it is essential they are flexible and adhere to the following principles (suggested by Drummond and Ensor, 2001):

- o **Involvement** – participants in the control process should be involved in the development of the control measures. If not, there is a danger that staff will fail to take ownership of the measures.
- o **Target setting** – objectives should be quantifiable and achievable. These targets should be agreed and communicated in advance.
- o **Focus** – recognize the difference between the source and the symptoms of the problem
- o **Effectiveness** – ensure that what is being measured is the right thing: 'what gets measured gets done'.
- o **Management by exception** – develop tolerance zones and take corrective action if results fall outside this zone.
- o **Action** – effective control systems should promote action rather than just identifying problems.

Problems with control systems

Developing relevant and effective control systems is a challenging task for marketers. Potential problems with control systems include:

- o They can be costly and it is important that the benefits of the system outweigh the costs
- o Rigid control measures have also been blamed for stifling creativity because people have to conform to pre-set targets
- o They can encourage a culture of inspection rather than of development and continuous improvement
- o The systems can tend to deal with the symptoms rather than exposing the underlying causes.

There are a variety of ways of classifying the various forms of control. For the purpose of this text control measures will be categorized as either financial or non-financial.

Financial control measures

Financial control measures are an essential part of the control process. Three main types of financial controls are discussed: ratios, budgets and variance analysis.

Ratios

Financial ratios are commonly employed as a means of control. Ratios are a simple and effective means of measuring performance. However, they should not be viewed in isolation. Ratios can be used for two main purposes:

o   Trend analysis – comparisons can be made over time
o   Comparative analysis – ratios can be compared with industry standards or the competition.

Ratios can be classified into four main categories:

o   Profitability ratios – concerned with measuring a firm's ability to produce profit
o   Liquidity ratios – concerned with the ability of a company to remain solvent
o   Debt ratios – concerned with a firm's ability to manage debt
o   Activity – relates to the effectiveness of a firm to generate activity.

For further discussion of ratios refer to Unit 5 – Financial analysis and techniques for developing a view of the future.

Budgets

These are the most commonly applied means of control. Forecasts are translated into budgets in an attempt to ensure that key financial targets are achieved. Budgets therefore translate the marketing strategy into financial terms. All plans, whether marketing, production or HRM, are translated into financial terms in the form of a budget. It is then possible to co-ordinate the activities of all departments into a single master plan. Budgets can be set in a variety of ways:

o   Based on the past – many organizations develop budgets based on previous budgets taking into account inflation, etc.
o   Objective and task (zero-based) – budgets are based on the cost of achieving a set of given objectives
o   Activity related – for example budgets are set as a percentage of forecasted sales
o   Competitive parity – budgets are based on what the competition are spending.

Budgets are an essential control measure but their value depends to a large extent on the appropriateness of the methods by which they have been set. Many companies are now recognizing that the budgeting system is perhaps the greatest barrier to change. Budgets tend to reinforce command and control management and undermine attempts at organizational change. The annual budgeting cycle can be inappropriate for companies facing rapidly changing markets. Budgets tend to encourage incremental thinking, the extrapolation of existing trends with little vision of the future and can even stifle breakthroughs in improvement.

Variance analysis

Variance analysis examines the variation between actual and planned results and can be applied to a range of activities. For example, actual expenditure is compared with budgeted forecasts to identify the reasons for the differences.

Non-financial controls

Non-financial controls can be applied at all levels within an organization – strategic, operation and tactical. The advantages and disadvantages of non-financial controls are summarized in Table 9.3 and Table 9.4 (adapted from Ittner and Larcker, 2000).

Table 9.3 Advantages of non-financial measures in providing improved control criteria

Alignment to long-term organizational strategies	Financial control measures tend to be aligned with annual or shorter term accounting measures. These are not directly linked to key competitive issues such as competitive strength or customer alignment
Closer linkage to the drivers of industry success	Drivers of success in many industries are linked to factors that cannot readily be measured in a company account. These include, for example, innovativeness, intellectual capital, organizational culture
Non-financial indicators provide improved indicators of future financial performance	The only financial indicator of investment into customer loyalty programmes, or in research and development activities, is a reduction in the current year's profits. Financial measures provide no indication of the potential future, beneficial impact. Non-financial measures can indicate improvements in customer loyalty levels and in customer perception of products
Measures beyond management control	Financial measures are generally assumed to be within management control. However, much is beyond management control and of great impact on the business. Non-financial measures can provide vital information on the marketing environment on 'uncontrollable areas', e.g. changes in the economy, in social values, in legal decisions etc.

Table 9.4 Disadvantages/problems of non-financial measures

Time and cost	Financial measures are relatively inexpensive control mechanisms in contrast to many non-financial measures, which require, in some cases, specially commissioned research to implement – for example consumer attitude measurement
Problems of comparison	A variety of measures is possible which creates problems of comparison. In addition, when confronted by many measures, which measures should be considered more important where measures indicate conflicting conclusions (e.g. customer satisfaction versus market share versus repeat purchases)
Lack of clear causal links	Lack of clarity in matching non-financial measures to tangible objectives. Xerox, for example, placed greater weighting on customer satisfaction surveys. Implicit in this is that customer satisfaction is linked to financial performance. Research found this not to be the case: consequently Xerox changed their emphasis to customer loyalty, which was found to be correlated with financial performance
Lack of rigour	One criterion against which to judge measures is statistical rigour, i.e. that results are repeatable and have assigned probabilities. Non-financial measures are frequently statistically unreliable and can potentially report random events

Performance appraisal

This is concerned with trying to maximize the performance of staff either individually or in teams. Performance appraisal focuses on the control and development of staff through the setting of objectives and the review of their performance. Areas of strengths and weaknesses may be identified and training needs developed to overcome the weaknesses. Many organizations implement an annual appraisal scheme for staff to review progress and establish objectives for the next year. Effective appraisals call for managers to have good people skills and the process should be seen as a positive and constructive experience. Three key skills are necessary:

o   Reviewing performance
o   Giving feedback
o   Counselling.

Benchmarking

Benchmarking is a technique in which individual processes within the value chain are compared between organizations. This could include competitors, market leaders or successful internal processes. The objective is to compare performance with that of market leaders with a view to identifying best practice and continual improvement. Benchmarking assesses small processes within the organization, consequently very different organizations may be used in the comparison. For example:

o   An airline may benchmark on food preparation and serving processes against a leading fast-food restaurant
o   A restaurant chain may benchmark on inventory management against a leading supermarket group
o   A large legal consulting firm may benchmark on customer relationship marketing against a leading financial services organization.

Definition

Benchmarking – A systematic and ongoing process of measuring and comparing an organization's business processes and achievements against acknowledged process leaders and/or key competitors, to facilitate improved performance (Drummond and Ensor, 2001).

Benchmarking may be considered in five stages:

o   The specification of the precise processes which are to be benchmarked and how these are to be measured
o   Selection of the organization against which to benchmark, e.g. the leading organization in the processes of interest
o   Identification of the differences in performance and the reasons for under-performance
o   Planning of how improvements are to be made to achieve best practice
o   Setting up of a monitoring and assessment programme to control the delivery of improved performance.

Case history

Benchmarking in practice

Plastic Engineering, based in Leamington Spa, Warwickshire, sells £8.5 million of safety systems such as brakes and steering columns to the motor industry each year. It has been under increasing pressure to cut prices to remain competitive against overseas manufacturers. The company decided to use the Benchmarking Index to give an objective measure of their performance against the opposition. The company provided all the relevant data and information and then received a Benchmarking report that compared the company's performance with that of 200 other plastic companies on a wide range of indicators such as delivery times, stock turn, productivity per worker and wastage rates. It also measured against a wider sample in areas such as customer and staff satisfaction.

The results confirmed much that the company already knew, but did not have the courage to face. They were in the best 25% of companies in the survey in the areas of product quality and customer satisfaction. However, the firm did not score well on management/staff communication, stock turn and productivity per worker.

As a result of these findings the company made major changes to its working practices. The old assembly line was replaced by team working. Functional divisions were replaced by cell manufacture, investment in training was doubled and exchange visits were organized with companies achieving best practice in areas targeted for improvement.

The changes brought valuable benefits. Plastic Engineering reduced its stock of raw materials by 19% by encouraging suppliers to deliver just in time. The shopfloor was less cluttered and the capital tied up in stock was cut from £240,000 to £200,000. Better housekeeping resulted in a 5% decline in wastage. The business improved its on-time delivery rate from 60% to 98% in six months. The Benchmark Index cost the company £400 and the managing director believed this was the best investment they ever made.

Source: Sumner Smith (2000), www.Lexis-Nexis.com

Balanced scorecard

The balanced scorecard is a framework, developed by Kaplan and Norton (1992), that acknowledges the various perspectives of different stakeholder groups, whilst at the same time linking objectives with performance measures. This model was outlined in Unit 6 – Strategic intent. However, it is worth revisiting it at this stage to highlight its role in the control stage of the planning cycle. Refer to Figure 6.5 for an overview of the various performance measures that may be used. The model suggests that objectives and subsequent performance measures should relate to four distinct areas: the customer perspective, the financial perspective, the internal perspective and innovation and learning. This approach highlights the importance of developing a balanced set of objectives and ensures that organizations do not place all their emphasis in one area, such as finance.

Marketing performance control

Kotler et al. (1999) identify four main types of controls for marketing activity:

o **Annual planning** – this involves evaluating the performance of the previous year's marketing activities such as sales, market share, customer satisfaction.
o **Profitability** – profitability is a major concern of any marketer. Profitability can be calculated not only by product but also by distribution channel, market segment or even individual customer.
o **Efficiency control** – this is concerned with optimization of assets. For example, return on promotional spend. Figure 9.7 illustrates some of the various measures that can be used to evaluate the marketing mix.
o **Strategic control** – it is imperative that marketing activity is ultimately helping to achieve organizational goals. This can be undertaken in the format of the marketing audit that will review all marketing activity.

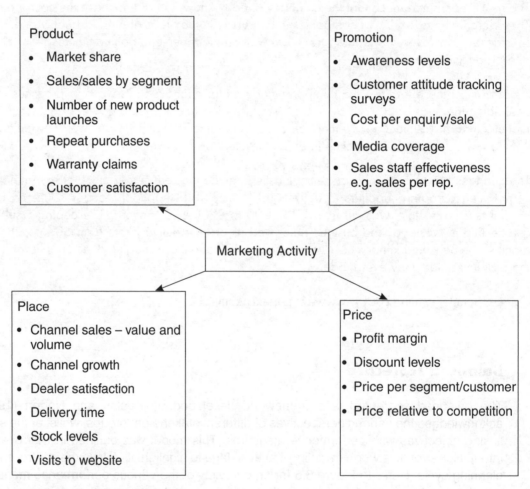

Figure 9.7 Controlling the marketing mix
Adapted from Drummond and Ensor, 2001, p.139

Extended knowledge

For further reading on control refer to: Drummond G and Ensor J (2001), Chapter 14.

Activity 9.5

Control mechanisms

Identify your own organization's control mechanisms. Classify them according to financial and non-financial controls.

How effective are these controls in helping to improve the marketing planning process?

What recommendations would you make to improve the control process?

Question 9.3

Control systems

Answer Question 7 from the December 2002 Planning and Control paper on control systems. Go to www.cimeduhub.com to access specimen answers for this question. Question 7 from the December 2001 paper was also on effective control systems.

Summary

o Marketing implementation is concerned with translating marketing strategy into action. This very important stage is often overlooked by many organizations. In some cases plans fail, not because they are inappropriate plans, but because they are poorly implemented.

o There are many barriers that exist to successful implementation of plans such as mechanistic planning cycles, focus on the short-term, rigid plans, lack of commitment to the plan, lack of time and other resources and lack of fit with organizational culture and structure.

o The development of an organizational culture that welcomes change is a key ingredient in the successful implementation of marketing plans. Managers need to be familiar with the process of change and the impact it has on people in order to effectively manage change.

o The development of a market orientation is an essential task of the marketing department. Without a customer-centred philosophy it is likely that any new plans will encounter problems.

o In order to achieve successful implementation of plans it is necessary to consider leadership, organizational culture, organizational structure, available resources, control mechanisms, skills, the strategy itself and the systems.

o Internal marketing is concerned with applying the principles and practices used for external marketing to the internal marketplace. This will ensure that internal marketing programmes will mirror those of the external marketplace. Internal marketing can play an important role in facilitating the successful implementation of plans.

- o The skills associated with project management, such as objective setting, planning, delegation, team building and crisis management, are all skills that can help to implement often complex marketing projects.

- o The final stage of the marketing planning process is the development of control mechanisms to monitor the success of marketing plans. The outputs of these measurements should be linked to action, in the form of either corrective action or the revisiting of marketing objectives. The results can also be used to inform future decisions.

- o Control mechanisms should be developed that measure not only efficiency but also effectiveness. Control measures can be categorized into either financial or non-financial control mechanisms.

- o Financial controls generally include the use of ratios, budgets and variance analysis. Non-financial controls can be applied at any level within the organization.

- o Benchmarking is a key non-financial control technique where organizations measure their performance, i.e. benchmark, against other organizations in an attempt to identify 'best practice'.

- o There are four main types of controls for marketing activity: annual planning, profitability, efficiency control and strategic control.

Further study and examination preparation

Extended knowledge

Bibliography

Aaker D (1998). *Strategic Market Management*, 5th Ed., John Wiley & Sons.

Beenstock S (1998). Ninety five percent of this man's staff say they love working for him. What's his secret?, *Management Today*, April.

Berry (1986). Big Ideas in services marketing, *Journal of Consumer Marketing*, Spring.

Bonoma T (1984). Making your Marketing Strategies Work, *Harvard Business Review*, 62:2, pp. 68–76.

Drummond G and Ensor J (2001). *Strategic Marketing Planning and Control*, 2nd Ed., Butterworth-Heinemann.

Ittner C and Larcker D (2000). A bigger yardstick – Company financial data has limitations as a measure of company performance, *Financial Times, Mastering Management* Series, 16th October.

Jobber D (2001). *Principles and Practice of Marketing*, 3rd Ed., McGraw Hill.

Kaplan R S and Norton D P (1992). The Balanced Scorecard: Measures that drive performance, *Harvard Business Review*, 70:1, pp. 71–79.

Kotler P, Armstrong G, Saunders J and Wong V (1999). *Principles of Marketing*, 2nd European Ed., Prentice-Hall.

Mazur L (1999). Unleashing employee's true value, *Marketing*, 29 April.

Piercy N (2000). *Market-Led Strategic Change*, 2nd Ed., Butterworth-Heinemann.

Sumner Smith D (2000). Firms get ahead by measuring themselves against the best, *Sunday Times*, 15 October.

Wilson G (1993). *Making Change Happen*, Pitman.

appendix 1
guidance on examination preparation

Preparing for your examination

You are now nearing the final phase of your studies and it is time to start the hard work of exam preparation.

During your period of study you will have become used to absorbing large amounts of information. You will have tried to understand and apply aspects of knowledge that may have been very new to you, while some of the information provided may have been more familiar. You may even have undertaken many of the activities that are positioned frequently throughout your Coursebook, which will have enabled you to apply your learning in practical situations. But whatever the state of your knowledge and understanding, do not allow yourself to fall into the trap of thinking that you know enough, you understand enough, or even worse, that you can just take it as it comes on the day.

Never underestimate the pressure of the CIM examination.

The whole point of preparing this text for you is to ensure that you never take the examination for granted, and that you do not go into the exam unprepared for what might come your way for three hours at a time.

One thing's for sure: there is no quick fix, no easy route, no waving a magic wand and finding you know it all.

Whether you have studied alone, in a CIM study centre, or through distance learning, you now need to ensure that this final phase of your learning process is tightly managed, highly structured and objective.

As a candidate in the examination, your role will be to convince the Senior Examiner for this subject that you have credibility. You need to demonstrate to the examiner that you can be trusted to undertake a range of challenges in the context of marketing, that you are able to capitalize on opportunities and manage your way through threats.

You should prove to the Senior Examiner that you are able to apply knowledge, make decisions, respond to situations and solve problems.

Very shortly we are going to look at a range of revision and exam preparation techniques, and at time management issues, and encourage you towards developing and implementing your own revision plan, but before that, let's look at the role of the Senior Examiner.

A bit about the senior examiners!

You might be quite shocked to read this, but while it might appear that the examiners are 'relentless question masters' they actually want you to be able to answer the questions and pass the exams! In fact, they would derive no satisfaction or benefits from failing candidates; quite the contrary, they develop the syllabus and exam papers in order that you can learn and then apply that learning effectively so as to pass your examinations. Many of the examiners have said in the past that it is indeed psychologically more difficult to fail students than pass them.

Many of the hints and tips you find within this Appendix have been suggested by the Senior Examiners and authors of the Coursebook series. Therefore you should consider them carefully and resolve to undertake as many of the elements suggested as possible.

The Chartered Institute of Marketing has a range of processes and systems in place within the Examinations Division to ensure that fairness and consistency prevail across the team of examiners, and that the academic and vocational standards that are set and defined are indeed maintained. In doing this, CIM ensures that those who gain the CIM Certificate, Advanced Certificate and Postgraduate Diploma, are worthy of the qualification and perceived as such in the view of employers, actual and potential.

Part of what you will need to do within the examination is be 'examiner friendly' – that means you have to make sure they get what they ask for. This will make life easier for you and for them.

Hints and tips for 'examiner friendly' actions are as follows:

o   Show them that you understand the basis of the question, by answering *precisely* the question asked, and not including just about everything you can remember about the subject area.

o   Read their needs – how many points is the question asking you to address?

o   Respond to the question appropriately. Is the question asking you to take on a role? If so, take on the role and answer the question in respect of the role. For example, you could be positioned as follows:

   'You are working as a Marketing Assistant at Nike UK' or 'You are a Marketing Manager for an Engineering Company' or 'As Marketing Manager write a report to the Managing Partner'.

   These examples of role-playing requirements are taken from questions in past papers.

o   Deliver the answer in the format requested. If the examiner asks for a memo, then provide a memo; likewise, if the examiner asks for a report, then write a report. If you do not do this, in some instances you will fail to gain the necessary marks required to pass.

o   Take a business-like approach to your answers. This enhances your credibility. Badly ordered work, untidy work, lack of structure, headings and subheadings can be off-putting. This would be unacceptable in the work situation, likewise it will be unacceptable in the eyes of the Senior Examiners and their marking teams.

o   Ensure the examiner has something to mark: give them substance, relevance, definitions, illustration and demonstration of your knowledge and understanding of the subject area.

o   See the examiner as your potential employer, or ultimate consumer/customer. The whole purpose and culture of marketing is about meeting customers' needs. Try this approach – it works wonders.

o   Provide a strong sense of enthusiasm and professionalism in your answers; support it with relevant up-to-date examples and apply them where appropriate.

o   Try to do something that will make your exam paper a little bit different – make it stand out in the crowd.

All of these points might seem quite logical to you, but often in the panic of the examination they 'go out of the window'. Therefore it is beneficial to remind ourselves of the importance of the examiner. He/she is the 'ultimate customer' – and we all know customers hate to be disappointed.

As we move on, some of these points will be revisited and developed further.

About the examination

In all examinations, with the exception of Marketing in Practice at Certificate level and Analysis and Decision at Diploma level, the paper is divided into two parts.

   o   Part A – Mini-case study = 40 per cent of the marks
   o   Part B – Option choice questions (choice of three questions from seven) = 60 per cent of the marks.

Let's look at the basis of each element.

The mini-case study

This is based on a mini-case or scenario with one question, possibly subdivided into between two and four points, but totalling 40 per cent of marks overall.

In essence, you, the candidate, are placed in a problem-solving role through the medium of a short scenario. On occasions, the scenario may consist of an article from a journal in relation to a well-known organization: for example, in the past Interflora, EasyJet and Philips, among others, have been used as the basis of the mini-case.

Alternatively, it will be based upon a fictional company, and the examiner will have prepared it in order that the right balance of knowledge, understanding, application and skills is used.

Approaches to the mini-case study

When undertaking the mini-case study there are a number of key areas you should consider.

Structure/content

The mini-case that you will be presented with will vary slightly from paper to paper, and of course from one examination to the next. Normally the scenario presented will be 400–500 words long and will centre on a particular organization and its problems or may even relate to a specific industry.

The length of the mini-case study means that usually only a brief outline is provided of the situation, the organization and its marketing problems, and you must therefore learn to cope with analysing information and preparing your answer on the basis of a very limited amount of detail.

Time management

There are many differing views on time management and the approaches you can take to managing your time within the examination. You must find an approach to suit your way of working, but always remember, whatever you do, you must ensure that you allow enough time to complete the examination. Unfinished exams mean lost marks.

A typical example of managing time is as follows:

Your paper is designed to assess you over a three-hour period. With 40 per cent of the marks being allocated to the mini-case, it means that you should dedicate somewhere around 75 minutes of your time to both read and write up the answer on this mini-case. Some students, however, will prefer to allocate nearer half of their time (90 minutes) on the mini-case, so that they can read and fully absorb the case and answer the questions in the context of it. This is also acceptable as long as you ensure that you work extremely 'SMART' for the remaining time in order to finish the examination.

Do not forget that while there is only one question within the mini-case, it can have a number of components. You must answer all the components in that question, which is where the balance of times comes into play.

Knowledge/skills tested

Throughout all the CIM papers, your knowledge, skills and ability to apply those skills will be tested. However, the mini-cases are used particularly to test application, i.e. your ability to take your knowledge and apply it in a structured way to a given scenario. The examiners will be looking at your decision-making ability, your analytical and communication skills and, depending on the level, your ability as a manager to solve particular marketing problems.

When the examiner is marking your paper, he/she will be looking to see how you differentiate yourself, looking at your own individual 'unique selling points'. The examiner will also want to see if you can personally apply the knowledge or whether you are only able to repeat the textbook materials.

Format of answers

On many occasions, and within all examinations, you will most likely be given a particular communication method to use. If this is the case, you must ensure that you adhere to the requirements of the examiner. This is all part of meeting customer needs.

The likely communication tools you will be expected to use are as follows:

- Memorandum
- Memorandum/report
- Report
- Briefing notes
- Presentation

- o Press release
- o Advertisement
- o Plan.

Make sure that you familiarize yourself with these particular communication tools and practise using them to ensure that, on the day, you will be able to respond confidently to the communication requests of the examiner. Look back at the Customer Communications text at Certificate level to familiarize yourself with the potential requirements of these methods.

By the same token, while communication methods are important, so is meeting the specific requirements of the question. This means you must understand what is meant by the precise instruction given. **Note the following terms carefully:**

- o **Identify** select key issues, point out key learning points, establish clearly what the examiner expects you to identify.
- o **Illustrate** the examiner expects you to provide examples, scenarios and key concepts that illustrate your learning.
- o **Compare and contrast** look at the range of similarities between the two situations, contexts or even organizations. Then compare them, i.e. ascertain and list how activities, features, etc. agree or disagree. Contrasting means highlighting the differences between the two.
- o **Discuss** questions that have 'discuss' in them offer a tremendous opportunity for you to debate, argue, justify your approach or understanding of the subject area – caution – it is not an opportunity to waffle.
- o **Briefly explain** this means being succinct, structured and concise in your explanation, within the answer. Make your points clear, transparent and relevant.
- o **State** present in a clear, brief format.
- o **Interpret** expound the meaning of, make clear and explicit what it is you see and understand within the data provided.
- o **Outline** provide the examiner with the main concepts and features being asked for and avoid minor technical details. Structure will be critical here, or else you could find it difficult to contain your answer.
- o **Relate** show how different aspects of the syllabus connect together.
- o **Evaluate** review and reflect upon an area of the syllabus, a particular practice, an article, etc., and consider its overall worth in respect of its use as a tool or a model and its overall effectiveness in the role it plays.

Source: Worsam, Mike, *How to Pass Marketing*, Croner, 1989.

Your approach to mini-cases

There is no one right way to approach and tackle a mini-case study, indeed it will be down to each individual to use their own creativity in tackling the tasks presented. You will have to use your initiative and discretion about how best to approach the mini-case. Having said this, however, there are some basic steps you can take.

- o Ensure that you read through the case study at least twice before making any judgements, starting to analyse the information provided, or indeed writing the answers.

- o On the third occasion read through the mini-case and, using a highlighter, start marking the essential and relevant information critical to the content and context. Then turn your attention to the question again, this time reading slowly and carefully to assess what it is you are expected to do. Note any instructions that the examiner gives you, and then start to plan how you might answer the question. Whatever the question, ensure the answer has a structure: a beginning, a structured central part of the answer and, finally, always a conclusion.

o   Keep the context of the question continually in mind: that is, the specifics of the case and the role which you might be performing.

o   Because there is limited material available, you will sometimes need to make assumptions. Don't be afraid to do this, it will show initiative on your part. Assumptions are an important part of dealing with case studies and can help you to be quite creative with your answer. However, do explain the basis of your assumptions within your answer so that the examiner understands the nature of them, and why you have arrived at your particular outcome. **Always ensure that your assumptions are realistic.**

o   Only now are you approaching the stage where it is time to start writing your answer to the question, tackling the problems, making decisions and recommendations on the case scenario set before you. As mentioned previously, your points will often be best set out in a report or memo type format, particularly if the examiner does not specify a communication method.

o   Ensure that your writing is succinct, avoids waffle and responds directly to the questions asked.

Part B

Again, with the exception of the Analysis and Decision case study, each Part B is comprised of six or seven more traditional questions, each worth 20 per cent. You will be expected to choose three of those questions, to make up the remaining 60 per cent of available marks.

Realistically, the same principles apply for these questions as in the case study. Communication formats, reading through the questions, structure, role-play, context, etc. – everything is the same.

Part B will cover a number of broader issues from within the syllabus and will be taken from any element of it. The examiner makes the choice, and no prior direction is given to students or tutors on what that might be.

As regards time management in this area, if you used about 75 minutes for the mini-case you should have around 105 minutes left. This provides you with around 30 minutes to plan and write a question and 5 minutes per question to review and revise your answers. Keep practising – use a cooker timer, alarm clock or mobile phone alarm as your timer and work hard at answering questions within the timeframe given.

Specimen examination papers and answers

To help you prepare and understand the nature of the paper, go to www.cimeduhub.com to access Specimen Answers and Senior Examiner's advice for these exam questions. During your study, the author of your Coursebook may have on occasions asked you to refer to these papers and answer the questions. You should undertake these exercises and utilize every opportunity to practise meeting examination requirements.

The specimen answers are vital learning tools. They are not always perfect, as they are answers written by students and annotated by the Senior Examiners, but they will give you a good indication of the approaches you could take, and the examiners' annotations suggest how these answers might be improved. Please use them. You can also access this type of information through the Virtual Institute on the CIM website using your student registration number as an access code.

Other sources of information to support your learning through the Virtual Institute are 'Hot Topics'. These give you scope to undertake a range of associated activities related to the syllabus and study areas, and will also be very useful to you when you are revising.

Key elements of preparation

One Senior Examiner suggests the three elements involved in preparing for your examination can be summarized thus:

- o Learning
- o Memory
- o Revision.

Let's look at each point in turn.

Learning

Quite often students find it difficult to learn properly. You can passively read books, look at some of the materials, perhaps revise a little, and regurgitate it all in the examination. In the main, however, this is rather an unsatisfactory method of learning. It is meaningless, shallow and ultimately of little use in practice.

For learning to be truly effective it must be active and applied. You must involve yourself in the learning process by thinking about what you have read, testing it against your experience by reflecting on how you use particular aspects of marketing, and how you could perhaps improve your own performance by implementing particular aspects of your learning into your everyday life. You should adopt the old adage of 'learning by doing'. If you do, you will find that passive learning has no place in your study life.

Below are some suggestions that have been prepared to assist you with the learning pathway throughout your revision.

- o Always make your own notes, in words you understand, and ensure that you combine all the sources of information and activities within them
- o Always try to relate your learning back to your own organization
- o Make sure you define key terms concisely, wherever possible
- o Do not try to memorize your ideas, but work on the basis of understanding and, most important, applying them
- o Think about the relevant and topical questions that might be set – use the questions and answers in your Coursebooks to identify typical questions that might be asked in the future
- o Attempt all of the questions within each of your Coursebooks since these are vital tests of your active learning and understanding.

Memory

If you are prepared to undertake an active learning programme then your knowledge will be considerably enhanced, as understanding and application of knowledge does tend to stay in your 'long-term' memory. It is likely that passive learning will only stay in your 'short-term' memory.

Do not try to memorize parrot fashion; it is not helpful and, even more important, examiners are experienced in identifying various memorizing techniques and therefore will spot them as such.

Having said this, it is quite useful to memorize various acronyms such as SWOT, PEST, PESTLE, STEEPLE, or indeed various models such as Ansoff, GE Matrix, Shell Directional, etc., as in some of the questions you may be required to use illustrations of these to assist your answer.

Revision

The third and final stage to consider is 'revision', which is what we will concentrate on in detail below. Here just a few key tips are offered.

Revision should be an ongoing process rather than a panic measure that you decide to undertake just before the examination. You should be preparing notes throughout your course, with the view to using them as part of your revision process. Therefore ensure that your notes are sufficiently comprehensive that you can reuse them successfully.

For each concept you learn about, you should identify, through your reading and your own personal experience, at least two or three examples that you could use; this then gives you some scope to broaden your perspective during the examination. It will, of course, help you gain some points for initiative with the examiners.

Knowledge is not something you will gain overnight – as we saw earlier, it is not a quick fix; it involves a process of learning that enables you to lay solid foundations upon which to build your long-term understanding and application. This will benefit you significantly in the future, not just in the examination.

In essence, you should ensure that you do the following in the period before the real intensive revision process begins.

- o Keep your study file well organized, updated and full of newspaper and journal cuttings that may help you formulate examples in your mind for use during the examination
- o Practise defining key terms and acronyms from memory
- o Prepare topic outlines and essay answer plans
- o When you start your intensive revision, ensure it is planned and structured in the way described below. And then finally, read your concentrated notes the night before the examination.

Revision planning

You are now on a critical path – although hopefully not too critical at this time – with somewhere in the region of between four and six weeks to go to the examination. The following hints and tips will help you plan out your revision study.

o You will, as already explained, need to be very organized. Therefore, before doing anything else, put your files, examples, reading material, etc. in good order, so that you are able to work with them in the future and, of course, make sense of them.

o Ensure that you have a quiet area within which to work. It is very easy to get distracted when preparing for an examination.

o Take out your file along with your syllabus and make a list of key topic areas that you have studied and which you now need to revise. You could use the basis of this book to do that, by taking each unit a step at a time.

o Plan the use of your time carefully. Ideally you should start your revision at least six weeks prior to the exam, so therefore work out how many spare hours you could give to the revision process and then start to allocate time in your diary, and do not double-book with anything else.

o Give up your social life for a short period of time. As the saying goes 'no pain – no gain'.

o Looking at each of the subject areas in turn, identify which are your strengths and which are your weaknesses. Which areas have you grasped and understood, and which are the areas that you have really struggled with? Split your page in two and make a list on each side. For example:

Planning and control	
Strengths	Weaknesses
Audit – PEST, SWOT, Models	Ratio analysis
Portfolio analysis	Market sensing
	Productivity analysis
	Trend extrapolation
	Forecasting

o Break down your list again and divide the points of weakness, giving priority in the first instance to your weakest areas and even prioritizing them by giving them a number. This will enable you to master the more difficult areas. Up to 60 per cent of your remaining revision time should be given over to that, as you may find you have to undertake a range of additional reading and also perhaps seeking tutor support, if you are studying at a CIM Accredited Study Centre.

o The rest of the time should be spent reinforcing your knowledge and understanding of the stronger areas, spending time testing yourself on how much you really know.

o Should you be taking two examinations or more at any one time, then the breakdown and managing of your time will be critical.

o Taking a subject at a time, work through your notes and start breaking them down into subsections of learning, and ultimately into key learning points, items that you can refer to time and time again, that are meaningful and that your mind will absorb. You yourself will know how you best remember key points. Some people try to develop acronyms, or flowcharts or matrices, mind maps, fishbone diagrams, etc., or various connection diagrams that help them recall certain aspects of models. You could also develop processes that enable you to remember approaches to various options. (But do remember what we said earlier about regurgitating stuff, parrot fashion.)

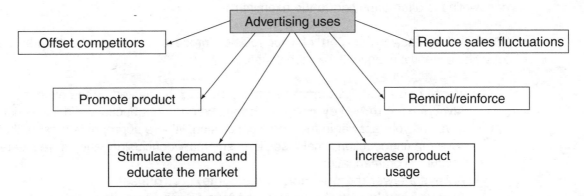

Figure A1.1 Use of a diagram to summarize key components of a concept.
Adapted from Dibb, Simkin, Pride & Ferrell, Marketing Concepts and Strategies, 4th edition, Houghton Mifflin, 2001

Figure A1.1 is just a brief example of how you could use a 'bomb-burst' diagram (which, in this case, highlights the uses of advertising) as a very helpful approach to memorizing key elements of learning.

o Eventually you should reduce your key learning to bullet points. For example: imagine you were looking at the concept of Time Management – you could eventually reduce your key learning to a bullet list containing the following points in relation to 'Effective Prioritization:'

 o Organize
 o Take time
 o Delegate
 o Review.

Each of these headings would then remind you of the elements you need to discuss associated with the subject area.

o Avoid getting involved in reading too many textbooks at this stage, as you may start to find that you are getting confused overall.

o Look at examination questions on previous papers, and start to observe closely the various roles and tasks they expect you to undertake, and importantly, the context in which they are set.

o Use the specimen exam papers and specimen answers to support your learning and see how you could actually improve upon them.

o Without exception, find an associated examination question for the areas that you have studied and revised, and undertake it (more than once if necessary).

o Without referring to notes or books, try to draft an answer plan with the key concepts, knowledge, models and information that are needed to successfully complete the answer. Then refer to the specimen answer to see how close you are to the actual outline presented. Planning your answer, and ensuring that key components are included, and that the question has a meaningful structure, is one of the most beneficial activities that you can undertake.

o Now write the answer out in full, time-constrained and written by hand, not with the use of IT. (At this stage, you are still expected to be the scribe for the examination and present handwritten work. Many of us find this increasingly difficult as we spend more and more time using our computers to present information. Do your best to be neat. Spidery handwriting is often offputting to the examiner.)

o When writing answers as part of your revision process, also be sure to practise the following essential examinations techniques:

   o **Identify and use the communication method** requested by the examiner.
   o **Always have three key parts to the answer** An introduction, middle section that develops your answer in full, and a conclusion. Where appropriate, ensure that you have an introduction, main section, summary/conclusion and, if requested or helpful, recommendations.
   o **Always answer the question in the context or role set.**
   o **Always comply with the nature and terms of the question.**
   o **Leave white space** Do not overcrowd your page; Leave space between paragraphs, and make sure your sentences do not merge into one blur. (Don't worry – there is always plenty of paper available to use in the examination.)
   o **Count** how many actions the question asks you to undertake and double-check at the end that you have met the full range of demands of the question.
   o **Use examples** To demonstrate your knowledge and understanding of the particular syllabus area. These can be from journals, the Internet, the press, or your own experience.
   o **Display your vigour and enthusiasm for marketing** Remember to think of the Senior Examiner as your Customer, or future employer, and do your best to deliver what is wanted to satisfy their needs. Impress them and show them how you are a 'cut above the rest'.

o Review all your practice answers critically, with the above points in mind.

Practical actions

The critical path is becoming even more critical now as the examination looms. The following are vital points.

   o Have you registered with CIM?
   o Do you know where you are taking your examination? CIM should let you know approximately one month in advance.
   o Do you know where your examination centre is? If not find out, take a drive, time it – whatever you do don't be late!
   o Make sure you have all the tools of the examination ready. A dictionary, calculator, pens, pencils, ruler, etc. Try not to use multiple shades of pens, but at the same time make your work look professional. *Avoid using red and green as these are the colours that will be used for marking.*

Summary

Above all you must remember that you personally have invested a tremendous amount of time, effort and money in studying for this programme and it is therefore imperative that you consider the suggestions given here as they will help to maximize your return on your investment.

Many of the hints and tips offered here are generic and will work across most of the CIM courses. We have tried to select those that will help you most in taking a sensible, planned approach to your study and revision.

The key to your success is being prepared to put in the time and effort required, planning your revision, and equally important, planning and answering your questions in a way that will ensure that you pass your examination on the day.

The advice offered here aims to guide you from a practical perspective. Guidance on syllabus content and developments associated with your learning will become clear to you as you work through this Coursebook. The authors of each Coursebook have given subject-specific guidance on the approach to the examination and on how to ensure that you meet the content requirements of the kind of question you will face. These considerations are in addition to the structuring issues we have been discussing throughout this Appendix.

Each of the authors and Senior Examiners will guide you on their preferred approach to questions and answers as they go. Therefore where you are presented with an opportunity to be involved in some activity or undertake an examination question either during or at the end of your study units, do take it. It not only prepares you for the examination, but helps you learn in the applied way we discussed above.

Here, then, is a last reminder:

- o   Ensure you make the most of your learning process throughout
- o   Keep structured and orderly notes from which to revise
- o   Plan your revision – don't let it just happen
- o   Provide examples to enhance your answers
- o   Practise your writing skills in order that you present your work well and your writing is readable
- o   Take as many opportunities to test your knowledge and measure your progress as possible
- o   Plan and structure your answers
- o   Always do as the question asks you, especially with regard to context and communication method
- o   **Do not leave it until the last minute!**

The writers would like to take this opportunity to wish you every success in your endeavours to study, to revise and to pass your examinations.

Karen Beamish
Academic Development Advisor

unit 1

Debriefing Activity 1.1

You should have had few difficulties in finding a range of different marketing definitions. They are probably all quite different but will have common characteristics. In general terms, the definitions focus on two aspects of marketing. Firstly, that marketing is a functional activity that is concerned with the operational aspects of marketing such as market research, promotion, pricing and product development. Secondly, that marketing is more than just a functional activity. It is a business philosophy that permeates the whole organization and puts the customer at the centre of its activity.

Debriefing Activity 1.2

The questionnaire focuses on five aspects of market orientation – customer orientation, competitor orientation, long-term perspectives, interfunctional co-ordination and organizational culture.

By undertaking an assessment of your own organization, you will be able to assess its level of market orientation. In particular, you will be able to identify areas of strengths and weaknesses. The results may confirm your existing thoughts or else identify areas that you had not necessarily paid great attention to in the past.

The questionnaire is not designed to produce a definitive judgement about the level of market orientation, instead it provides a framework for discussing the key issues relating to market orientation.

You would probably find that if different individuals from different departments and backgrounds completed the questionnaire you would have different results. This is not a deficiency of the questionnaire, rather it relates to personal experiences and attitudes.

Debriefing Activity 1.3

A suggested approach is provided in the context of motor vehicle distribution.

Driving change
Two main change drivers may be identified for this sector. These include, technology (the Internet) and the legal environment. In the European context, European regulation (EC) 1475/ 95 on motor vehicle distribution and after sales servicing expires on 30 September 2002. This

means that the legal right of manufacturers to control most motor vehicle distribution, through 'official', manufacturer dealerships, will end. Legislators have the option to sanction a range of legal relationships, between the manufacturer and the distributor. At one extreme, they may prevent the manufacturers from participating in car distribution and retailing. At the other extreme, they may make a few changes to the existing system.

Impact of change

Internet – impact will be to increase competition (by facilitating the entry into this market of new competitors) and to reduce prices (through increased price transparency). Margins will be reduced in this sector and this will create additional problems for traditional, official car dealerships. They tend to be located in central areas of cities, incurring high rents, and also maintain large numbers of sales staff.

Legal changes – the current industry structure is regarded as anti-competitive. It is highly probable that new legislation will require greater competition. Increased competition from legal reform, and from the Internet distributors, will result in an intensively competitive car dealership sector. Downward pressure in prices will encourage the so-called 'car supermarket' distributors to take a larger hold of the market.

Result of change

Assume that any remaining 'official' dealerships continue to offer full 3-year warranties and servicing. Other car distributors are likely therefore to market cars which have only a standard 1-year warranty. Opportunities will therefore arise for 'garage services' companies to enter the warranty servicing market and for financial service providers to offer warranties for the second and third years of the life of the car.

Debriefing Activity 1.4

These changes are having a major impact on the way in which companies are run. For example, the role of the manager is changing from an individual who assigns tasks to subordinates to one that tries to maximize the effectiveness of the staff. Workers are now not seen as mindless robots but as individuals that can think for themselves. Many layers of middle management have been stripped out and been replaced with decentralized rather than top-down decision-making. Teamworking is beginning to replace individualistic performance. The ability of a company to control operations is no longer sufficient. A key role is now about managing relationships. These factors all have an impact on how companies can meet the needs of the diverse range of customers that they serve.

Debriefing Activity 1.5

All organizations will have their own personal planning processes. The nature of their planning and control cycles will vary according to a number of factors such as organizational size, culture, nature of the business (fast moving or slow moving), number of staff involved, top-down or bottom-up approach, responsibility for planning, etc. Types of planning may include corporate planning, marketing planning, marketing mix planning and other functional types of planning such as HRM, Research and Development and contingency planning. Time frames for planning will also be influenced by the type of industry in which an organization is working. Planning cycles may be monthly, six-monthly, annually, five-yearly or even longer in some situations. In some organizations, planning is highly mechanized while in others it can often be ad hoc without formal planning cycles. Refer to Unit 9 for further information on control mechanisms and how the planning process can be improved.

Debriefing Activity 1.6

Organizational structure can have a major influence on the effectiveness of planning and communication and also the corporate culture. Highly hierarchical structures often result in effective vertical communication and planning. However, they can inhibit cross-departmental communication and develop a culture of competition between departments or different business units. In contrast, flatter organizations can aid communication across the company and can reduce the layers of bureaucracy often associated with highly hierarchical organizations. Matrix structures can be effective in breaking down departmental barriers but problems can sometimes arise because teams are faced with conflicting messages from two different managers.

The culture of an organization has a major influence over the planning process and must be considered when developing plans. Culture relates to the 'way we do things around here'. It is often very difficult to change and can be a long and painful process.

unit 2

Debriefing Activity 2.1

In an exam situation you often find your mind goes blank when asked for examples. This activity will provide you with a wealth of examples that you can refer to in the Planning and Control exam.

Debriefing Activity 2.2

All organizations approach environmental scanning in different ways. There are those organizations that have a rigorous and formal approach whilst others adopt more of an ad hoc and informal approach. There is no one 'best' method. The important aspect is how organizations translate the information they collect into action. Your recommendations may relate to a number of issues such as the way in which the information is collected, the means by which it is processed and the method by which it is disseminated.

Debriefing Activity 2.3

It is not enough to just identify the trends in the macroenvironment. Companies must be ready and able to take action in order to take advantage of opportunities or to deflect the threats created by changes in the external environment. This activity will highlight your company's ability to monitor and respond to these changes.

Debriefing Activity 2.4

This activity will provide you with numerous examples of ways in which companies are adopting the 'societal marketing' concept. You can then use them as practical examples in the exam if required.

Debriefing Activity 2.5

This model can prove very helpful in understanding the dynamics of the industry within which you are operating. It will help to identify where the balance of power lies and will highlight the threat of new entrants and substitute products.

Debriefing Activity 2.6

This activity will help you to understand the structure of your industry and also identify those companies with whom you are competing directly.

Debriefing Activity 2.7

This activity will provide a structured approach to competitive analysis. It is helpful to consider different strategic business units or products in turn because it is likely that you will be competing with different companies in different markets. This framework will help to identify your key competitors, also those companies that are worth attacking and those to be avoided.

Debriefing Activity 2.8

This activity may reveal how little your company knows about your competitors. It may also provide you with some valuable information that you could use in your work. It may surprise you as to how much information is readily available in the public domain. This task will probably prove more difficult if you operate in a business-to-business environment, where there is less published information. However, marketers have to be ingenious when trying to gather information about competitors.

Debriefing Activity 2.9

Lager/Beer
Lager/Beer culture/subculture will influence whether consumers will drink Lager or Beer in the first place. For example, Muslims do not drink alcohol. Social class may be important because higher social class drinkers may choose 'premium' brands that might be seen as less 'vulgar' than ordinary brands.

Social factors will be important in this instance because lagers/beers are often consumed in social settings. Reference groups can be a powerful influence. The consumer may choose a brand that matches their reference group or may want to be seen to be as different. The drinker may also select a brand that they think an aspirant group might choose.

Personal influences such as age and life-cycle stage may influence choice of Lager/Beer. A particular brand may be selected to reflect a particular lifestyle. Disposable income may influence which brands a drinker can afford to buy. A consumer may purchase a brand to match their personality – outgoing and individualistic or conservative and wanting to blend in with the crowd.

Psychological factors such as perception relate to how the drinker interprets advertisements and how the consumer's understanding of the brand may enhance their self-image. Attitudes towards various brands and beliefs about the kind of people who buy them will vary, as will attitudes to product attributes such as country of origin, strength or ingredients.

Financial services
Financial services are going to be less influenced by social factors because they are not consumed in public and are not necessarily perceived as status symbols.

Cultural factors will be important because some cultures/subcultures value financial services to a greater degree than others. Social class may influence peoples' attitudes to financial services. For example, higher social classes often seek delayed gratification whilst lower social classes look for immediate gratification and are therefore less likely to purchase pensions or life assurance.

Social factors such as the family may play an important role. Purchasers may seek advice of friends or colleagues. It is likely that the purchase will be made by a decision-making unit.

Personal influences such as age, stage in the life-cycle, occupation and economic circumstances will be highly influential.

Psychological factors such as perception relate to the purchaser's interpretation of promotional campaigns.

There are enormous implications for marketing managers for both of these products. They will have to be marketed differently because they are influenced by very different factors.

Debriefing Activity 2.10

Repetitive buying behaviour – may include products such as washing powder, baked beans, rice, pasta, milk, eggs

Variety seeking – may include products such as shampoos, books, CDs

Buyer dissonance reduction – may include products such as life assurance and pensions

Complex buying behaviour – may include products such as holidays, cars, house extensions.

Debriefing Question 2.4

It is essential that marketing managers have a detailed understanding of buyers – how they buy, why they buy and their likely responses to the various elements of the marketing mix. When entering an overseas market, it is essential that a detailed analysis of the factors which influence buyer behaviour be undertaken. The following factors are important:

- o Cultural factors
- o Social factors
- o Personal factors
- o Psychological factors.

The purchase of fashion goods will be particularly influenced by these factors. It may be possible to identify segments of consumers that cross cultural boundaries or it may be necessary to tailor the marketing mix to meet the needs of the local market.

Debriefing Activity 2.11

The members of the decision-making group include:

- o Initiator
- o User
- o Buyer
- o Influencer
- o Decider
- o Gatekeeper.

All members perform different roles. However, the decision-making unit is not necessarily a fixed entity and the members of the DMU may change as the decision-making process continues. This is more likely for a more complex or new purchase. The more important the purchase decision, the more complex the DMU will be, involving numerous members.

The marketer's task is to identify and reach the key members in order to convince them of the product/services benefits. It could be assumed that the key member is the purchaser. However, in many cases they may have little influence over the decision and other members may be of more significance. Relationship marketing is of prime importance in organizational markets and the key marketing task is to nurture relationships with the influential DMU members. For highly technical purchases, suppliers may work with engineers, who may have a great deal of influence over the decision, to help solve problems and ultimately to win orders.

Many decisions are ultimately made by committees that are largely inaccessible to sales staff. However, if a supporter of the product can be identified within the DMU, this person could act as an advocate and influence the final decision.

The influential members of the DMU may change as the decision-making process continues and marketers should attempt to identify these. For example, at the beginning of the process the key member may be the gatekeeper. This person may be responsible for gathering information on potential suppliers. It is important that they are targeted, may be through advertising or direct mail.

unit 3

Debriefing Activity 3.1

Refer to list of assets and competencies identified by Hooley et al. (1998). This is a useful starting point for identifying unique capabilities. You may find that it is easy to identify one factor that is obviously the source of your competitive advantage, or you may discover that it is a combination of assets or competencies that gives the organization its unique capabilities. To identify your strategic group consider the various criteria that you could use to categorize the organizations in your industry. Criteria could include: size of the company, assets and skills, scope of the operation, breadth of the product range, choice of distribution channel, relative product quality or brand image.

Debriefing Activity 3.2

This activity will reveal the effectiveness of your internal marketing auditing process. Many organizations fail to regularly review their activities and as a result continue to pursue strategies, processes and activities that fail to keep abreast with changing environmental conditions. This can result in strategic drift. Alternatively, you may find that your organization does undertake regular reviews of internal marketing activities but that they are ineffective. This may be due to lack of objectivity or simply that it is highly mechanistic and is of no real value to the organization.

The types of actions that you may have identified are likely to be highly diverse but could include redesigning the marketing information system, reorganization of sales staff responsibilities, review of target markets, etc.

To ensure the internal marketing auditing process is effective, it is important that it is regularly undertaken by 'objective' people in a systematic manner. However, it should be much more than purely a form-filling activity, to be of any real value. An effective internal marketing audit should help to answer the following questions:

- Where are we now?
- How did we get there?
- Where are we heading?

Debriefing Activity 3.3

- New product and service developments are lower in the last 5 years, but the rate of successful market launches has risen from 29% of developments to 57%
- Sales per new development have risen from £5 million to £8 million
- Although 30% of sales, in the last 12 months, are from products launched in the last 5 years (up from 18% three years ago) only 13.5% of these sales are new (incremental) sales. The remaining 16.5% are sales that have cannibalized current products. This is an indication of poor planning
- The payback period for new developments is lengthening.

Debriefing Activity 3.4

This activity looks very straightforward. However, in reality you may find it quite difficult to access the information that you require. It may be that your organization does not collect sales data in a suitable format. If this is the case, consider how data would be best collected and organized to allow you to undertake this kind of analysis. It may also be difficult to decide what you regard as a 'new' product or service. Is an existing product new if it is repackaged? However you define a new product/service, the important thing is that you continue to use this definition in your analysis, to ensure that you are comparing like with like.

unit 4

Debriefing Activity 4.1

If you operate in a service company you will probably find this quite a challenging activity. You will have to be flexible in your definitions of each of the activities. You may want to refer to the December 1999 Planning and Control case study, easyJet, because students were asked to apply the value chain.

This activity will enable you to identify sources of competitive advantage. For example, does your advantage lie in your ability to manufacture products more efficiently than competitors, is your level of customer service superior to others or do you have the ability to innovate and get new products/ideas to market faster than competitors?

The value chain is very inwardly oriented, rather than being focused on the external environment (in particular the market and customers). It is also worth remembering that in most industries a single organization rarely undertakes all the value-creating activities and therefore any analysis should recognize the wider value system.

Debriefing Activity 4.2

This portfolio of articles will ensure that in the exam you are armed with a number of current examples to exemplify your points.

Debriefing Activity 4.3

Dr Martens firstly has to decide whether they wish to stay in the market. Refer to the financial and non-financial criteria listed in the text that must be considered when making this decision. If they decide to exit the market then they must decide whether to eliminate the brand overnight or withdraw gradually.

It is more likely that you will decide that it is worthwhile trying to rejuvenate the brand. This could include seeking new markets/segments, repositioning the product, new product development, new communications strategy, new distribution strategy, etc. Be creative with your ideas!

Debriefing Activity 4.4

Examples of products/services that have reached maturity/decline phase are numerous. This activity will arm you with real-life examples of products and strategies that you can use in the exam. Refer to the options given by Wilson and Gilligan (1997) and consider which applied to your chosen product.

Debriefing Question 4.2

The PLC is one of the best-known models in marketing and is arguably capable of providing a broad framework for strategic thinking. This question requires you to:

- Focus upon the strategies that are suited to the decline stage
- Identify the criteria that should be used in choosing between alternatives.

A good answer would include the following components:

- **Introduction** – a brief explanation of the PLC and its characteristics
- **Reasons for decline** – technological advances, changing customer needs, increase in competition, etc.
- **Options** – non-deletion, eliminate overnight (divest), increase price or reduce promotion (milk) or stay and attract competitor's customers
- **Evaluation of alternatives** – could include inventory level, notification of customers, resource implications, legal implications, impact on associated products and services, entry barriers, industry attractiveness, competitor activity, marketing objectives, substitute products, overall product portfolio, number of replacement products, nature of market, market exit costs, degree of customer loyalty, importance of product to distributors
- **Conclusions.**

Debriefing Activity 4.5

Examples of products that have been adopted rapidly are mobile phones, digital TV, Internet access. Examples of products that have been slowly adopted (or not at all) are Sinclair C5, some financial service products, electric cars.

The reasons as to why there are differences in rate of adoption relate to factors such as level of newness, ability to trial the product, the relative cost, additional costs that may be incurred and the complexity of the product.

Debriefing Activity 4.6

Below is a worked example for a hypothetical financial services company.

	Product/SBU 1 Pensions			Product/SBU 2 Current Accounts			Product/SBU 3 Insurance		
	Weighting	Score	Rating	Weighting	Score	Rating	Weighting	Score	Rating
Market Attractiveness									
1. Market growth rate	3	10	30	3	1	3	3	3	9
2. Market size	3	8	24	3	6	18	3	7	21
3. Profit opportunity	2	7	14	2	2	4	2	4	8
4. Strength of competition	2	6	12	2	1	2	2	3	6
Total	10		80	10		27	10		44
Competitive Strength									
1. Market share	4	8	32	4	3	12	4	7	28
2. Cost advantages	1	7	7	1	5	5	1	5	5
3. Relationships	2	8	16	2	1	2	2	5	10
4. Distribution capabilities	3	8	24	3	2	6	3	4	12
Total	10		79	10		25	10		55

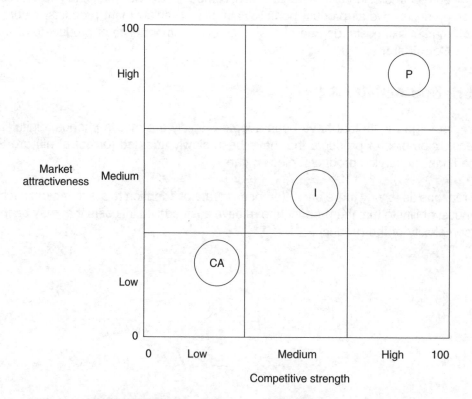

CA: Current Accounts I: Insurance P: Pensions

unit 5

Debriefing Activity 5.1

Ratio calculations of topline financial variables more commonly used in strategic planning

Type of ratio	Example topline ratios
	1. **Profitability ratios** • gross profit margin $= (GP/Sales) \times 100$ $\dfrac{408,000 \times 100}{1,160,000} = 35\%$ • net profit margin $= (NP/Sales) \times 100$ $\dfrac{40,800 \times 100}{1,160,000} = 3.5\%$
Fundamental strength of the business	2. **Capital structure ratios, also termed 'gearing' ratios** • debt ratio $=$ total debt/total assets where: total debt $=$ current liabilities $+$ long-term liabilities total assets $=$ fixed assets $+$ current assets $= 96,900$ $\dfrac{+ 60,000}{729,000 + 190,400} = 1 : 5.9$
	3. **Liquidity** • current ratio $=$ current assets/current liabilities $190,400/96,900 = 1 : 1.96$ • liquid ratio $=$ (current assets $-$ stock)/current liabilities $(190,400 - 85,000)/96,900 = 1 : 1.09$
Operational efficiency of the business	4. **Asset utilization** • stock turnover ratio $=$ cost of goods sold/stock at cost on balance sheet $(752,000/85,000) = 1 : 8.85$ • debtor turnover $=$ sales turnover/debtors $(1,160,000/64,600) = 1 : 18$ • credit turnover ratios $=$ cost of goods sold/trade creditors from the balance sheet $(752,000/51,000) = 1 : 14.7$
Investment performance	5. **Investment performance ratios** • Price to earnings ratio (P/E ratio) $=$ market price per share[1]/earnings per share[2] $165p/5.7p = 29$

[1] From stock market (assumed to be 165p)
[2] Declared annually or twice per year by the company.

Detailed information as follows:

- Dividend payments (taken from profit and loss account) total £38,000 (i.e. 10p per share preference shareholders $=$ £4,000, and £34,000 ordinary shareholders).
- Number of shareholders (taken from Balance Sheet) $= 670,000$
- Earnings per share $=$ £38,000/670,000 $= 5.7p$

Debriefing Activity 5.2

This is a very straightforward, digestible site, developed specifically as an introduction to practical accounts analysis for students. Accounts have been standardized to facilitate comparison and they are accompanied by a textual summary. A facility exists to tabulate selected ratios in order to compare companies in the data set.

Debriefing Activity 5.3

In many small departments, the forecast level of sales for the marketing plan, e.g. is based on informal consensus forecasting. Key channels intermediaries, and company sales and marketing staff, are asked for their views on the level of competition, demand and the strength of products offered by the business. The methodology may be described as qualitative trend extrapolation, where last year's sales and market share information is adjusted based on the views of the 'experts' consulted. It is a valid approach that is relatively quick to undertake and encapsulates complex views of the future. The approach is normally used for annual forecasts, frequently including monthly sub-forecasts.

unit 6

Debriefing Activity 6.1

This exercise will not provide definitive answers about the appropriateness of your selected mission statements. However, what it does is to focus your mind on the important elements of a mission statement. Too often, mission statements consist of bland generalizations that could be applied to any company. It is not an easy task to develop an appropriate and motivating mission statement but at least Piercy's framework provides a starting point.

Debriefing Activity 6.2

Figure 6.2 provides a useful framework for identifying the various influences on a company's mission statement. You may find that your organization's mission is mainly influenced by the desire to make a profit and satisfy shareholders. Alternatively, you may work for an organization that is greatly concerned about the environment or human rights and will therefore be more influenced by business ethics. In reality, you will probably find that most of the organizations are influenced by all the factors but to a greater or lesser degree.

Debriefing Activity 6.3

This activity will force you to consider different types of objectives that exist and the relationship between the various levels of objectives within the organizational hierarchy. It will also illustrate the difficulties in writing appropriate SMART objectives. This will prove particularly helpful when you come to preparing for the Analysis and Decision case study exam.

Debriefing Activity 6.4

You will probably find that one perspective is more dominant than others once you have analysed your objectives. In many organizations the main priority is profit and therefore the financial perspective will tend to dominate. In companies greatly concerned with customer service and satisfaction, many objectives will relate to the customer perspective. It is quite rare to find organizations that give equal priority to all four areas of the business. It may be interesting to compare your answer to this activity to your answer in Activity 6.1 which asked you to look at the influences on the mission statement. This will reveal whether there is actually any synergy between the mission statement and its objectives.

Debriefing Activity 6.5

This activity should highlight the number of different stakeholders that your organization has. The number and diversity of the groups may surprise you. It is now possible to appreciate the difficulties facing organizations when they have to try to meet the needs of these diverse groups of people. Different organizations will give greater emphasis to the needs of some groups rather than others.

unit 7

Debriefing Activity 7.1

This exercise will provide you with the opportunity to apply this theoretical framework to a practical example. You will probably find that many companies do not fall conveniently into one of the three categories. Instead, they will probably use a combination of the three strategies. This model is helpful in focusing your mind on the generic strategies that companies may use to gain competitive advantage and the dangers of failing to have a clear and consistent strategy. The activity will also provide you with examples that you may be able to use in the exam.

Debriefing Activity 7.2

Davidson's approach provides a useful framework to identify various means of attaining a sustainable competitive advantage. This activity will encourage you to collect examples that you may be able to refer to in the exam.

Debriefing Activity 7.3

You may have selected companies such as Coca-Cola and Pepsi, Tesco and Sainsburys, McDonald's and Burger King, Caterpillar and Komatsu, Unilever and Procter and Gamble (to name but a few). Research has shown that it can often be very expensive to attack a market leader, and may end in disaster. For example, Laker Airways attacked the major airlines in the 1970s on a low-price platform. The other airlines reacted by cutting their prices. This forced Laker out of business because the company did not have a lower cost structure than their competitors.

Debriefing Activity 7.4

This model should not be new to you and it is likely that you have had to apply it to practical situations before. The purpose of this activity is to revise the model and to ensure that you understand the practical implications of the model. It is a useful model for identifying the various growth strategies open to an organization. However, it does not really address the issue of what competitive advantage an organization should pursue.

Debriefing Activity 7.5

You should have no problem sourcing articles on strategic alliances. There appears to be an abundance of companies that have recognized that to sustain their competitive advantage they will have to join forces with other firms. The motivations for these alliances will vary considerably but will probably relate to the factors identified in this unit.

Debriefing Activity 7.6

A good example of a declining market is the tobacco market in western countries. Different tobacco companies have adopted different strategies in response to their declining market. Strategies could include:

- ○ Targeting new customers, e.g. in developing countries where smoking is still accepted
- ○ Diversifying into other markets such as food products
- ○ Divesting their business, e.g. selling their brands to competitors and withdrawing from particular market sectors
- ○ Continuing as before and hoping that competitors will exit the market leaving them as the profitable survivor.

Debriefing Activity 7.7

This activity will provide you with contemporary examples that you may be able to use in the exam.

unit 8

Debriefing Activity 8.1

This Web site obviously provides you with a snapshot of the types of questions that are used to build up the VALS profiles. Consider the extent to which you match the characteristics of your category – fulfilled, experiences, believers, strivers, makers or strugglers. You have probably concluded that some of the characteristics are relevant to yourself and others are not. This is likely to be true of all lifestyle segmentation methods because they are looking for common characteristics (which is challenging given that we are all individuals). The key question relating to segmentation is 'do those individuals in a particular segment behave in a similar manner?' It is likely that this method of segmentation will be more appropriate in some markets than others – for example, financial services, cars and holidays (i.e. those that relate to a person's lifestyle). There are obvious limitations of this type of framework due to the generalizations that are made. The questionnaire is more appropriate for Americans than for European citizens, which has implications for companies that are operating internationally. It is likely they will encounter problems relating to cultural differences when trying to develop cross-cultural segmentation bases.

Debriefing Activity 8.2

Answers to this activity will vary greatly and it is impossible to give a definitive answer. Instead refer to the following ways in which markets can be segmented and identify those which you believe to be the most useful.

Consumer markets:

Customer characteristics

- ○ Demographic
- ○ Geographic
- ○ Geodemographic
- ○ Psychographic.

Behavioural characteristics

- ○ Benefits sought
- ○ Usage frequency
- ○ Usage status
- ○ Purchase occasion
- ○ Attitude towards the product
- ○ Buyer readiness stage.

Organizational markets – see Figure 8.6

Debriefing Activity 8.3

The three companies are all adopting a concentrated market segmentation strategy but the segments they are targeting are very different.

Club 18–30 holidays

Club 18–30 is segmenting obviously on age, but it could be argued that they are also adopting on benefit segmentation. Not all 18–30 year olds will seek out the types of holidays offered by Club 18–30, i.e. a two week package holiday featuring sun, sand, sea, drinking, night clubbing in predominately Mediterranean resorts. It is essential that Club 18–30 targets like-minded customers because the social aspect is a key part of the service offering. These 'co-consumers' will have a large influence on customer satisfaction and therefore they must be looking for the same type of holiday.

The Web site is filled with vibrant colours, fast moving images and little text. The types of people it features are the company's target market and will therefore attract a particular type of individual. The Web site features naked men and a woman 'frolicking' on the beach. This image projects clearly the type of holiday potential customers can expect! The Web site helps to achieve the desired positioning of a holiday company that is for young, single, social individuals that are seeking out a beach type holiday with like-minded people.

Voyage Jules Verne

This company appears to be segmenting the market using multi-dimensional segmentation bases. They are segmenting on age i.e. targeting the older age group, possibly the 55+ market but with those that are in the high income bracket. Lifestyle segmentation could be useful in this context. The holidays are on average longer than the normal two weeks. It is likely that their core customers are retired and have greater opportunity to take longer and more frequent holidays. The cost of the holidays is high, reflecting the more exotic destinations and the luxury end of the market they are targeting. However, it is not all retired people because a great many retired people do not have the level of disposable income necessary to travel with Jules Verne.

This Web site of Voyage Jules Verne compared with that of Club 18–30 uses more muted colours and contains lots of text about all the holiday packages that could be selected. There is a wide range of different holiday styles available such as holidays specialising in geology, astronomy, botany and photography. This reinforces the idea that they are segmenting on lifestyle. VJV focuses on the 'sense of occasion' surrounding a holiday. The Web site provides information on the history of the company and lots of other information which encourages a feeling of trust. VJV are positioning themselves as a high quality provider of exclusive tailor-made holidays that are off the beaten track.

The Discerning Traveller

This company is targeting a niche market. It only offers 'individual self-led hiking holidays' in Britain for either 3, 5 or 7 nights. It appears to be segmenting on lifestyle or benefit segmentation bases. It would only appeal to keen walkers that are looking for a UK based holiday. The company suggests suitable routes, books the accommodation and carries the luggage between the hotels/B&Bs. It successfully positions itself by providing lots of images of lovely scenery and detailed itineraries. The major difference between this holiday provider and the other two companies is that it is designed for customers to travel alone. VJV and Club18–30 both offer 'package' holidays where the co-consumers will have an influence on the holiday experience. In contrast, The Discerning Traveller is targeting customers who are happy to travel independently.

Debriefing Activity 8.4

Virgin is operating in a diverse range of market sectors ranging from trains, planes, mobile phones, weddings, financial services, health clubs, wines, cars and car hire. The ability of Virgin to stretch its brand into so many unrelated markets is probably related to the brand values of the Virgin brand. Brands such as Coca-Cola and Guinness have very strong brand images that relate directly to the product itself, whereas the Virgin brand is not tied strongly to one product and is often regarded as the 'people's brand' (as an alternative to conventional brands) and particularly relates to Richard Branson himself. This has enabled Virgin to stretch into many unrelated markets.

It is difficult to judge the impact that the problems of Virgin Trains has had on the Virgin brand. Many of the problems associated with Virgin Trains are not in fact due to Virgin itself but due to problems with Railtrack. Some customers appreciate this and feel that Richard Branson has a huge task ahead and as a result see Virgin Trains as a completely separate entity. However, it is undeniable that for some people the performance of Virgin Trains has had a negative umbrella effect on the overall Virgin brand.

Debriefing Activity 8.5

There will be many factors that will have influenced the level of success that a repositioned/revitalized brand has achieved such as:

o   Relevancy to the target market
o   Credibility of the brand
o   Level of promotional support
o   Extent to which the product/service continues to meet a need
o   Achieving correct pricing strategy.

You will probably be able to identify many other factors that are specific to your chosen examples. You must also consider what you mean by 'successful'. For example, when VW repositioned the Skoda brand they did not see an immediate increase in sales. It has been a very long process from raising awareness of the newly designed brand to changing perceptions and then seeing an increase in sales in the end. Therefore, initial success could not be measured by sales figures alone. It was necessary to measure awareness and customer attitudes in the early days following the relaunch of the Skoda brand.

Debriefing Activity 8.6

Drummond and Ensor (2001) suggest that there are six enablers that help to create a culture that embraces change and innovation:

- o External inputs
- o Teamwork
- o Exchange of information
- o Senior management support
- o Support and systems
- o Reward.

unit 9

Debriefing Activity 9.1

This activity will identify whether your organization can effectively implement the strategies it has developed. Many organizations find the implementation stage the most challenging and often find it difficult to translate plans into actions. The reason for your choice of quadrant will be influenced by factors such as organizational culture, effectiveness of communication, staff motivation, abilities of managers, sufficient resources (human, time and physical), planning process, staff rewards, etc.

Debriefing Activity 9.2

The internal barriers that you have identified will probably resemble those factors identified in Unit 9 – Implementation and control. The challenge facing many organizations is how to overcome these barriers. Unit 9 – Implementation and control identifies a number of strategies that companies can adopt to try to improve implementation of plans such as internal marketing, project management and change management.

Debriefing Activity 9.3

This model provides a representation of the stages people move through when faced with change. Different individuals will progress through the stages at different paces and some may not pass through all the stages in a linear manner. This model will highlight the need for managers to help staff to accept as rapidly as possible, for example by promoting the benefits of the change and offering incentives to adapt. It is inevitable that some people will continue to resist change and may in fact choose to leave the organization, rather than accept changes.

Debriefing Activity 9.4

Many organizations continue to overlook the fact that happy, motivated and committed staff can improve profitability. For example, motivated staff may provide a greater level of customer service and therefore customer retention may improve. Committed staff that are happy with their work will be less likely to leave the organization and therefore, staff training will be worthwhile. Highly motivated staff may be more inclined to suggest new ideas, because they feel valued. These examples show that there is a link between internal and external marketing.

The intranet is an ideal tool for communicating with all staff and also other external parties. It ensures that all staff can access relevant information. This is particularly useful for organizations that operate on a number of sites or even in a number of countries. The one problem with intranets is that organizations have to avoid overloading users with information. This can result in users being bombarded with messages and choosing not to use the intranet in the intended way.

Debriefing Activity 9.5

Use the checklists provided to classify the types of control mechanisms employed in your organization. You may find that many control mechanisms are concerned with measuring efficiency rather than effectiveness. It is important that organizations develop relevant controls because 'what gets measured gets done'. Control measures should be linked to objectives. The balanced scorecard is a useful approach for ensuring that objectives are balanced and that they are linked into appropriate control measures.

appendix 3
curriculum information and reading list

Syllabus

Aims and objectives

The aim of the unit is to enable students to develop a sound theoretical and practical understanding of marketing planning and control.

The objectives are to:

- o Enable students to understand the theoretical concepts, techniques and models that underpin the marketing planning process
- o Build practical skills associated with the management of the planning process
- o Enable students to justify their strategic decisions and recommendations
- o Develop an understanding of the barriers that exist to effective implementation of strategy
- o Appreciate the need to tailor marketing plans and process to allow for the specific sector and situational factors that apply to any given organization
- o Develop an awareness of the techniques that underpin innovation and creativity in organizations.

Learning outcomes

Students will be able to:

- o Understand and critically appraise a wide variety of marketing techniques, concepts and models
- o Conduct and evaluate a detailed marketing audit, both internally and externally
- o Identify the elements that can be used to create competitive advantage.
- o Compare and contrast strategic options
- o Specify a clear rationale when choosing between strategic alternatives
- o Prepare effective and realistic marketing plans
- o Initiate control systems for marketing planning
- o Understand and evaluate the processes that can be used to overcome barriers to effective implementation of marketing strategies and plans
- o Evaluate a range of techniques that facilitate innovation in organizations.

Indicative content and weighting

3.1 Market-led approach to planning (10%)

3.1.1 *Adopting a market-led orientation*

- Marketing orientation
- Role of marketing in market-led strategic management
- Drivers of change in the business environment.

3.1.2 *The strategic marketing process*

- Corporate strategy/marketing interface
- The basis of planning and control: the structure of planning and the cycle of control
- The nature of strategic, tactical and contingency planning.

3.2 Analysis (25%)

3.2.1 *External analysis*

- Environmental analysis
- Industry analysis
- Market analysis
- Competitor analysis

    1. Competitive intelligence
    2. The competitive intelligence cycle
    3. Sources of competitive information

- Customer analysis.

3.2.2 *Internal analysis*

- Resource-based approach: organizational assets, capabilities and competencies

    1. Technical resources
    2. Financial standing
    3. Managerial skills
    4. Organization
    5. Information systems

- Asset-based approach:

    1. Customer-based assets
    2. Distribution-based assets
    3. Alliance-based asset
    4. Internal assets

- Marketing activities audit:

    1. Marketing strategy audit
    2. Marketing structures audit
    3. Marketing systems audit
    4. Productivity audit
    5. Marketing functions audit

o   Innovation audit:

1. The organizational climate
2. Rate of new product development
3. Customer satisfaction ratings
4. The innovation/value matrix
5. The balance of cognitive styles of the senior management team.

3.3 Techniques for analysis and strategy development (20%)

3.3.1 *Techniques for developing a future orientation*

o   Trend extrapolation
o   Modelling
o   Intuitive forecasting
o   Individual or genius forecasting
o   Consensus forecasting

1. Jury forecasting
2. Delphi forecasts

o   Scenario planning
o   Market sensing
o   War gaming
o   Synthesis reports.

3.3.2 *Auditing tools*

o   Portfolio analysis
o   Value chain
o   PIMS
o   Experience curves
o   Financial

1. Ratio analysis
2. Productivity analysis
3. Segmental analysis
4. Balance sheet evaluation
5. Profit and loss accounts

o   SWOT analysis
o   GAP analysis.

3.4 Strategy formulation and selection (30%)

3.4.1 *The strategic intent*

o   Mission
o   Objectives
o   Stakeholders
o   Customer/competitor orientation
o   Evaluation of balanced scorecard.

3.4.2 *Approaches to creating strategic advantage*

- o Generic strategies
- o Developing sustainable advantage

  1. Superior product or service
  2. Perceived advantage
  3. Global skills
  4. Low-cost operator
  5. Superior competencies
  6. Superior assets
  7. Scale advantages
  8. Attitude advantages
  9. Legal advantages
  10. Superior relationships

- o Alliances and networks
- o Offensive/defensive strategies
- o Competitive positions and strategy

  1. Strategies for market leaders
  2. Strategies for market challengers
  3. Strategies for market followers
  4. Strategies for market nichers

- o Product/market strategy

  1. Product/market matrix
  2. PLC
  3. PIMS
  4. Portfolio analysis

- o Strategies for declining and hostile markets
- o Strategic wear-out and renewal.

3.4.3 *Developing a specific competitive position*

- o Strategic alignment process
- o Assets/competencies
- o Segmentation and targeting

  1. Evaluation of balanced scorecard

- o Positioning
- o Branding strategy

  1. Brand equity
  2. Brand evaluation
  3. Brand name strategy
  4. Brand extension
  5. Brand stretching
  6. Brand revitalization
  7. Brand repositioning

- o Innovation and product development
- o Building customer relationships.

3.4.4 *Strategic marketing plans*

- o Process and structure of marketing planning
- o Strategic and tactical marketing decisions.

3.5 Implementation and control (15%)

3.5.1 *Key elements of implementation*

- o Leadership
- o Internal marketing
- o Project management

     1. Systems
     2. Skills

- o Management of change.

3.5.2 *Key elements of control*

- o The dimensions of effective marketing feedback and control systems
- o Basic control concepts and their application throughout the planning and implementation process
- o Financial control

     1. Budgets
     2. Ratios

- o Benchmarking.

Further study

Students are encouraged to read as widely as time permits to gain different perspectives on the syllabus. It is essential that students keep up-to-date particularly in the area of information technology by reading broadsheet newspapers and appropriate magazines.

The *Financial Times* has regular features on information and communications technologies relevant to marketing applications that you may find useful. If you want to find out more on a specific topic then use electronic databases available in many libraries, e.g. MINTEL, FT Profile, McCarthy, etc.

Reading list

Core texts

Ensor, J and Drummond, G (2001) *Strategic Marketing: Planning and Control*, 2nd Edition. Oxford: CIM/Butterworth-Heinemann.

Hooley, G, Saunders, J and Piercy, N (1998) *Marketing Strategy and Competitive Positioning*, 2nd Edition. Hemel Hempstead: Prentice-Hall.

Aaker, DA (2001) *Strategic Market Management*, 6th Edition. Chichester: John Wiley.

Syllabus guides

CIM (2003) *CIM Companion: Planning and control.* Cookham: Chartered Institute of Marketing.

BPP (2003) *Planning and Control.* London: BPP Publishing.

Meek, H, Meek, R (2003) *Strategic Marketing Management: Planning and Control Coursebook.* Oxford: Butterworth-Heinemann.

Supplementary reading

Adkins, S (1999) *Cause-related Marketing.* Oxford: Butterworth-Heinemann.

Davidson, H (1997) *Even More Offensive Marketing.* West Drayton: Penguin.

Doyle, P (2002) *Marketing Management and Strategy,* 3rd Edition, Harlow, FT/Prentice-Hall.

Janszen, F (2000) *The Age of Innovation.* Harlow: Pearson.

Jobber, D (2001) *Principles and Practice of Marketing.* 3rd Edition. Maidenhead: McGraw-Hill.

McDonald, M (2002) *Marketing Plans.* 5th Edition. Oxford: Butterworth-Heinemann.

Mercer, D (1998) *Marketing Strategy: The challenge of the external environment.* London: Sage.

Piercy, N (2001) *Market Led Strategic Change.* 3rd Edition. Oxford: Butterworth-Heinemann.

Pringle, H and Thompson, M (2001) *Brand Spirit: How cause related marketing builds brands.* Chichester, John Wiley.

BPP (2002) *Planning and Control practice and revision kits.* London, BPP Publishing. *Planning and control: Success tape.* Learning cassettes by BPP Publishing.

Index